Robert Browning and His World

Robert Browning

and His World:

The Private Face [1812–1861]

BY MAISIE WARD

CASSELL · LONDON

920
20194 BRO

CASSELL & COMPANY LTD
35 Red Lion Square, London WC1
Melbourne, Sydney, Toronto
Johannesburg, Auckland

© *Mary J. Ward* 1967
First published in Great Britain 1968
S.B.N. 304 93167 5

o C

Printed in Great Britain by
Lowe & Brydone (Printers) Ltd., London
F.368

For two Franks—

my husband and my grandson

Acknowledgments

I am grateful for permission to use quotations from the following published works: from *New Letters of Robert Browning* to Kenneth Leslie Knickerbocker, Yale University Press and John Murray; from *Letters of the Brownings to George Barrett*, to Paul Landis and University of Illinois Press; from *Dearest Isa*, to Edward C. McAleer and T. Nelson & Sons, Ltd.; from *Learned Lady*, to Edward C. McAleer and Oxford University Press.

I am also grateful to John Murray for the general permission to quote from the following collections of letters on which he owns the copyright: *Letters of Elizabeth Barrett Browning to her Sister*, edited by Leonard Huxley; *Robert Browning and Julia Wedgwood*, edited by Richard Curle; and *Robert Browning: A Portrait* by Betty Miller. For permission to quote from *Poetry of Experience* by Robert Langbaum my thanks to the author and Chatto & Windus; from *Religious Trends in English Poetry Vol. IV* by Hoxie Neale Fairchild, to the author and Oxford University Press. Further, for permission to quote from *Essays in London and Elsewhere* by Henry James, to Harper and Row; from *The Middle Years* by Henry James, to Wm. Collins Sons & Co. Ltd. Lines from *Little Boxes*, words and music by Malvina Reynolds copyright 1962 by Schroder Music Company, Berkeley, California, used by permission.

For permission to quote from *Letters to Robert and Elizabeth Browning from Owen Meredith*, edited by Aurelia B. Harlan and J. Harlan Junior, I thank Baylor University—to which I also owe a deep debt of gratitude for access to much valuable unpublished material, especially *The Poet Robert Browning and His Kinsfolk* by his cousin, Cyrus Mason, from which I was allowed to quote freely; to the Henry W. and Albert A. Berg Collection of the New York Public Library; to the Astor, Lenox, and Tilden Foundations for quotations from Elizabeth Barrett Browning's childhood letters and her letters to her sister, Arabel, and to Sophia Eckley; to the University of Texas for access to the drawings and notebooks of Robert Browning's father and permission to use two unpublished letters of the poet to Sarah Flower; to

Wellesley College for access to much interesting correspondence—and an examination of the Love Letters still in the box where Browning placed them a century ago; to the Pierpont Morgan Library for permission to quote from Mrs. Jameson's letters to Lady Noel Byron; to the Victoria and Albert Museum for a photostat of, and permission to quote, Mill's discussion of *Pauline* with Browning's annotations; and to the Trustees of the British Museum for permission to quote from the Kenyon typescript containing passages and complete letters omitted from the printed volume of *The Letters of Elizabeth Barrett Browning*.

In all these libraries I have received most courteous attention. I would like to thank especially Hannah French, Research Librarian at Wellesley; Dr. John Gordan and Mrs. Szladits at the Berg Collection and Professor Herring at Baylor. To Mrs. Veva Wood of the Armstrong Library, Baylor University, I find it hard to express my gratitude adequately, for her unremitting help and co-operation during my two visits to Baylor and in subsequent correspondence.

I am most grateful to Professor Edward C. McAleer, who has long been helping me by advice and the loan of books, and who has read this first volume in manuscript and made valuable suggestions; to Professors Park Honan and Robert Langbaum for rapidly reading and commenting on the proofs, in the middle of a busy semester; to the Rev. Dr. William Whitla for a very thoughtful reading of proofs; and to Mr. H. C. Duffin for a useful correspondence arising out of his book *Amphibian*. Also, to the helpful staff of the Public Library of Newark, New Jersey for their help over many months of reading and research.

Contents

Illustrations

Introduction

I guess I'm half a quack,
For whom ten lines of Browning whack
The whole of the Zodiac.

D. G. ROSSETTI

POETS' CORNER

"Do you object to all this adulation?" Browning was asked when surrounded by admiring undergraduates.

"Object to it! No; I have waited forty years for it, and now—I like it."

The chief regret felt by Henry James, present in Westminster Abbey for the funeral at which England paid "her greatest honour to one of her greatest poets," was that Browning could not write about it: "His own analytic spirit would have rejoiced . . . the pictorial sense would have intertwined itself with the metaphysical. . . . Passion and ingenuity, irony and solemnity, the impressive and unexpected, would each have forced their way through . . . even perhaps to the dim corners where humour and the whimsical lurk."

Looking around him, James seemed to see in the dark chapels and crowded transepts a "company in possession," gazing with cold eyes on this newcomer with his "bewildering modernness." Yet the very fact of his "lying there among the classified and protected makes even Robert Browning lose a portion of the bristling surface of his actuality." Among the great writers, among the oddities gathered in the Abbey, "none of the odd ones have been so great and none of the great ones so odd . . . there is no poetic head of equal power—crowned and recrowned by almost importunate hands—from which so many people would withhold the distinctive wreath."

Browning is today labeled a Victorian, with every implication of the stuffiness attached to the word, but James found his distinguishing mark to be his difference: "a tremendous and incomparable modern," with "boldnesses and overgrowths, rich roughnesses and humours . . . what he takes into the Abbey is an immense expression of life—of life rendered with large liberty and free experiment, with an unprejudiced intellectual eagerness to put himself in other people's place, to participate in complications and consequences; a restlessness of psychological research that might well alarm any pale company for their formal orthodoxies."

Browning would have enjoyed "prefiguring and playing with the mystifications, the reservations, even perhaps the slight buzz of scandal in the Poets' Corner to which his own obsequies might give rise! . . . we leave our sophisticated modern conscience, and perhaps even our heterogeneous modern vocabulary, in his charge among the illustrious."[1]

When Browning said he had "waited forty years" for appreciation, he forgot one brief interlude. Criticism had gone far toward establishing him by warm praise of *Paracelsus;* but after the "incomprehensible" *Sordello,* it turned against him and so remained for another thirty years. From then onward the "importunate hands" that were crowning him went on to heap the wreaths perhaps too incessantly, too indiscriminately. Nor was it only the poetry. The "immortal lovers" were called so once too often. The Brownings, like Aristides, are suffering today for being painted by their admirers as too good to be true and too admirable to be endurable.

WHAT THEN DOES
MR. BROWNING MEAN?

When Kingsley asked the question: "What then does Mr. Newman mean?" it was a double-edged one calling for a twofold answer. As a challenge to Newman's thought the *University Sermons* already contained the answer, though expressed too subtly and too profoundly for Kingsley. As a challenge to his integrity it called forth the *Apologia*. At Baylor University I saw Browning's high desk from the Casa Guidi, and I wondered: Did the poet really stand to write or was a tall stool the answer? Then imagination displaced the poet for the priest. Newman did, we know, stand far into the night penning, with the tears his generation so freely shed, the answer that was the history of his mind. Yet who shall say that after the *Apologia* had been written John Henry Newman had really made plain what Henri Bremond much later could still call "The Mystery of Newman"?

There is quite as certainly a Mystery of Browning, possibly insoluble, but certainly not to be penetrated on the intellectual level by those who, as he himself complained, read poetry as a substitute for a cigar or a game of dominoes. As Swinburne pointed out, the best hours of the day, the clearest state of the mind, are called for. Those inured to modern poetry will find Browning's less formidable than did their grandparents; the thing they will not find is that he ever improved matters by talking in prose. Browning knew very well, when he resolutely refused to talk about his own poetry, that he would only make it more difficult by trying to "explain." It was poured out (the best of it) in hours of high exaltation: How could he say anything but "What I have written I have written"?

Browning, says Robert Langbaum, "was actually telling his age that they were asking the wrong questions of the universe; he was himself reaching for the right questions for which the proper vocabulary has been supplied only in our time through the philosophies of existentialism and symbolic form." And he dissents from the attempt made by so many to discuss as separate propositions Browning the poet and Browning the thinker. "Are we to conclude," he asks (in *Victorian Poetry*, Spring, 1965), "that while Browning may have a future as a poet, he can have none as a thinker? We cannot if we believe that poetry is a form of thought."

While we stammer, the poet can find full utterance; while we build, as Browning himself told Ruskin, the tidy rows of houses erected "so cleverly" in many a suburb, his is a Stonehenge of rough half-hewn rocks, or a cathedral perhaps only half finished.

Langbaum is pointing toward a new understanding of Browning's poetry as belonging to our age more than to the nineteenth century. But of late much other writing has been done about Browning which asks what he means in the second sense in which Kingsley challenged Newman. A tendency is rife to treat him as a psychological patient with the critic as his analyst. He was noisy and healthy—a sure sign of his insecurity and fundamental ill health. He married a woman six years older than himself—"a fact which even those with the least possible touch of Freudianism may find relevant." He was self-assertive, yet he would gossip about everything but "never about Robert Browning." His apparent masculinity was really "over compensation." This and much more does Richard Altick assert, with a confidence few psychologists would feel in analyzing a man they had never seen, never questioned; a man nearly eighty years dead.

Two things might help if such an analysis is to be attempted: first the testimony of wife, friends, enemies, and casual contemporary gossip; but all this gives much the picture Browning's critics are bent on destroying.

Second, and even more important, is his poetry; and it is astonishing how little awareness of this is shown in much contemporary writing. "Browning," we read, "had no real interest in anything that went on in the world except as it touched Robert Browning." There are less extreme cases than this, but certainly many critics appear not to have read *as poetry* the poems which have excited other poets from Rossetti through

Swinburne to Ezra Pound and Robert Lowell. They approach Browning as a man might approach the Venus de Milo, observing with cool realist's eye that the arms are broken, but observing almost nothing else!

Too bad Browning did not simplify the critics' task by being a womanizer, a homosexual, drunkard, or drug addict.[2] All that remained was to discover some sort of intellectual weakness plus an unhealthy relation with his mother. Professor Altick in *The Browning Critics* and Mrs. Miller in *Robert Browning: A Portrait* find this in his marriage to an older woman: she was a mother figure. Jeannette Marks in *The Family of the Barrett* discovered even more convincingly that Elizabeth Barrett underwent a "transference" when her father and her doctor disappointed her—and found a father figure in Browning. A sort of double incest?

All this is a bit confusing perhaps, but not really as startling as a recent remark assuming that Browning was haunted through life by a teen-age betrayal of Shelley. Dying at the age of seventy-seven, did Browning, a reviewer wonders, "hear the cock crow for the third time"?

He would have rubbed his eyes to see himself thus cast as Peter to Shelley's Christ. There is no slightest trace at any time in his life of this sense of guilt. In his teens he came close to idolatry of Shelley and continued, though to a modified degree, to admire the poet all his life, blenching only over Shelley the man when finally realizing his conduct toward his wife Harriet.

The theory of Browning's betrayal derives almost certainly from Mrs. Miller's book in which Browning, cast as the anti-hero, is portrayed as failing in all the great relations of his life: his integrity to his ideals; his behavior as son, husband, father. Wonderfully ingenious and brilliantly written, the book received the reviews usually accorded a best-selling novel.

A year after Browning's death William Sharp (better known as Fiona MacLeod) had published a *Life*, a little over-enthusiastic but containing valuable elements. In the next year came *Life and Letters*, by Mrs. Sutherland Orr, who had the advantage of close personal friendship with the poet. Between her book and Mrs. Miller's we have only *The Life* begun by W. Hall Griffin and completed by

H. C. Minchin. I owe something to them all, and still more to such learned writers as De Vane; and to the insights of men like Dowden, Herford, Raymond, Edwin Muir, and Langbaum. Despite many errors of detail, Chesterton casts a brilliant light on the poet; both Robert Lowell and Robert Langbaum have told me they think his the best book in the vast Browning literature. An enormous amount of fresh material has become available, scattered over the world, laid up in libraries, or buried in obscure periodicals.

The books and articles actually being published seem endless—letters especially, and really valuable criticism; but I was surprised at the rich vein of unpublished material not fully explored.

There are in the British Museum the four large volumes of the Kenyon typescript (considerably expurgated in the published edition); the letters to Browning's son, Pen, at Balliol College; the correspondence with Dr. Furnivall, founder of the Browning Society, in the Huntingdon Library. Add to these the letters at the University of Texas—to Pen's tutor, Gillespie, and his art teacher, Heyermans; to the Mr. Natrop with whom Pen shared a studio and who introduced him to Rodin; the letters to Millais at the Pierpont Morgan Library and to Kenyon at Wellesley College. From these we get a change of proportion as compared with the letters to women, continually pouring in later years from Browning's pen. Ladies with abundant time for writing certainly got in return the lion's share, but Browning also had many men friends. Much of this material belongs in my second volume; but for this one I gained light from Baylor University's *The Poet Robert Browning and His Kinsfolk*, written by his cousin, Cyrus Mason; the three hundred unpublished letters in the New York Public Library's Berg Collection from Elizabeth to Arabel Barrett and to Mrs. Eckley—besides her own childhood letters and youthful self-portraiture.

Ideas have changed as to the function of the biographer—at once narrowing and widening it. The duty of a full mastery of the material and as rich and balanced a presentation of it as possible is today often played down in favor of an attempt to do the impossible in penetration of motives and thoughts hidden in the subconscious. An exaggeration of good has swung into a greater exaggeration of evil—colored usually by an imperfect apprehension of the psychiatry of the moment. Even if psychiatry were more stable than it is, its use can lead to a theorising which I feel to be doubtfully legitimate in a critic, and wholly illegitimate in a biographer. Only a novelist has the right to create a character; when faced with "dry, puzzling, authentic fact," one sometimes envies him. Above all some problems must be left as the problems that they are. The biographer is not a judge. His task is different from that of the painter. He has not just to deal with given features—item two gray eyes and the rest. From an immense mass of material he must try to make so fair a selection that the reader can use it to form his own picture. Just as acquaintances quarrel over a man's character, so should readers.

I do not for a moment disclaim that warm sympathy with my subject once considered desirable in a biographer. Without sympathy, empathy is impossible. Yet it remains a dubious compliment when everybody agrees that the picture given is "convincing," when no loophole is left for another view.

Robert Browning's poetry, his personality, his family and friends were primarily his world, but much else is needed to understand a man living in an era so different from ours, one who inside his own period lived in three immensely various worlds. There was the middle-class dissenting English society of his boyhood; the Italy, so ancient and so new, of his younger manhood; the aristocratic English world of his fifties into his old age—each as different from the others as any of them are from the English, or American, world of today.

I have been tempted to some such titles as *Triumphant Failure* and *Success* instead of the two that have emerged. For Browning's greatest work was undoubtedly done when nobody wanted it, and his noblest period was that when he was proud to be, as Elizabeth called him, lover, husband, and nurse; or as others less kindly said, *"le mari de Madame."* Apart from an occasional crank, it is only after her death that he is depicted as bad-tempered, snobbish in society, prolix in the poetry now in such demand. Even then this is a minor note in a general chorus of admiration, though a note that must be listened to. The earlier Brown-

ing does not pose the riddle offered by the later, and especially empha-
sized by his younger contemporary, Henry James, in his theory of the
two Brownings, poet and socialite. Yet in this sharp-cut distinction the
subtle critic was perhaps for once oversimplifying.

I have tried to study the backgrounds of all Browning's worlds, to
grow intimate with some of the leading characters who were his friends
or critics—Fox, "Weaver Boy" and minister; Mill and Macready, Rossetti, Tennyson, Disraeli, and Gladstone; Mrs. Jameson and Lady
Ashburton; Thackeray's daughter and many others, besides a multitude
of diarists from England and the United States—to see through their
eyes as well as through Browning's poetry the man as he appeared and
as he was.

After traveling, reading, meditating, not only on the facts but on
many interpretations new and old, I believe that there is still a lot to be
said for the old Browning tradition. But the note of inquiry should be
struck again and again, should even be held down firmly on dubious
points. No canonization can proceed until the devil's advocate has been
allowed, indeed urged, to bring out every dark spot in the alleged saint's
life. Well, I do not propose to canonize Browning; the extremists on
both sides shall speak—and nearly everyone who knew him was an
extremist.

One cannot meditate on a man for years without forming views or
at least surmises about his character. But these too belong to my second
volume. They can make sense to the reader only if tested, as they have
been formed, after the study of a completed life. I do not believe it possible to reach a total understanding of anything, let alone any person,
in this strange, terrible, beautiful, mysterious world. Dealing with
genius, especially, analysis is often baffled. Mystery need not be a fog;
it may be a piercing clarity to which our fogbound sight must be ad-
justed. Genius can co-exist wth weakness, weakness with strength.
Juvenal's *maxima reverentia* is due not to the young alone but to every
human soul—reverence and pity.

As you read a poet, you see that he, who is deeper in the mystery
of life than we, sees more mystery there; that the tension between the
greatness of what he sees and the limits of language and of his own

personality bring struggle, physical and mental exhaustion, perhaps neurosis.

> All I could never be
> All, men ignored in me,
> This I was worth to God . . .

P.S. BY WAY OF APOLOGIA

I have been writing this book for more than four years and in this period have flown round the world twice and had a major operation in Sydney, Australia. With my earlier biographies—of my parents, Chesterton, the young Newman—all the material was at hand. But I have written this book in Australia, England, France, Italy, and the United States. The impossibility of carrying a library by air, of ever having all my authorities in one place, the increasing weight of notes sent across two oceans and not always reaching their destination, plus the use of nine or ten different stenographers—all this has made the job of checking peculiarly onerous. I hope the learned scholars, of whom I stand in awe, will be lenient as to "commas and dots to i's."

On the other hand I have never believed in a multitude of references; they mean nothing to the general reader and are not particularly useful to students. When the source of a quotation is shown in the text, or when its matter is uncontroversial I have added no note. All the letters quoted to Arabel and to Mrs. Eckley are in the Berg Collection. In general the notes are directed towards helping students with guidance on further reading.

I could not have completed my work without the generous help of librarians, some of whom have passed into the second category of personal friends, to all of whom acknowledgment is made on pp. iii and iv. My gratitude is truly heartfelt.

Robert Browning and His World

1 The Browning Family

This curse of class difference confronts you like a wall of stone. Or rather it is not so much like a stone wall as the plate-glass pane of an aquarium; it is so easy to pretend that it isn't there, and so impossible to get through it.

GEORGE ORWELL

S ELDOM can anyone have been subjected to an odder series of conjectures as to his ancestry than was Robert Browning. The story of the family's descent, on which were based tales of chivalry told by an uncle to himself and his sister, had been current, Browning said, in his father's family. Mrs. Orr declares that *he* neither accepted nor repudiated it. He did, however, in later years, use on some of his letter paper the coat of arms which his son flaunted at the Palazzo Rezzonico. The painter Rudolf Lehmann noted in Browning a surprising "punctiliousness on the subject of his and his family's pedigrees." Cyrus Mason, son of Mr. Browning's sister, presents in his biography such evidence as there is of their family descent—and it is weak indeed.

It is unquestioned that their common grandfather, another Robert Browning, came from Dorset to London in the eighteenth century, and that *his* father had died at Pentridge, having occupied a house which was afterward a coaching inn. This is confirmed by Sir Vincent Baddeley K.C.B., a more distant cousin, in an interesting article in *The Genealogists' Magazine* (March, 1938). But Cyrus Mason is not content with leaving his great-grandfather as the first known ancestor. Seizing on the name Browning, the county Dorset, and the Christian names John,

Robert, and William, he links his own and the poet's great-grandfather with another family, possessors of various manors granted by Edward III in another part of Dorset. One of them was Sheriff of Dorset and Somerset under Edward IV. These were "fighting men from Poole," whose name began as Bruning, then became Brownyng, and finally Browning. None of this does Sir Vincent Baddeley regard as proved.

Mason is on surer ground when showing that his grandfather was an educated man, describing the books eighteenth-century Robert[1] and his brother brought with them to London, and the ease with which Robert, the elder, got a post at the Bank of England, rising to a position of heavy responsibility and turning into a "somewhat pompous" city man. "A substantial resident of Peckham," he became "a staunch supporter of the Church of England," regarding it as "the soundest buttress of the British constitution."

To this man's younger brother, Reuben, Browning's father owed the cultivation of literary and artistic tastes, his own father regarding "students of literature, art or music as little better than vagabonds." Reuben remained a Nonconformist, though his brother considered this faith "only suitable to the spiritual wants of petty tradesmen or the religious guidance of people struggling against poverty, certainly not for well-placed gentlefolk."

Rushing to the opposite extreme from Cyrus Mason, Furnivall, cofounder of the Browning Society, did something so incredible that, were not Sir Vincent Baddeley an actual eyewitness, one would refuse to believe it. Building on the fact that their former home was now an inn, Furnivall declared that Browning's great-grandfather was the innkeeper, *his* father having been first page at Corfe Castle, then footman and butler there. He was made to withdraw the footman story, but subsequently, says Sir Vincent, he erected a tombstone with an inscription devised by himself:

Robert Browning of Woodyates in this Parish died Nov. 25, 1746.
He is the first known forefather of Robert Browning poet.
He was formerly footman and butler in the Bankes family.
"ALL SERVICE RANKS THE SAME WITH GOD."
BROWNING

Sir Vincent called on the churchwardens and Council of the Parish, had the tomb altered, and the quotation deleted! It was not so easy to delete men's memories of what they had read or heard—this, or Furnivall's other stories of Jewish descent, of colored ancestry, of anything or everything of speculative interest.

Of Jewish ancestry the poet would have been proud; his admiration for that great race was frequently expressed. By colored blood—called at that date "a touch of the tar brush"—he would inevitably have been embarrassed. Furnivall was, however, more convinced of this than of the possible Jewish element; and Jeannette Marks, after careful research in Jamaica and St. Kitts, believes it to be a possibility. For John Tittle, Browning's maternal great-grandfather, was, she says, "ignored" in the strangest manner by his mother, Lucy Tittle. He had a difficult character, "ambitious, imprudent, impulsive," and had embroiled himself with his brother to whom father and mother were clearly devoted and to whom most of their property was bequeathed. But Mrs. Marks feels we must look to some deeper reason for their attitude, and at that date especially the color question could be that reason.

Could—but need not. For John became a clergyman with "an indifferent or tollerable (sic) good parish" in St. Kitts, also sharing a plantation with a man who had "vile principles" and did not pay him his dues; he sent by every ship complaints about everybody to the Bishop of London—accompanied by gifts. He married Margaret Strachan. His daughter, Margaret Tittle, was Browning's grandmother and through her Dr. Furnivall suggested a possible way for the element of color to have come. But surely her portrait is almost aggressively Aryan.

Browning might have laughed at this; yet he might also have squirmed, for he was a man of his age. And in that age Disraeli's picture in *Sybil* does not at all exaggerate the pedigrees constructed by the Heralds' College for the *noveaux riches,* or the enormous importance attached to descent. The poet preserved, Mrs. Orr tells us, "the old framed coat of arms handed down to him from his grandfather"; and wore a signet ring engraved from it, the "gift of an uncle." And she adds that the older members of the family accepted as a certainty this very problematical pedigree.

There was certainly some excuse in the fact that, if the thing mattered at all, the reality was seldom the same as the appearance. In how
many English villages even today do the ancient owners' descendants
live in a cottage while the rich—and now titled—manufacturer owns
their ancestral home! Browning's great-grandfather *may* have kept an
inn, and may too have had the right to bear arms centuries old. The inn,
at whatever date it became one, was a chief ground of Moulton Barrett's
objection to Browning as a son-in-law. But if, as was later alleged,
Browning's own son wanted to marry an innkeeper's daughter at
Dinant, the poet (though with other good reasons for objecting) may
well have been haunted by the proverb: "Three generations from shirt
sleeves to shirt sleeves."

To return to what we know: Margaret Tittle's son (father of the
poet) married Sarah Anna Weidemann, a Scot from Dundee, de-
scended from a German, spoken of by Mrs. Orr as a shipowner, and hail-
ing from Hamburg. Mrs. Miller could not find his name in any list of
Dundee shipowners. She discovered in the *Register of Sasines* a William
Wiedemann, Mariner. A friend, checking for me at Hamburg, could
not find the name on any list still existing.

Browning's father was an interesting and rather eccentric character. "Lovable beyond description," said D. G. Rossetti, "a complete
oddity." His nephew describes his exaggerated interest in anatomy,
declaring that on his wedding day he disappeared and was found dis-
secting a dead duck; that for the same purpose he once kept a rat "too
long" in his desk at the bank. He had "a taste for the horrible," but also
a taste so strong for poetry that the family suspected him as the author
of some of his son's verses. Actually it was a painter's career he had
longed for, and much remains to suggest that there was truth in the
view of others besides his half brother, Reuben, and his nephew, Cyrus,
that he might have brought fame to the family a generation earlier than
his son. As it was, Cyrus, obviously disliking his cousin, perhaps envying
his good luck, declares that this uncle of his *planned* to educate his son
to be a poet. It was apparently a family decision, for Cyrus had never
heard his own mother, another aunt (perhaps Mrs. Silverthorne), or

Browning's parents suggest any other future for "young Robert." Cyrus clearly believes that it was by no power born in him but sheerly by parental teaching and family fostering that this particular poet was made.

Not knowing their relative ages, one cannot tell whether all this means that by the time Cyrus was old enough to begin observing, the die had been cast for a poetic career. Certainly the impression is strong that during Robert's early childhood Mr. Browning would have liked to see his son become the successful painter that he himself might have been. He was always drawing: groups in the street, clients calling at the bank, individual heads. They often carry a caption which makes one feel he might have become an Osbert Lancaster, commenting cynically on the world of politics, high finance, and law. There are quite a number of these captioned drawings at Baylor University and Wellesley College.

Rossetti greatly admired Mr. Browning's sketches, saying that he had "a real genius for drawing," though "caring for nothing except Dutch boors." He and all his friends agreed that he *could* not draw a pretty face. There is indeed at Wellesley what I can only hope was a caricature of his daughter Sarianna. How could she have borne to see it or he to keep it? Reuben Browning put the effect of these drawings rather quaintly by saying that they always awakened "the admiration and risible qualites of the company."

Good as they are, these collections do not compare with the richness and variety of the drawings at the University of Texas; these were made for Alice Corkran and are described by her in *Chapters from the Story of My Girlhood* and also in an article in *The Bookman* of April, 1896.

In his old age Mr. Browning became intimate wth the family of an English journalist in Paris with two daughters, Henriette and Alice, to whom he meant more than many a grandfather. The two small girls would sit on each side of Mr. Browning at a large littered table while he drew and painted. One quite lovely thing is a map of *Pilgrim's Progress*, depicting Vanity Fair, The City of Destruction, The Wilderness, the Slough of Despond, The Valley of the Shadow of Death, The

Delectable Mountains. All delicately colored, they are explained in tiny exquisitely written notes.

Seen by *The Bookman* as having an "eye for faces not less keen than his son's," Mr. Browning relates *The Ghost Story* as going on "amid a series of interruptions and cross questions, each new personage interpolating a remark which prevents the last speaker from proceeding ... believers and unbelievers ... hit off with delicious fun ... London of the thirties comes alive." And already spiritualism is rife—"a very small party ... nobody danced but a hat and a table."

Notebooks crammed with reading lists, chiefly historical, and notes of English, Scotch, French history, complicated genealogies, odd bits of verse, complete this collection:

> I write the wonders for the News
> I criticize for the reviews.

Thackeray's daughter gives a rather horrific account of her childish fright at the sketches Mr. Browning poured out of the ill-treated slaves on his mother's plantation; but of the dozens of drawings I have seen, only one could be called even faintly frightening. Neither Alice nor Henriette Corkran, who knew him so intimately, seem to have seen any. "Often," says Henriette, "he would stop in front of cabarets and draw groups of workmen, drinking, smoking, gesticulating. ... His sketches were admirable, they were so full of life. ... The grotesque appealed strongly to Mr. Browning."

It would be surprising, however, if he had not at times drawn those men and scenes which had made so deep an impression on him in boy-hood—and it may have been some of these sketches that impressed Cyrus as horrible. Browning told Elizabeth Barrett that his father shivered and turned pale at the recollection of the cruelties he had witnessed and even at the sight of blood. For the poet's grandfather, the "pompous" one of Peckham, having lost his first wife and married again, had sent his eldest son out to work in the West Indies. When he refused to have a part or lot in the horrible institution of slavery, this singular parent not only disinherited him of the estate which should have come to him from his mother, but also sent him a bill for his education. It was, by this time, too late to follow his artistic bent, and to serve in the Bank of England was at least better than to rule a slave compound. But Cyrus Mason believed it was the lack of culture not the slavery that caused his uncle to leave Jamaica.

The only prose work I have read of Mr. Browning's is dull enough —the story being at once wildly improbable and pedestrian in its telling. But his drawings and comic verse are a very different matter, and the son may well have caught the trick of absurd double and even treble rhyming from his father.

More than once they chose the same subject to write about. With the "Pied Piper" we know that the story was in Wanley's *Wonders of the Little World* and in other books in Mr. Browning's library, and his cartoons show how he came to write and illustrate a poem on a spiritualist medium. When Browning began on the Piper, the admiring father abandoned his own version unfinished. But a few lines of it are worth quoting:

> There is at a moderate distance from Hanover—
> A town on the Weser of singular fame:
> A place which the French and the rats often ran over—
> But though my tale varies
> Yet sage antiquaries
> Are all in one story concerning its name—
> 'Tis Hammelin (but you had better perhaps
> Turn over your atlas and look at the maps)
> Which, without flattery
> Seemed one vast rattery . . .

As a boy, Mr. Browning had shared with John Kenyon—also of Jamaican origin—the organizing of mock combats among their schoolfellows "exciting themselves to battle by insulting speeches derived from the Homeric text." He told Henriette Corkran that in boyhood he had known by heart the first book of the *Iliad* and the Odes of Horace, and it seemed to her that he also knew by heart "the Bible and history generally." When his son was a baby, he would send him to sleep by humming odes of Anacreon, and he taught him grammar by setting in grotesque rhymes the words to be remembered.

Mr. Browning was in fact a born educator. He looked, Henriette thought, much more like a poet than his son and had, even in his seventies, "great vivacity and freshness of mind." A picture emerges as we watch this older Robert Browning—at once guiding and yielding, probably both with a good deal of wisdom. Most of our knowledge of him comes through the poet, but something also from his half brother, Reuben, who describes him as a walking encyclopedia. He could find his way in the dark to the right bookcase in his huge library, and to the right book, and bring it back into the light for any needed reference, which he also turned up with miraculous speed. At Baylor are some of the volumes he had bound with added pages for his own notes. He knew rare books so well that he could tell which bookseller had the Codex or Elzevir in question and what price it was likely to fetch.

Mr. Browning's work at the bank appears to have been as much of practical everyday life as he cared to be bothered with. We learn that he changed the restaurant at which he lunched because they insisted on his choosing what he would eat. Cyrus Mason says he was shaved daily by his wife and that both wife and daughter disliked his absorption in verses, drawing, and learned books. Probably day-to-day "practical" matters were left to the two able-bodied women, at home all day with servants to wait on them, while husband and father earned the income he allowed them to spend—except for what went on his treasured library. But a bibliophile with tastes for drawing, verse-making, and conversation has not done too badly if, in addition to all this, he has earned the family living and done more than his share in the production and education of a poet.

How seriously to take Cyrus I am not sure, yet as the poet's cousin and near neighbor he was in a position to observe, and if we allow for a certain bias, his observations are worth noting. The Browning household was, he says, "maintained in some style with my uncle's salary." He himself found it "genteely dreary" and the family enveloped in "a misty pride."

Another aunt, Mrs. Silverthorne, and her three sons were very fond of "young Robert," but no one who knew the Brownings ever seems to have mentioned the Masons.

Cyrus and his mother noted with displeasure that Robert's sister, Sarianna, would walk to the chapel she attended followed by a maid carrying her books. He felt that "each of the occupants" of the house was "constantly self-absorbed," Uncle Robert studying a learned book or making grotesque drawings, Aunt Robert with her roses "or some household punctilio," Sarianna full of her own importance and her chapel, and (apparently dating the observations and explaining the sting), "the poet so preoccupied with his love affair that he found no opportunity to show any attention to kinsfolk."[2]

One suspects that the Brownings were bored to death by the Masons, and it might be refreshing to hear the Silverthorne opinion of both families and their mutual relationship! But one thing emerges—a clear picture of parents nurturing in a son, on whom all their hopes were set, the genius in which they so fully believed. "Young Robert," Cyrus says (whether from his own observation or that of his mother), "was developed by his father into an acknowledged genius."

Of Browning's mother—Sarah Anna, elided for her daughter into Sarianna—we know so little that speculation is as easy as it is futile. Carlyle described her as "the fine type of a Scottish gentlewoman." Mr. Kenyon declared that she would not need to go to heaven as she made heaven around her. Her religious views were narrow, and Mrs. Orr says that "in all her goodness and sweetness she seems to have been somewhat matter-of-fact," with nothing of the artistic qualities of her son and husband save her musical talent. Both Sarianna and her brother loved their mother with a deep affection, and Alfred Domett describes the family as most happy and united. Browning himself spoke of his mother as "a divine woman." He and she, while not alike intellectually, were curiously close physically. In the famous Love Letters he often tells Elizabeth how neuralgic headaches would affect them both simultaneously, and simultaneously depart.

The family way of life was certainly comfortable. We learn casually of Browning's pony in the stable, of a large garden, of Mr. Browning's collections of prints, his library of six thousand books, many of them very valuable, including a first edition of *Paradise Lost*. He was, of course, clever at picking up these treasures, though too generous in parting with them. Browning's masters in music, Italian, fencing, and the rest must have cost money, and so must the excellent bindings in which his father reclothed the books, to which he had added blank pages.

There was a degree of ease not today associated with a salary of £250 rising to £320. Indeed these figures need very considerable translating to discover their equivalent in our present inflated money.

It was not as simple as I had expected to find enlightening books on household expenses of more than a century ago. All those offered to me at the London Library and the British Museum dealt with tons of meat, hundreds of bundles of carrots, and the like. Translating, I got the impression that meat would have retailed at between threepence and fivepence a pound, a dozen bottles of wine at less than the cost of one bottle today. (Certain imported or hothouse luxuries were, of course, much more expensive. Cyrus was impressed by his uncle having, in Jamaica, often exchanged a pineapple for a sheet of writing paper while in London pineapples cost three to five guineas.)

I found two further sources of information, Dickens and the London School of Economics, a graduate of which told me I should be well within the mark if I multiplied by ten the income figure of 1830 or thereabouts. This would give Browning's father at his top earning point over £3,200 a year in today's money, *free of income tax* before we add anything for interest from his inherited money.

As to Dickens, information is scattered through all his books: The clerks' lunch in *Bleak House* cost threepence each for meat, a penny for marrow pie; the waitress was tipped a penny. In *The Old Curiosity Shop* Kit Nubbles, earning £6 a year, takes his mother, his small brother, his fellow servant, and her mother out to a play and an oyster supper; yet Kit was no lad to spend his entire quarter's wage of thirty shillings on one evening's entertainment.

In *Our Mutual Friend* Bella Wilfer's husband had a salary of thirty shillings a week, which enabled her to keep a neat little maid in a neat little cottage. And in *A Christmas Carol* the entire Cratchit family were living on fifteen shillings a week of Scrooge's money, while the eldest boy dreamed of the splendors of a first job at five shillings. Eighteen shillings a week was the full board paid by the youngest gentleman at

Mrs. Todgers' very exclusive boardinghouse, and her efforts to avoid offending Mr. Pecksniff were censured by him as worshiping the golden calf of Baal. "Oh calf, calf," he repeated mournfully, "Oh Baal, Baal."

Yet, however comfortable a family might be on an average clerk's salary, it would not be easy to get out of it fairly large sums in ready cash —the regular payments of £16 a time which Mr. Browning produced for the printing of the son's earlier books, still less the £100 which made him a foundation member of London University, the £100 he later lent to facilitate Browning's marriage and journey to Italy. (Cyrus Mason declares, but Mrs. Orr seems to deny, that this was supplied by Uncle Reuben.)

A salary, however, was not all the money there was in the family. Although Mr. Browning was disinherited and therefore relatively poor, some money had been willed to him by his "Uncle Tittle" and "Aunt Mill." Mrs. Miller says this can have been very little, as the Tittles were cordwainers in Jamaica and made shoes for the Barrett family there. They were, and no doubt did. *But a century earlier.* For by 1739 their carriages along with the Barretts' were to be seen at the welcome to Admiral Vernon; and the head of the family was buried in 1742 under the velvet pall reserved for the most important citizens. There is indeed as we have seen some mystery about Browning's direct ancestor, but, while much less wealthy than his brother, he also owned both property and slaves. Earthquakes and the destruction of papers make the details difficult to trace, but certainly none of the family ever returned to the humble origins in which Mrs. Miller leaves them.[3]

Browning's father had renounced the property that involved slaveowning. His aunt and his uncle were making him some compensation. One wonders what is the relevance of the footnote quotation from "Andrea del Sarto" with which Mrs. Miller emphasizes her treatment of Browning's relationship to his parents:

> My father and my mother died of want,
> Well, had I riches of my own? . . .
> Some good son
> Paint my two hundred pictures—let him try.

2 The Boy Browning

My Father, who knew better than turn straight
Learning's full flare on weak-eyed ignorance,
Or, worse yet, leave weak eyes to grow sandblind,
Content with darkness and vacuity.

"DEVELOPMENT"[1]

ONE OF Browning's earliest memories was of watching his mother holding a parasol over her head while she searched for a spotted frog in the strawberry bed. He had insisted on the frog as a condition for taking his medicine, and this very compliant parent had yielded. Swallowing the nauseous mixture the child improvised:

Good people all who wish to see
A boy take physic look at me.

Robert Browning was born May 7, 1812, at Camberwell where the family lived up to his twenty-fifth year. Today long swallowed by London, it was then surrounded by open fields. Pleasant walks led to Dulwich, to London itself or, farther afield, through woods and country lanes.

Animals were a passion with Browning and he had an extraordinary influence over them. He amassed in his private collection owls and monkeys, magpies and hedgehogs, an eagle, and two large snakes. There was also a toad, left in its own habitat but coming out to greet him as well as a toad can, and following him about the garden. A story of a lion kicked to death by an ass upset him so much that he hid the book; and both his two years younger sister and he cried so bitterly over the story of a parrot, set free but dying of hunger and cold, that their parents had to change the end of the story before reading it to them again. It is a rather remarkable case of heredity through at least three generations, inherited from his mother who could even tame butterflies, passed on to his son who could safely persuade a large snake to remain draped around his model for Dryope. Among the reasons for the break-up of his son's marriage was the menagerie of beasts and overvocal birds at the Palazzo Rezzonico.

Park Honan in *Browning's Characters* has a fascinating chapter on Imagery, tracing among other forms the use made by Browning of animal imagery. Dr. Honan found in "Caliban's" 295 lines sixty-three references to animals. And while in this instance their chief effect was "that of picturing Caliban's animality generically," similar imagery is used by Browning in illustration of individual character. In *The Ring and the Book* Guido is likened to a wolf-in-sheepskin, scorpion, wildcat, dog and hawk, and many other beasts; Caponsacchi is "lamb-pure," "lion-brave"; Pompilia a white ermine, a fawn, a bird. And the lawyer Archangeli, only concerned with what brings himself nourishment and enjoyment ("for lambkins we must live") mentions more animals "in terms of food than in terms which relate them to the attributes of other characters."

A lion the Browning children had seen in captivity in the famous Royal Menagerie reappears in "The Glove," with black mane and glowing eyes.

> And you saw by the flash on his forehead,
> By the hope in those eyes wide and steady,
> He was leagues in the desert already,
> Driving the flocks up the mountain.

We can imagine the little Brownings as they listened to the roar from the cages and passed through the rooms of the Menagerie "painted with exotic scenes" to add to the drama. Not that Browning needed much help in creating drama for himself. His mother recorded the first real walk on which she took him, when he poured out descriptions of houses and other property owned by him with so much topographical detail that she remarked, "Why, sir, you are quite a geographer."

Born, would one say, to be a naturalist? But when only two years and three months old he had drawn a cottage—colored with currant juice, for paint on brushes was poisonous if sucked—which his father dated and treasured. Surely Robert's works would one day be hung on the walls of the great galleries. Long before the authorized age of fourteen, Mr. Browning took his son to the Dulwich collection—the one place in their neighborhood where any art existed, and the predecessor by twenty-four years of the National Gallery, which was opened only in August, 1838. There the boy would sit in front of a single picture for a good hour at a time. Would he then be an artist? Well, perhaps; but young as he was on his first effort at painting, he may have been yet younger when he rushed down from his bedroom to listen to his mother's playing and when she stopped sobbed out "Play, play." One of his own earliest memories, before his small hand could stretch an octave, was of her playing Avison's "Grand March in C."

"I was studying the grammar of music," he told a friend, "when most children are learning the multiplication table." And it was this musical bent that he was satisfying in part as he pulled himself up to the table before he could walk unaided and went round and round it improvising verses. Of the career of a musician he certainly thought in youth—but it was by no means the only thought. (One would love to know what prompted an entry in his journal at the age of seven "married two wives this morning.")

It is almost bewildering to see a boy so young dragged in so many different directions, for music and painting were not mere dilettante tastes; each was entered upon passionately. From infancy, says Mrs. Orr, he had "an unresting activity and a fiery temper. He clamoured for occupation from the moment he could speak." But later on this occupation might be one of pure mind and feeling—essentially contemplative. Besides the quiet gazing at a single picture, he could, says William Sharp, lie "beside a hedge or deep in meadow grasses and there give himself up so absolutely to the life of the moment that even shy birds would alight close by," would momentarily perch on the form lying so still beneath their wings.

This power of stillness and of gazing can only have grown gradually, for Mrs. Orr declares that it was for relief from his restless and endless activity that his parents sent him to his first school, an old-fashioned "dame" school. Reading and writing were taught there, but Browning's removal was soon requested. He was so far in advance of the other children that their parents were all threatening to withdraw them. He could read at four or five, and his sister told Mrs. Orr that when the other parents complained of favoritism on the teacher's part, she rather acidly retorted that if she could give their children "Master Browning's intellect," she could easily satisfy them.

The title "Master Browning" reminds us of the historical period, which should always be kept in mind if a biography is to be intelligible. One cannot be invariably exact, but a good soaking in novelists from Jane Austen to Dickens, George Eliot and Thackeray, and an attention to the biographies of the period will help, to say nothing of the memories we have who are old, of the still earlier memories of our great-aunts and uncles. (One of mine distinctly remembered the rejoicings after the battle of Waterloo.)

Waterloo was fought when Browning was three years old; enclosure of the common lands was on foot; the Industrial Revolution in full swing, the French Revolution a living and frightening memory to many Englishmen; the aristocracy still held all power; education was for the few and with its absence went the absence of democracy.

The social climate, perhaps especially in the middle-class dissenting world in which the Brownings lived, tended to be stuffy and this stuffiness produced curious reactions. Mrs. Orr tells the story of Browning as a very small boy taking a keen dislike to a visitor. She had spoken sneeringly of "Lovers' Lane" and he, with no least idea of what a lover was, decided to show her something worse by appearing before her as a devil. This meant—and Mrs. Orr refers to it with unnecessary delicacy—clad in nothing at all except a tail (How did he stick it on?) and making the most hideous face he could contrive. Instantly he was "snatched up" and carried away. As late as the beginning of this century

I have observed a child's bewilderment over the incomprehensible agitation of grownups. Mrs. Orr does not seem to realize the direct result in the odd sensitiveness Browning continued to feel about being seen in a state of even partial undress.

But this childhood is a record of sheer love and indulgence from both father and mother, and with the father especially an opening of windows on all sides of the mind. For above the urges we have noted—indeed often half creating those urges—were Mr. Browning and his books:

> My Father was a scholar and knew Greek.
> When I was five years old, I asked him once
> "What do you read about?"
> >   "The siege of Troy."
> "What is a siege and what is Troy?"
> >   Whereat
> He piled up chairs and tables for a town,
> Set me a-top for Priam, called our cat
> —Helen, enticed away from home (he said)
> By wicked Paris, who couched somewhere close
> Under the footstool, being cowardly,
> But whom—since she was worth the pains, poor puss—
> Towzer and Tray,—our dogs, the Atreidai,—sought
> By taking Troy to get possession of
> —Always when great Achilles ceased to sulk,
> (My pony in the stable)—forth would prance
> And put to flight Hector—our page-boy's self.
> This taught me who was who and what was what:
> So far I rightly understood the case
> At five years old: a huge delight it proved.

At five, a pure game; at eight the question: "How would you like to read yourself the tale?" introduced him to Pope and to a Greek primer at which he "duly drudged, / Grew fitter thus for what was promised next— / The very thing itself, the actual words."

In an early eighteenth-century edition of Dryden's translation of Juvenal, Browning wrote: "My father read the whole of the Dedicatory

Preface aloud to me as we took a walk together up Nunhead Hill, Surrey, when I was a boy." For the hundred pages of this preface the eager boy was keeping pace physically and mentally with an even more eager father. Entranced by pictures, friend of beasts and lover of nature, passionate addict of music—but books still came first. There was *Robinson Crusoe* in a first edition; but Quarles' *Emblems* and Wanley's *Wonders of the Little World* were his earliest favorites—rare books both, dating from the seventeenth century. It would be unthinkable to give either to a child today.

The introduction to *Emblems* in the edition of 1777 tells us that the book had been "generally known and well received for more than a century past." It is a work of intense piety with references to Augustine, Gregory, Jerome, Cyprian, Bernard, and many less-known writers of the early and medieval Christian periods. There are biblical allusions innumerable and a severe moral note throughout:

> Think ye the pageants of your hopes are able
> To stand secure when earth itself's unstable?
> Come dunghill worldlings . . .

Strange little woodcuts depict the soul as a child, Cupid and Mammon, devils with pitchforks, angels, et cetera. The devil is shown in the chariot of the world driving it fiercely, and again standing between the contestants in a game of bowls. And what, I wonder, could a child make of the lines about earth's motherhood?

> The ubrous breasts, when fully drawn, repast
> The thriving infant with their milky flood,
> But being overstrained return at last
> Unwholesome gulps composed of wine and blood.

The attraction of this book must have lain in the meter and the many new words. The rhythm varies; the vocabulary is a large one; there are Titans, spangled nymphs, Astrea, Cupid, Stygian night, and other fascinating puzzles. The classics were as familiar to Quarles (graduate of Cambridge, barrister, chronologer to the city of London) as they were quickly becoming to his young reader: "The busy mint / Of our laborious thoughts is ever going / And coining new desires."

Wanley's *Wonders of the Little World* sounds innocent enough, but it is much more astonishing for a child's reading. It shows "by many thousands of examples . . . what MAN hath been from the First Ages of the World to these Times in respect of his Body, Senses, Passions, Affections, His Virtues and Perfections, his Vices and Defects." All this and more is set out on the title page as "collected from the writings of the most approved Historians, Philosophers, Physicians, Philologists and others by Nathaniel Wanley Vicar of Trinity Parish in the City of Coventry, London 1678."

The many pages of contents are hair-raising. To summarize a few: Infants heard to cry in mother's womb . . . carried dead in womb for some years . . . petrified in womb. Persons who have made entrance to the world in a different manner from the rest of mankind.

Of giants, pygmies, dwarfs . . . Of persons who have renewed their age and grown young again. Of persons who have changed their sex.

Of the strange rigours in punishments used by several persons and nations. (This heading is implemented by stories of torture too horrible to do more than glance at.)

Of unusual diseases . . . "This world is a kind of great hospital . . ." Of unusual ways of dying . . . Of people supposed dead returning . . . Of strange ways murders are discovered.

Of force of imagination and phantasie. Of people seeing in the dark . . . Of varieties in senses: hearing, touch, taste (The story is here told of a man who ate two live mice which gnawed his vitals).

Of the Passion of Love . . . Of extreme Hatred . . . Of Fear . . . also of Panick Fears.

Had Browning read all the pages that followed one can imagine him as suffering from "panick fears." It is hard to tell; much passes over a child's consciousness which would pierce the adult's, but does it pierce later? And what did he make of the Passion of Jealousy, illustrated by a man who "caused himself to be gelded" so that he could be entirely certain, if his wife had a baby, that he was not its father? His biographers have found in Wanley the roots of a good many of Browning's poems; but till I held the huge volume in my hands I never guessed what else he was poring over in those mysterious years of childhood.

It was certainly in Wanley that he first read "The Pied Piper" and "The Cardinal and the Dog." The haunting notion in that poem—of evil in the shape of a black dog—occurred again in the story of the magician Agrippa from whom he borrowed the introduction to *Pauline*. Always keenly alive to the struggle between good and evil, alive too to the dangers of the occult, he found in Wanley the character of Paracelsus—chosen for his second great poem. The story in *The Ring and the Book* of Pope Stephen feeding to the fish the fingers of his dead predecessor, the very name of a "garden fancy" *Schnafnaburgensis* (which means simply a native of Aschafenburg), were dropped by Wanley into a memory which, as Browning himself once said, lost nothing committed to it except "names and the battle of Waterloo." And we can scarcely doubt the book's share in awakening Browning's lifelong interest in abnormal psychology.

But this library of his father's fed also tastes that with many boys would have inhibited learning—music and painting. Avison's book on musical expression set on foot a whole train of thought about shifting tastes in music. How early, I wonder, did John Relfe, "musician in ordinary to the King" become "Master of mine, learned, redoubtable"? He lived at Camberwell, and taught Browning musical theory—and this introduced yet more books. For Relfe had written a learned *Principles of Harmony* and other works through which Browning learned to write accompaniments, later destroyed by him, but above all his musical poems about music: "A Toccata of Galuppi's" and "Abt Vogler."

Then there was Gerard de Lairesse, the painter, on the flyleaf of whose book *The Art of Painting in all its Branches*, Browning wrote: "I read this book more often and with greater delight when I was a child than any other: and still remember the main of it most gratefully for the good I seem to have got from the prints and the wonderful text." We owe to the Griffin-Minchin biography and to De Vane's work on Browning's *Parleyings* a realization of how important were these books, and the others there discussed, to Browning's development. This is in part the answer to a question that fascinated Chesterton: Why did he so frequently choose unimportant or forgotten people to write about? Partly perhaps from a democracy which knew that no man is unimpor-

B*

tant; but chiefly because he had met these people at the impressionable age of earliest encounters.

The *Biographie Universelle* in fifty volumes was also on his father's shelves and here were garnered more facts about Paracelsus, the subject of his proposed tragedy "Narses," ideas for *King Victor and King Charles* and for *The Return of the Druses*. "One would almost surmise," says Griffin, "that he had read its fifty volumes through."

Miserably undated as this childhood is, we only learn that the days of fullest absorption and happiest occupation were rudely curtailed when Browning became, at eight or nine, a weekly boarder in a school of which the junior part was taught by the Misses Ready and the senior by their brother the Reverend Thomas Ready.

Alfred Domett, later one of Browning's closest friends, had two older brothers who were his schoolfellows, and one of them remembered "young Browning in a pinafore of brown Holland such as small boys used to wear in those days." Six years older than Browning, he recalled how they "used to pit him against much older and bigger boys in a chaffing match to amuse themselves with the little bright-eyed fellow's readiness and acuteness of repartee."

But to Browning the weekly boarding spelt undiluted misery. On hearing the decree, he chose, says Mrs. Orr, a leaden cistern in the school for his "place of burial." It had on it a raised image of a face. He imagined this face as his epitaph, passing his hands over it again and again and chanting, "In memory of unhappy Browning." Time softened the pain of the endless weekly exile, but not the intense dislike of the school. At first the big boys bullied him, he later told Domett, but the thing went much deeper than that. The teachers were kind enough, and he remembered with shame having written verses in praise of the headmaster which enabled him to get away with many small tricks. On Prize Day, although he tells us he never won a prize—a difficult feat says Mrs. Orr, so many were given—he was chosen to recite. But he probably reserved his energies for the weekend and the holidays. It would be characteristic if he chose deliberately not to compete—it is likely enough that he had no equals with whom to compete: what other

boy of eight was reading Pope's *Iliad* and beginning to learn Greek?
Who might be reading the *Biographie Universelle?* How many of them
had a father knowing Greek, Latin, French, Spanish, Italian, and Hebrew and taking very good care to pass on his learning to his children?

And how many books did they own? How many had they read?
Even an ordinary child going from an immensely cultured home to a
second-rate school detests and despises it. Let the masters be as kind as
they will, it does not make up for mediocrity. Browning stated his com-
plaint to Domett quite simply, "he says they taught him nothing there."
Hearing of a "heavy" sermon preached by Thomas Ready, seven years
after he had left school, Browning improvised

> A *heavy* sermon—sure the error's great
> For not a word Tom utters has its weight.

Browning was in fact suffering from the change described by Chesterton when instead of learning—such joy at home—he was being
taught by someone he did not know something that he did not want to
know.

But at some date in his school life came a curious interlude.

In Sotheby's catalogue of the sale of Browning material in 1913,
Lot 1047, is a two-volume edition of the plays of Nicholas Rowe with
Elizabeth Barrett's signature in each volume, and on a flyleaf of Volume I "Robert Browning (who at school revived 'The Royal Convert'
and acted Aribert therein etc.)"

Nicholas Rowe (1674–1718), a friend of Pope, who called him a
delightful companion often "drinking and drolling" late into the night,
wrote many plays in which the leading actors of the day appeared. "He
seldom pierces the breast," said Johnson, "but he always delights the ear
and often improves the understanding." *The Royal Convert* was first
staged in 1707.

If the play was put on without cuts, Browning had an immense
part to learn—but at twelve or fourteen the memory is at its best. Aribert is the brother of Hengist, king of Kent, son of that Hengist who
first invaded Britain. He is secretly married to a British Christian,
Ethelinda, and has himself become a Christian. King Hengist is be-

trothed to Rodogune, a Saxon princess. But unfortunately he has fallen
in love with Ethelinda, while Rodogune is passionately enamored of
Aribert.

Through five acts of noble sentiments, threats, and denunciations
a double theme is played: religion and love. Aribert, prepared "To
scorn / And trample on their ignominious altars" is threatened by his
brother:

> "'Tis well Sir! Impious boy!
>   One to the priests."
> (*Exit a Gent*)
> "Bid 'em be swift and dress their bloody altars!"
> (*The Priests bind Aribert, and lead him to the altar, while
> the solemn musick is playing.*)

The young Christian pair exchange pages of noble sentiments about
the superiority of the heaven for which they are bound, interspersed
with occasional sighs for a little happiness on earth. It looks as though,
if Aribert would give up Ethelinda to his brother and turn to Rodogune,
their religion could be forgiven them. But Aribert asks his brother the
meaning of

> This frantick, wild demand? What should I yield,
> Give up my love, my wife, my Ethelinda
> To an incestuous brother's dire embrace?

Of course it all ends well—but the plot and the language remind
one that even the pious nonconformist world of that date was not yet
Victorianized.

Clearly this "revival" was a regular school play, possibly the finale
to Browning's five or six years in the school. We can imagine the scene
in Belloc's words:

> The upper school had combed and oiled their hair,
> And all the parents of the boys were there

to witness young Browning, to listen to stilted denunciations of pagan-
ism and passionate proclamations of a readiness for martyrdom, and an

exaltation of Britannia, with Saxon, Celt, and Roman welded into one triumphant ruler of the waves.

The endless soliloquies and speeches may well have later affected adversely Browning's own plays; his considerable acting powers probably showed themselves, but it may be that the false note struck in the noble speeches of Aribert were, with other elements in the boy's small world, preparing him for the disruptive influence two years later of his introduction to the poet Shelley.

A memory with which Browning made even his pious mother laugh reluctantly, had been that of the Misses Ready drilling the smaller boys in brushing their hair to the accompaniment of Dr. Watts' hymns; Browning would illustrate "with voice and gesture the ferocious emphasis with which the brush would swoop down in the accentuated syllables":

> Lord 'tis a pleasant thing to stand
> In gardens planted by Thy hand. . . .
> Fools never raise their thoughts so high,
> Like *brutes* they live, like BRUTES they die.

But the fact of the mother's reluctance to laugh poses another question: In all the delights of learning—to which were added as the years went on dancing lessons, fencing lessons, riding lessons—was there one supremely irksome element, to feel which irksome was to feel wicked: religion?

As a small child Browning describes himself as "passionately religious." Preaching once to his even smaller sister, he reduced her to tears, and then, turning, said to an imaginary official, "Pew opener, remove that child." He read the Bible, probably with the interest that he gave to every book. But the chapel to which Congregationalists or other Nonconformists would repair depended far too much on the abilities of the incumbent of the moment. Few men can pray with thoughts and words suited for other minds. And Browning had certainly been unfortunate in the ministers of his earlier life. Speaking of one of them, the Reverend George Clayton, another minister, Edward White, said he felt impelled as a boy to gnaw the pew top as he listened to lengthy "prayers which were newspapers, entering into every particular of births, marriages and deaths and foreign travel, of deacons and the like." Clayton was said to be of "the old school" and "to have stiffened and starched" those who sat under him. Edward White's brother relates how Browning, stationed with his parents in the front of the gallery, "did not care to conceal his something more than indifference to the ministrations to which he listened weekly, and which once brought down upon him a rebuke from the Pastor in open Church!"

No better than George Clayton and George Ready was the Reverend Mr. Irons, to whose chapel the Browning family chiefly repaired— to be "ironed" as some of their friends put it. Domett recalls in his diary going up Camberwell Grove to test how far off he could hear "Mr. Irons bawling out his sermon." From a distance he could clearly hear the words, "I am very sorry to say it, beloved brethren, but it is an undoubted fact that Roman Catholic and midnight assassin are synonymous terms."

According to "Christmas-Eve" a sermon might have ten headings, and it may have been Browning's own boyhood that evoked the picture of how, whatever their intrinsic value,

> . . . Such truths looked false to your eyes,
> With his provings and parallels twisted and twined,
> Till how could you know them, grown double their size
> In the natural fog of the good man's mind, . . .
>   The zeal was good and the aspiration;
> And yet, and yet, yet, fifty times over,
>   Pharaoh received no demonstration,
> By his Baker's dream of Baskets Three,
> Of the doctrine of the Trinity,—
> Although, as our preacher thus embellished it,
> Apparently his hearers relished it.

Religion then had begun to be weariness, as so often in adolescence, and in Browning's case with considerable reason. Like school it was a waste of the hours he longed to have—for everything.

At thirteen Browning was still at the Ready school; was, one supposes, still taken to church on Sundays to be starched or ironed, but there was possible a good deal of that absence of mind which has been defined as presence of mind on something else.

That his biographers should rejoice over the destruction of *Incondita*, written when he was twelve or thirteen, is bewildering. The poems could not be other than immature, but his was a fascinating and pregnant immaturity. How much went into these verses of flowers and birds, of music and vivid pictures—of Men and Women? Were there any of the horrors of Wanley's *Little World?* As Clayton or Irons droned on, were other verses made in his mind—to emerge later in his lyrics? Were pictures formed for "The Flight of the Duchess" as he walked past the gypsy camps in Dulwich wood? For he would, says William Sharp, his earliest biographer, "join company with any tramps, gypsies or other wayfarers."

There were fairs at Camberwell and Greenwich and at Peckham just opposite Mr. Ready's school. "For three days each summer," writes Mr. Hall Griffin, "the Walworth Road from Camberwell gate to the village green—a goodly mile—was aglow after sunset with candles beneath coloured shades on the road-side stalls." There was the canvas-covered avenue with its gingerbread booths, there was music and dancing . . . there was the ever-popular Richardson's Theatre—"appreciated, it is said, by the poet in his younger days."

In our era of mass illumination one longs sometimes for the more subdued glow of the candles throwing up the color of their shades or sparkling with the brilliants of their chandeliers—made brighter by the surrounding darkness, today totally excluded.

Much of these younger days of Browning's must have found their echo in poems so greatly admired by the boy's father that he sought a publisher for them—but in vain. *Incondita* he had called them, for his mind was still like the beginnings of creation not yet formed and ordered, but present also was the beginning of the light that would become sun, moon, and stars as the spirit of God moved over the waters.

Two sisters, Eliza and Sarah Flower, are mixed up with the story of *Incondita* and much speculation has been poured out over Browning's feelings toward them. Was he in love with either or both? And if so at what date? For while he knew them both from early childhood, they were respectively nine and seven years older than he was and from the age of sixteen to that of twenty he appears to have lost sight of them. Browning's first two biographers knew him personally—Mrs. Orr by far the better—both in later life. Sharp suggests that he had "more than one episode of the heart." Mrs. Orr is convinced that, *if* Browning was ever in love before he met Elizabeth, it was with Eliza Flower—and of course such a love in a precocious adolescent between the age of twelve and sixteen is not at all improbable. After that the break of four years seems to have been complete. We know so little. Yet so much has been written about all this, from Hovelaque's treatment of Browning's youth —dwelling especially on *Pauline, Paracelsus* and *Sordello* and opting for a Browning fascinated by both sisters, but chiefly the younger—to Mrs. Miller's skilful reconstruction of the Flower and Fox families, at the later date when Browning was a fairly frequent visitor but much wrapped up in his own poetical career.

Eliza and Sarah Flower were daughters of the then famous Benjamin Flower, editor of *The Cambridge Intelligencer*. Most shamefully had he been imprisoned and fined for breach of privilege, in a prosecution brought by the House of Lords for a comment on the political inconsistency of a bishop. A young schoolmistress Eliza Gould, given the choice between abandoning *The Cambridge Intelligencer* or her job, unhesitatingly left her pupils and repaired to Newgate where she found Flower and "bestowed her heart on the spot and her hand upon his release." She had died in 1810 and Benjamin had tried to be both father and mother to the girls, bringing them up in an atmosphere of idealism and poetry rather than of the strict attention to needlework and household management then deemed the chief essential in a girl's education. Harriet Martineau, who had emerged from her own subjection to this, who lived in the same world, political and social, is said to have painted their portraits both in *Deerbrook* and in *Five Years of Youth or Sense and Sentiment*.

"When the sisters sat in the balcony their voices would ring out clear and sweet by the hour together." To this singing Browning may have listened with renewal of the transport his mother's playing brought in babyhood: "I knew the Flowers when I was five or six years old," he wrote many years later, "earlier I do think. When I got older, perhaps at twelve or thirteen, I wrote a book of verses which Eliza read and wrote to me about." Eliza made a copy for herself and showed it to William Fox—"which verses," says Browning, "he praised not a little, which comforted me not a little." Nonetheless "in a few months . . . I saw the proper way, and put my blessed poems in the fire."[2]

Fox, who had come to know the Flowers the previous year on a tour in Scotland, was in February, 1824, opening a new Unitarian Chapel in South Place Finsbury. Brought up, as he put it, on "the sour milk of Calvinism," on a poor Norfolk farm where his father had suffered under the iniquitous game laws—being prosecuted for killing a pheasant which was devouring his grain—William Fox himself began life as a bank clerk, went on to the ministry, and became finally a publicist and politician. He never forgot his origins and what they had taught him, and during his campaign against the Corn Laws (which should, Miss Martineau said, be described more clearly in terms of the bread they were keeping from the poor) he signed himself "The Norwich Weaver Boy." But at this date Fox was primarily a minister. He had, his biographer says, "a miraculous gift of preaching," not unhelped by his piercing eyes and his melodious voice. He was regarded as a "safe man," who made no attempt to arouse in his congregation "unseemly ecstasy." (Carlyle described him as having "a tendency to pot-belly and snuffiness.") The Flower sisters were producing hymns for the Chapel—Sarah writing the verses and Eliza supplying the music. Untrained though Eliza was, her reputation became a high one, and Browning wrote twenty years later: "I put it apart from all other English music I know, and fully believe it is the music we have all waited for."

That Browning should first have striven for the publication of *Incondita* and so soon afterward destroyed it is surely not unconnected with the fact that in the year 1826 he first read a volume of Shelley's verse.

In *Browning and Shelley: A Myth and Some Facts*, Frederick Pottle tells the fascinating story of his own search for this volume, long supposed to have been a pirated edition of *Queen Mab,* but in fact containing almost all else. "It is," he writes, "a little duodecimo volume bound in light drab boards. . . . The back is missing and the covers have been carefully stitched in again with coarse linen thread—by Browning's mother? I hope so." Inside the cover is written: "This book was given to me, probably as soon as published, by my cousin J. S. The foolish markings, and still more foolish scribblings show the impression made on a boy by this first specimen of Shelley's poetry. June 2nd 1878 'O World, O Life, O Time.'"

A facsimile page shows us how Browning worked at effacing most of the "foolish scribblings" of his fourteen-year-old frenzy of admiration. His mother procured for him the poems of Keats, and the rest of Shelley —almost certainly including *Queen Mab,* which made him a vegetarian. Pottle quotes: "No longer now / He slays the lamb that looks him in the face." But it was poetry that transfigured the world of boyhood's imagination, and Keats with Shelley became embodied for Browning in two nightingales that still sang in the gardens of Camberwell.

For long it was supposed that nothing of *Incondita* remained. Both Flower sisters died of tuberculosis (or consumption as it was then called) in early middle age and Browning recovered and destroyed the copy made by Eliza. But Sarah too had been busy copying, and two poems of some length survived and can be read today in Browning's collected works: "The First-Born of Egypt" and "The Dance of Death." For a boy of his age they are almost as remarkable as Sarah thought them and, while certainly imitating Byron, show also the influence of his Bible reading, of Wanley's gloomy pages—and it may well be of some boyhood experience of his own. For although it would be many years before the Flower sisters died, hardly a family at that date went untouched by fever or consumption. Of nine children often five, four, or fewer became adults. Typhoid, cholera, famine, and rabies dispute in one poem their right to be crowned lord of death—while the last of Egypt's ten plagues pictures the horror of a night which begins with "sunset glories flooding the pale clouds / With liquid gold," and ends

with the death of each family's first-born, from Pharaoh's heir to the
child in "poverty's lone hut"—as

> . . . each one owned
> In silence the dread majesty—the might
> Of Israel's God, whose red hand had avenged
> His servants' cause so fearfully.

Curious topics to be chosen by the boy who in manhood would be
unthinkingly dismissed as a facile optimist. Curious, too, that Browning on recovering these poems might have thrown them also into the
fire—but did not. Certainly as he grew older he grew more interested
in his own past, and it may be he felt on seeing them again that they
were not, for a boy, such poor stuff as he had remembered.

3 Pauline

Amid his wild-wood sights he lived alone.
As if the poppy felt with him! Though he
Partook the poppy's red effrontery
Till Autumn spoilt their fleering quite with rain.

"SORDELLO"

Browning's education from the age of fourteen was carried on
at home apart from a brief attendance at the new London University
during its opening term. His abrupt return thence is by Professor
Saintsbury deemed the sheerest of blessings: to those two terms he
chooses to attribute Browning's strange usages in Greek nomenclature
. . . Alcestis would just be Alkestis . . . but, "nymph," he complained,
was "numph" and "psyche" presumably "psuche."

London University was a new and bold experiment, but there can
be little doubt that Browning would have gained something from any
university. He was beginning to outgrow his father's tutelage and had
little companionship, least of all companionship of the intellect.

There were his Silverthorne cousins, reputed as "wild lads," with
one of whom, James, he shared a love of music and a passionate enthusiasm for the theater. They would walk from Camberwell to Richmond
to watch Edmund Kean—one such occasion being commemorated in
Pauline, obscurely enough to be missed by John Stuart Mill. James
was the one witness present at Browning's wedding, and in his memory
was written "May and Death." There was his young half-uncle, Reuben. There were the two Dowson brothers to one of whom, Christopher,

is addressed a very early letter of Browning's (1830): he married Mary Domett, whose brother Alfred became one of the poet's closest friends. Such scattered friendships are no real substitute for a public school or university relationship. They did gradually coalesce, around an eccentric Captain Pritchard, into a group calling themselves The Set or The Convivialists, but for some years Browning was altogether more lonely than was healthy for mind and body.

A curious problem existed for folk like the Brownings in the England of that day. The aristocracy, the gentry, had a certain education and society as of right; the Norwich Weaver Boy had won it by main force. But a boy in the comfortable middle class who, Nonconformist in religion, could not go to Oxford or Cambridge, had no great incentive to struggle for entry into a world he did not know when he had outgrown his own.

Perhaps Cerutti, Browning's Italian tutor, a political exile, introduced him in imagination to the country which he was to call later his university. "The Italian in England" might have been written after years of residence in Italy; surely friendship with a man who had *known* was its chief inspiration. Working under Relfe on the theory, and under his other teacher on the practice, of music, Browning wrote accompaniments which he later destroyed.

But much was postponed in his development during these years, much that should have flowered was half frosted. It is strange, Mrs. Orr comments, how Shelley established himself in Browning's imagination both as a maligned and persecuted man and as a "lofty spirit, one dwelling in the communion of higher things," but perhaps not as inconsistent as she felt it that the influence was a subversive one. For Browning was also reading Voltaire—and he was very ready to be subverted. Atheism was the natural if not really the logical outcome of a course of Ready, Clayton, and Irons. And most adolescents are ready for rebellion.

Browning's vegetarianism lasted for about two years till the weakening of his eyesight persuaded him back to normal food; but before being cured himself, Browning had affected Sarah Flower with his religious disquiet. Feeling that she could not communicate with her father, Sarah wrote to William Fox "a regular confession of faith, or

rather the want of it . . . the heinous sin of unbelief. . . ." She still believed in God, but "I would fain go to my Bible as I used to—but I cannot. The cloud has come over me gradually, and I did not discover the
darkness in which my soul was shrouded until, in seeking to give light
to others, my own gloomy state became too settled to admit of doubt.
It was in answering Robert Browning that my mind refused to bring
forward argument, turned recreant and sided with the enemy."

At home it was, said Browning's sister, the least amiable period of
his life. Probably the two years on bread and potatoes damaged other
things besides his eyesight, and the spiritual struggle—to be revealed in
Pauline—was showing in daily life. He himself never spoke of this
time except in words of strong self-condemnation. Sarah Flower, after
recovering from her "gloomy state," wrote one of the best-known hymns
in the English language: "Nearer, My God, to Thee."

Many years later Browning, writing to Julia Wedgwood, analyzed
what he believed from his own experience to be the common attitude
of the young toward the religious teaching given to them—an undoubt-
ing acceptance combined with a "practical atheism, . . . they have not
a natural need for what you artificially give them . . ." Children have
what to a child appear "better ways of their own for righting matters:
whereas the real instinct is developed with mature years, and, then only,
substitutes itself for the previous motives which are losing their virtue
of impelling or repressing one—hence the new birth: while this life
suffices, I don't see that another incentive to push on through its insufficiency, in the shape of a conceived possibility of a life beyond, is ever
given us."

When in 1864 he speaks of "thirty-five years ago," it would seem
to be not so much the child as the sixteen- or seventeen-year-old boy to
whom he refers as "the wise person of my perfect remembrance and
particular dislike."

Part of this self-reproach was probably over his behavior in leaving
London University so abruptly. He was only sixteen when he went
there. He was, according to his father, immensely keen to go, and his
education at home had been strong in Latin and Greek. Had he been
going to Oxford, meeting men from Eton and Winchester, it would

have been very different. But I think we can be fairly certain that in London the professors, however able, would have been obliged to gear their classes to students from schools similar to the one where Browning had raged with boredom. He might well have been learning again what his father had already taught him!

Mr. Browning had entered his son only for Classics and German, and had taken lodgings for him in the college neighborhood. After one term Browning gave up both the early-morning German class and the lodgings. At the end of the second term he threw up the whole thing, his father thus incurring the loss of £100 with which he had become a foundation member of the University.

No explanation has ever been given. Browning at that date, as he later said, did only that which seemed good to him in his own eyes.[1] He was a spoiled only son with adoring parents, who watched him in bewilderment, and it probably did not console them greatly to find that he was reading and digesting the whole of Johnson's Dictionary. William Sharp casts a vivid light on how a youthful poet is supposed to act when he describes Browning in what was still the countryside, walking about, his hat in his left hand, waving his right, declaiming biblical poetry. His hair was waving in the wind and he was quite oblivious to a following of small children. Many years la er Sharp heard Browning say, in reply to the remark that only in Italy did romance still remain: "Ah well, I should like to include poor old C mberwell."

This was the time when even Mrs. Orr calls him wild, and Sharp says "he would join company with any tramps, gypsies or other wayfarers." The fair at Camberwell with its crowds and its music, the lights in the surrounding blackness, the sudden glimpses of wild loveliness perhaps meant more to the youth of sixteen than to the boy of twelve. Was Browning's poem more than forty years later the re-creation of earlier meetings with a more glamorous Fifine?[2]

We know almost nothing about these years of genius on the boil, of the confusions of adolescence, and the coming of manhood.

Browning was only twenty years younger than Shelley and was subjected to many of the same influences. Shelley before him had studied Paracelsus and was familiar with the literature of the occult.

Both he and Browning attended medical lectures. And Shelley's mottoes to *Queen Mab* in Latin, Greek, and French, with long notes in all three, gave Browning a pattern which he followed in *Pauline,* published in March, 1833, just before his twenty-first birthday: "an account," says William De Vane (in the *Handbook*), "of his victory over the forces of doubt, skepticism and self-centeredness, and his winning to faith, hope and love . . . thoroughly autobiographical."

Never was a poem addressed to a woman who remains as unreal as this one, despite the French note at the end in which she herself speaks. She is nothing except the patient listener to the story of a boy's wanderings, conflicts, aberrations, and aspirations. "If she *existed* and loved him," said John Stuart Mill, "he treats her most ungenerously and unfeelingly." But Mill saw Pauline as "evidently a mere phantom," a recipient of the poet's self-revelation.

It is not surprising, one critic commented, that Pauline should have advised him to destroy a poem in which she, nominally its object, bore so minute a part. But Pauline's doubts as to whether or not the poem ought to be destroyed were, of course, Browning's own—and in astonishingly fluent French this boy was writing, under Pauline's name, a criticism of his own work that went deeper than that of Mill or of any other outside commentator.

Already his intellect was what Herford would later describe as "God intoxicated," and the poem is a confession to the God to whom he is returning. E. I. Watkin in *Poets and Mystics* sees Browning in "Christmas-Eve" as expressing a true mystical experience, and so perhaps is he in *Pauline:* a direct recognition of reality—of the supreme Reality—by a man's whole nature, not step by step in what he calls "reason's pedantry," but with a wide opening of the eyes of the mind, an *intense reception* of their vision.

> And what is that I hunger for but God?
>
> My God, my God, let me for once look on thee
> As though nought else existed, we alone!
> And as creation crumbles, my soul's spark
> Expands till I can say,—Even from myself

I need thee and I feel thee and I love thee.
I do not plead my rapture in thy works
For love of thee, nor that I feel as one
Who cannot die: but there is that in me
Which turns to thee, which loves or which should love.

The last two lines summarize what has recently come to be called the "betrayal" of Shelley. In what lay the betrayal? Not certainly in the abandonment of atheism. As Mrs. Miller notes (p. 19), "the least significant as well as the least durable result of his passionate preoccupation [with Shelley] was the adolescent atheism and vegetarianism which for a time accompanied it." What many critics agree with her in seeing is a rejection by Browning of "the fearless spiritual independence of Shelley," which the boy had recognized as measuring "the very nature of integrity itself." And Browning, it is felt, admits it with the words "I flung all honour from my soul."

But in *Pauline* these words, addressed as a confession to Shelley, have no reference whatever to a rejection of "spiritual independence." He is speaking of the wickedness into which he had fallen:

> I lost myself
> In deeds for which remorse were vain, as for
> The wanderings of delirious dream; yet thence
> Came cunning, envy, falsehood . . .

The effect of this stage of life is still with him in "sin and lust and pride." He cries out, "Why have I girt myself with this hell dress? / Why have I laboured to put out my life?"

Chesterton saw in the poem only the common experience of youth, which to every boy seems a secret horror of his own. Half imagination perhaps? A yielding to the mysterious promptings of sex? At that date especially this would have involved him in "falsehood and cunning"— to say nothing of "envy"!

Apart from the phantom Pauline, two persons are addressed in the course of the poem, God and Shelley, each with intense devotion. To God there are longer passages like the one just quoted, and sudden flashes:

> Air, air, fresh life-blood, thin and searching air,
> The clear, dear breath of God that loveth us . . .

And Shelley is there—*not as a past ideal betrayed, but as a present inspiration*, linked with the God to whom Browning has returned. The poem's final paragraph is addressed to him "Sun-treader, I believe in God and truth/ And love." Yet "I would lean on thee/ Thou must be ever with me." Earlier in the poem he has said "Thou art still for me as thou hast been." Clearly, whatever he felt at fourteen, he does not at twenty regard atheism as of Shelley's essence.

I have never seen a discussion of the relation between *Pauline* and the Dramatic Monologues of Browning's later writing. Before *Paracelsus,* and *Sordello,* it is a clear move toward them, as toward that "poem R. B." which he hoped one day to write. Indeed *Pauline* is "R. B. aetat.* 20" (which may be one of the reasons for his profound dislike of it).

Shelley's effect on him was first the feeling of "a key to a new world":

> I was vowed to liberty
> Men were to be as gods and earth as heaven . . .

He did not stay in the "bliss" of this, not because (as Mrs. Miller thinks) it was in conflict with "the standard of an all-too-tenderly loved mother"—*she is one person we do not find in the poem*—but because, "looking on real life/ The life all new to me," he found that men were not like that, earth not like that.

It is not always easy to follow the struggle as he tells it. One truth emerges which he learned in the course of it—that logic is not man's sole guide, or profoundest guide, to reality; there is intuition, there is love. This has been seen as a degradation of reason, with the consequence that he was deliberately "delivering falsely or imperfectly the message with which he had been entrusted." Seen thus it has been given as the reason for his "life-long obsession with the psychology of the charlatan, the quack." But thus to see it shows an unawareness of common experience at one end and of Existentialism at the other. Life *is* larger than logic. Poetry must utter the response to reality of the whole man; poet or philosopher must not stop short because bare intellect can go no further.

Twenty years later, in the period of his richest thought, Browning wrote an introduction to what proved some spurious letters of Shelley's. Men, he said, should not "confound, any more than God confounds, with genuine infidelity and an atheism of the heart, those passionate impatient struggles of a boy towards truth and love. . . . Crude convictions of boyhood, conveyed in imperfect and unapt forms of speech— for such things all boys have been pardoned. They are growing pains accompanied by temporary distortion of soul also."

How much was this an apologia for Shelley, how much for himself? Browning at twenty was again a Christian—but not a Christian of the Irons-Clayton-Ready school.

This recoil from his immediate past, this return to reality, could not work its cure in an instant. Many years must pass, shocks be experienced, a man's work done. But *Pauline* is of interest for several reasons: It looks back and forward. We see in it the boyhood out of which Browning has passed, the adolescence through which he is passing, wild confused ambitions, a sense of power and of beauty. It expresses all that the title *Incondita* claimed for his earlier verse. It should be studied by all who desire to understand Browning—more clearly than he understood himself.[3]

Against the background of chintz curtains, rose-gardens, much tenderness, much dull respectability, an incredibly varied library, and deadly sermons, the young poet was fighting the wild beasts of his imagination, oblivious of the world around, awakening suddenly when the work was done to the need of getting it known. His whole being was set on his poem and its success when he wrote the letter that introduced him once again to William Fox.

Describing himself as "an oddish sort of boy" whom Fox may perhaps remember, he recalls that he had been "at that time a sayer of verse and a doer of it, whose doing you had a little previously commended after a fashion," at a time when such commendation was "more thought of than all the gun, drum and trumpet of praise would be now" (at the age of twenty!)

This same boy, having heard of Fox as a contributor to the *Westminster*, ventures to send him "a free and easy sort of thing which he wrote some months ago 'on one leg' . . . should it be found too insignificant for cutting up, I shall no less remain, dear Sir,

Your most obedient servant
R. B."

Browning's feeling, whatever it was, for Eliza Flower had had time to subside. And, adds Mrs. Orr with circumspect Victorianism, "her affections were probably engaged." It was certainly an unusual situation. Benjamin Flower had died in 1829 and had left Fox as trustee and guardian to the two girls, already women. This was less surprising at a period when the "gentler sex" were supposed incapable of managing their own affairs, but Fox was only forty-six, married and with children of his own. Mrs. Fox, a faded and ineffectual woman, was watching helplessly the growth of a love between her husband and Eliza. (She herself was also Eliza and so was their daughter. Fox always called Eliza Flower "Lizzie.")

By his account to his mother there had never been a great deal of affection on his side and no effort on his wife's to shoulder her share of a rather heavy burden. Florance, the eldest son, was deaf and dumb. Fox had to cope to a great extent with the children, besides preaching, much lecturing and writing. From about 1826 he had been editing the *Monthly Repository* (which in 1831 he bought) and endeavoring to transform it into an intellectual organ for the Unitarian body and beyond it.[4]

It may well have been a relief to him to throw himself into the congenial task of discovering a new poet. He had recognized Tennyson ahead of the world—and now, *Pauline*, "though evidently a hasty and imperfect sketch, has truth and life in it, which gave us the thrill, and laid hold of us with the power, the sensation of which has never yet failed us as a test of genius."

Fox recognized that much was left for the future to unveil: "Archimedes in the bath had many particulars to settle . . . but he first gave a glorious leap—and shouted *Eureka!*"

Dr. Lounsbury in *The Early Literary Career of Robert Browning* has pointed out what a drug on the market poetry was at that date and how impossible it was to launch with the public a new poet however great. But he notes that Browning later always depicted his fate with the critics as worse than it was. He did now have a cordial mention in the *Athenaeum* which indicated the general literary despondency of the moment: "The day is past for either fee or fame in the service of the muse; but, to one who sings so naturally, poetry must be as easy as music to the bird, and no doubt it has a solace all its own."

Browning was intensely grateful to Fox, who added to his own tribute the good intention of getting a review from John Stuart Mill, a great friend of his, whose emotional situation with Harriet Taylor bore a strangely close resemblance to his own.

Harriet Taylor, friend also of the Flowers, had been to all appearances happily married to a rather dull, good-natured merchant, when she sought the advice of her minister, Mr. Fox, on some philosophical problems. He, strangely enough, suggested his young friend, John Stuart Mill, as a good counselor. Mill was at the moment thinking of marriage and it was said, according to his biographer, that "he thought of Eliza Flower, an elfin creature, musical and poetic." But at a first visit to the Taylor house he fell in love with Harriet, whose closest friend and confidante was Eliza.

"We dined," says Carlyle, "with Mrs. (Platonica) Taylor and the Unitarian Fox one day, and the husband." But "Mrs. Taylor herself did not yield unmixed satisfaction, I think, or receive it." She was, he said, "pale, passionate and sad looking." Jane Carlyle felt she "could really love 'Harriet' if it were safe and she were willing; but she is a dangerous woman and engrossed with a dangerous passion."

In both these relationships Mill-Harriet and Fox-Eliza the lovers proclaimed their innocence, but this was to give a special meaning to the term. One feels it strongly with Mill and his Harriet as she played cat and mouse with her husband, unwilling to relinquish him, yet determined to keep Mill. She had at first tried to hold the friendship on an intellectual level only, but felt, she soon claimed, a duty to humanity as well as to her family: Mill *needed* her affection. But the poor man surely needed either less or a great deal more, and Carlyle's description of him gives promise of a vitality later drained out of "the saint of rationalism," leaving him a somewhat dry and desiccated figure. He was, says Carlyle, "slender, rather tall and elegant . . . earnestly smiling eyes, modest, remarkably gifted with precision of utterance, enthusiastic yet lucid, calm."

Fox, settling an income on his wife, moved in 1834 into another house where he lived with Eliza Flower and two of his own children, joining forces with Sarah now married to William Adams. The third Fox child remained with his mother. Harriet Martineau and other friends were in no way placated by the protestations of innocence either of Eliza and Fox or of Mrs. Taylor and Mill. Unitarians and rationalists were at that date especially eager to show that intellectual emancipation did not mean a lower moral standard than that of Christians. Miss Martineau's anger indirectly affected Browning, for the sub-editor of Mill's periodical had met him at her house. So Mill refused later to review *Sordello*. But at this earlier date he set himself to read and review the anonymous *Pauline*.

Counted by years Mill was only six ahead of Browning, but in experience the gap would be hard to measure. Browning's father had made the learning of letters and all other beginnings within a child's scope a delightful game. But Mill, taught by a stern self-made father to read English at two, Greek at five, was next set to instruct his younger brothers and sisters. "I never was a boy," he told Caroline Fox,[5] "never played at cricket. It is better to let Nature have her own way." He was at twenty-six advanced in his profession, leader of a group of young radicals and a figure notable enough to have attracted strongly that searcher out of disciples, the prophet Carlyle. To him Mill confessed that, despite—or perhaps because of—his stern father's stern religion, he himself could not believe in God. Carlyle replied, "Patience, patience, time will do wonders for us." Patience Mill had, and although it never achieved this particular end, it did make him do with immense thoroughness any job he undertook.

Pauline, commented Saintsbury many years later, owes much to Shelley, but is yet instinct with Browning's own genius. This Mill saw only in flashes; the copy annotated by him shows that he sought a second opinion: "The passages [he wrote] where the meaning is so imperfectly expressed as not to be easily understood will be marked 'X.'" Another hand is to be seen in the "beautiful" and "most beautiful" written here and there. But quite unmistakably in Mill's own hand are several acknowledgements of poetic power. After one regret over obscurity, he adds "the meaning if I can guess it right is really poetical." And again of the verses about the young witch: "curious idealization of self-worship, very fine though." Three descriptive pages won the commendation of being "finely painted and evidently from experience."

These were slight efforts toward the favorable review with which he had hoped to oblige Fox, and it may well be that he did his best. Browning used to speak later as though Mill's review would have changed the book's fate for the better. It did not appear, for *Pauline* had already been briefly dismissed by another reviewer as "a pure piece of bewilderment" under the heading "Other Books."

The density of thought, the multiplicity of imagery and description in the poem might have baffled even a sympathetic reviewer. The "living hedgerows," "the quick glancing serpent," "tall rushes and thick flag-knots," "the pale snake," the wild mice, the stream so noiseless till "it joins its parent-river with a shout"—one is in the woods with Browning or gazing at the clouds or sea. Nor is there absent the element which later reviewers in the full tide of Victorianism called sensuality. The trees bend over the water "as wild men watch a sleeping girl." Pauline's neck "looks like marble misted o'er / With love-breath." For, however abstract as a person, Pauline is as woman "so close by me, the roughest swell / Of wind in the tree-tops hides not the panting / Of thy soft breasts. . . ."

We do not know whether Browning actually saw the abortive review. He did see what Mill had half advised Fox not to show him—the annotated copy, beginning on the title page itself, "too much pretension in this motto"; "not I think an appropriate image"; "not even poetically dramatical"; "Query meaning?"; "more prose than poetry"; "explain better"; "self-flattery."

Browning leaves most of these comments untouched, but occasionally fights back vigorously.[6] On the lines: ". . . so much was light / Lent

back by others, yet much was my own," Mill objects to the recurrence of
" 'so,' according to the colloquial vulgarism in the sense of therefore or
accordingly, from which occasionally come great obscurity and ambiguity—as here."

"The *recurrence*," says Browning "of 'so' thus employed is as vulgar
as you please: but the usage itself of '*so* in the sense of accordingly' is
perfectly authorised—take an instance or two from Milton." And he
proceeds to take ten instances giving each reference from *Paradise Lost*.
Browning's tone in this to-and-fro is a thoroughly good-tempered one.
But Mill tends to righteous wrath, especially over the last lines of the
poem. Here the poet, from speaking to Pauline turns to Shelley, and
then to his readers, begging them to "love me and wish me well." Beneath this line is printed "Richmond October 22, 1832."

Mill writes, "This transition from speaking to Pauline to writing a
letter to the public with *place* and *date* is quite horrible."

The word Richmond is underlined in ink and marked with a cross.
Beneath it Browning writes "Kean was acting there: I saw him in
Richard III that night. . . . There is an allusion to Kean p 47. I don't
know whether I had not made up my mind to *act* as well as to make
verses, and music, and God knows what—que de Chateaux en Es-
pagne."

The lover, the musician, the painter, the actor, all experience
packed into one life—a first attempt at his undying ambition to pull the
infinite into the finite—all this was struggling in the young Browning.
And he saw himself triumphing over old age as he witnessed Kean triumphing, at a time when the world knew he was drinking himself to
death.

> I will be gifted with a wondrous mind,
> Yet sunk by error to men's sympathy,
> And in the wane of life, . . .
> And lo, I fling age, sorrow, sickness off,
> And rise triumphant, triumph through decay.

All this suggests to the irreverent James Thurber's *The Secret Life
of Walter Mitty*—or perhaps just a poet's enlargement of every boy's

dreams. Browning had in the poem passed on from himself as an instrument of God in the rescue of Andromeda ("By the dark rock, and the white wave just breaking / At her feet; quite naked and alone") to himself as the great actor he has just witnessed. We can almost see the boy that he was, walking home under the stars and seeing Robert Browning as the supreme interpreter of Shakespeare.

A year had passed and here was the first of his dreams—*the* real dream, for a poet he supremely meant to be—rudely shattered. A bale of sheets came from the publisher: *Pauline*, Browning says, did not sell a copy. But far worse was this annotated horror Fox had sent him. On the final page Mill wrote at length:

> With considerable poetic powers, the writer seems to me possessed with a more intense and morbid self-consciousness than I ever knew in any sane human being. I should think it a sincere confession, though of a most unlovable state, if the "Pauline" were not evidently a pure phantom . . . the psychological history of himself is powerful and truthful—*truth-like* certainly, all but the last stage. *That,* he evidently has not yet got into. The self-seeking and self-worshipping state is well described—beyond that, I should think the writer had made, as yet, only the next step, viz. into despising his own state. I even question whether part even of that self-disdain is not *assumed.* He is evidently *dissatisfied,* and feels part of the badness of his state; he does not write as if it were purged out of him. If he once could muster a hearty hatred of his selfishness it would *go;* as it is he feels only the *lack* of *good,* not the positive evil. He feels not remorse, but only disappointment; a mind in that state can only be regenerated by some new passion, and I know not what to wish for him but that he may meet with a *real* Pauline.
>
> Meanwhile he should not attempt to show how a person may be *recovered* from this morbid state—for *he* is hardly convalescent, and what should we speak of but that which we know?

This final condemnation is weakened by two blind spots in Mill himself: he did not understand the outpouring of a poet who cannot, like a philosopher or a scientist, weigh and measure each word; he did not understand the Christian who had seen once more his lode star "A need, a trust, a yearning after God." And who now is bewildered "that I could doubt / Even his being—e'en the while I felt / His presence . . ."

The poem shows a recognition of "All my sad weaknesses, this wavering will, / This selfishness . . ."

Mill wrote his condemnation at the end of the book, but on the first page Browning added:

> The following Poem was written in pursuance of a foolish plan which occupied me mightily for a time, and which had for its object the enabling me to assume and realise I know not how many different characters:—meanwhile the world was never to guess that "Brown, Smith, Jones and Robinson" (as the spelling books have it) the respective authors of this poem, the other novel, such an opera, such a speech etc., etc., were no other than one and the same individual. The present abortion was the first work of the *Poet* of the batch, who would have been more legitimately *myself* than most of the others: but I surrounded him with all matter of (to my then notion) poetical accessories, and had planned quite a delightful life for him.
>
> Only this crab remains of the shapely Tree of Life in this Fool's paradise of mine.

This must surely have been written a little later, looking back dispassionately, not when the bale from the publishers and Mill's biting words struck simultaneously.

The blow was a doubly heavy one, for on the moral side his own conscience reinforced it. He *was* self-centered, self-conscious, selfish, already aware of what he could not later bear to recall, but also he had now revealed this ugly self of his to a world which must have appeared at that moment made up of John Stuart Mills. So *Pauline* became an abortion, to be destroyed, to be forgotten. And he seems to have convinced himself that as poetry too it was worthless. He found it almost impossible to show it to Elizabeth: "Will you and must you see it?" he asked plaintively. And he would not put it into collections of his work until menaced by the fear of a pirated edition—and even then it was heavily edited. Rossetti discovered it fourteen years later, was convinced that only the author of *Paracelsus* could have written it, and copied it out by hand.

In 1896 a copy of *Pauline* was sold for $700, in 1929 another is said to have fetched $1,600. What would they command today?

4 *Paracelsus*

*Measure your mind's height
by the shade it casts!*

"PARACELSUS"

BROWNING had not, like the prodigal son, asked for the immediate gift of an inheritance that would later be his, for he never spent anything "living riotously." But he was supported at home while he worked at what he believed to be his vocation. Was he wrong? We can perhaps dismiss a criticism which has been made of his three expensive journeys. One was made on a cargo boat, one in the Russian Consul General's carriage, and I think we may assume that the Consul paid all expenses for his "secretary" as Browning was termed. And surely a passage in the Love Letters refers to the third of these journeys—the second to Italy. Quoting Shelley on "those globes of deep red gold—/which in the woods the strawberry-tree doth bear," Browning tells Elizabeth that "when my Uncle walked into a sorb-tree . . . and I felt the fruit against my face, the little ragged bare-legged guide fairly laughed at my knowing them so well—'Niursi—sorbi!'" Browning, travelling with Uncle Reuben, was not likely to have been dipping deep into the parental exchequer.

Cyrus Mason's statement that the Browning parents had decided their son should be a poet and a poet only was probably based, in part at least, on the rejection of such jobs as would be normal for a youth of his social position at that date. Mr. Browning had refused an offer from the Bank of England which he himself had so longed to avoid. There can be little doubt that the Silverthorne uncle, father of Browning's favorite cousin, would have found a place for him in his brewery. But this would have meant no less drudgery, no better future prospects than the bank, and if Mason's view of the worldliness of the family is correct, they would certainly have aimed at something more socially acceptable.

Mrs. Orr tells us that Browning had considerable dramatic power and also that his father considered law as a possible career for him. And Cyrus Mason writes: "There were many serious discussions as to the propriety of 'young Robert' entering upon matters connected with the theatre." This may of course refer to a later date when he was writing plays, but to his mother if not to his father the acting profession would have been religiously anathema. The law had been chosen by Browning's two friends, Alfred Domett and Joseph Arnould, but their experience is so typical as to explain why, although attracted, the Brownings decided against it.

Domett had not long been called to the Bar before realizing the wearing delays during which a man's family must support a young barrister, and the slim chances of success without powerful connections. He decided for more rapid success and a wider life in New Zealand. His story may be read in *The Diary of Alfred Domett*, and in the *New Zealand Dictionary of Biography*—his mediation between the colonials and the British Government, his brief period as Prime Minister. One can only hope that Browning would have opposed his friend's deplorable support of the colonists in their grabbing of Maori land and their treatment of these highly developed people as savages. Domett combined this with writing romantic poetry about their legends and, after his return to England, Browning arranged for its publication.

Arnould's experience began later, for he was a Fellow of his College at Cambridge until he married. He was more successful than most young barristers, but only on private means could he keep a wife and family. For a long period he earned in fees only about £50 a year. His big success, too, came outside the home country, when he was invited to India and made Chief Justice of Bombay. Browning's future brother-in-law, George Barrett, would struggle (or saunter) on for years before he gave up the Bar for the farm.

It is fascinating to speculate on the effect Australia or New Zealand would have had on Browning had one of these countries instead of Italy become his "University"—whether his poetry would have gained or lost. The years saved of futile struggle to become a playwright might have been a gain, the grandeur of the physical scenes a revelation. But what of the world of men and women?

Browning himself was attracted by the diplomatic service, but had a boy in his social position the faintest chance of entering that stronghold of privilege? And if he had, could his parents possibly have paid out the large allowance often required for so long? Robert Lytton was *for eight years* an unpaid attaché at expensive embassies; and he, with immense social advantages, still felt that having been neither at Oxford or Cambridge was a crippling drawback.

But the effort was made and an ambiguous letter conveyed the impression that Browning had been accepted. In a letter to Sarah Flower (dated only Camberwell, Feb 4) he writes: "I don't go to Persia, and the Right Hon. Henry Ellis etc., etc. may go to a hotter climate for a perfect fool—(that at Bagdad in October, 127 Fahrenheit in the shade)."

This letter and another, dated "Wednesday mg" suggest high spirits despite repeated failures: ". . . on Saturday I waited on Murray, or rather Murray's son, and on presenting the kind puff of Mr. [illegible initial] I learnt that 'King Pandion he is dead: and all his peers wrapped up in lead', i.e., Lord Byron is 'no mo' and Poetry is 'no go.' Mr. Fox said much last Sunday of a Printing press at work just now in the S. Sea Isles. . . . Do you think Hokey-Pokey-Wankey-Fum would offer terms?"[1]

It was not so rare then for a man to be just a poet. There was Wordsworth, there was Tennyson, following Byron and Shelley.

Byron and Shelley were rich men by inheritance; Tennyson had his Cambridge friends to further his career. Browning's father told him that his sister, Sarianna, was taken care of and that there would be enough for him, but obviously enough would not be a feast. He was accepting, and his father for him, a narrow financial future, unless—

and probably both hoped for this with some confidence—his poetry had big sales. It seems likely that Reuben and the Silverthornes and Masons disapproved, that it was with aunts and uncles that the battles were fought to which he alludes in the Love Letters.

Mrs. Miller describes Browning's former schoolfellows working at their desks, his old friend Fox returning from a day at his office with the remark that now he felt like an honest man, and contrasts this with Browning's idleness. *"Pauline,"* she writes, "was published in March, 1833 . . . 'Beneath a flowering thicket lay Sordello.' " She adds the footnote "And there he still lay in May 1844, when *Sibrandus Schafna-burgensis* finds him reading in the garden, at ease 'under the arbute and the laurestine.' "

She quotes Browning telling Elizabeth that he was never obliged to do a given thing at a given time, but she does *not* quote Edmund Gosse, told by Browning that "freedom led to a super-abundance of production since on looking back he could see that he had often, in his unfettered leisure, been afraid to do nothing."

In success or failure, wrote Arnould to Domett, "the effect on him will be the same, viz to make him work, work, work."

Summing up the verse he actually published (to say nothing of what was written and destroyed) in the ten years which follow his twentieth birthday: *Pauline* 1,031 lines, *Paracelsus* 4,152, *Strafford* 2,200, *Sordello* 5,800, *Pippa Passes* 1,722, *King Victor and King Charles* 1,626, *The Return of the Druses* 1,780, *A Blot in the 'Scutch-eon* 1,324.

Most important of all was the volume of *Dramatic Lyrics* with its sixteen poems, in which we find the first and one of the most perfect of Browning's dramatic monologues, "My Last Duchess."

All this was indeed to "work, work, work" and this creative effort of his whole being was made no easier by frequent crippling headaches. Conrad declared that he would far rather move heavy sacks all day long under a burning sun than write his novels. Chesterton claimed that a day's office work was nothing beside the exhaustion of original writing. Newman spoke of his writing as "getting rid of pain by pain."

The Russian Consul General, Chevalier George de Benkhausen, invited Browning in March, 1834, to go with him on a "special mission" to his own country. There were no trains in much of Europe and from Rotterdam they traveled night and day as fast as horses could take them through the Low Countries and eastern Prussia. At Tilsit Browning saw snowdrops in blossom, but Russia was icebound: "the huge inns with their double-windowed, stove-heated dining-rooms, festooned with ivy and other climbing plants, which grew as if in a hot-house," sheepskin-clad peasants, scattered villages wooden-gabled, the frozen Dwina, the hills and valleys of Livonia, the sandy soil and pinewoods of Esthonia—all ending in what was then St. Petersburg. Unfortunately Browning destroyed his letters home, but the memory remained with his sister "how strangely he was impressed . . . above all by the endless monotony of snow-covered pine forests, through which he and his companion rushed for days and nights at the speed of six post-horses, without seeming to move from one spot."

He saw the breakup of ice on the Neva, the long-booted, gaily shirted workmen held back by police with poleaxes as they pressed to watch the huge ice field split and crack and whirl away in broken fragments. And then the Tsar drank a goblet of water, the wooden bridges swung into place and the city feasted the coming of spring.

Russian music fascinated Browning and half a century later, meeting Prince Gagarin in Venice, he sang some of the airs he had picked up on this short visit, so that the Prince exclaimed in astonishment at such musical memory "better than my own, on which I have hitherto piqued myself not a little."[2]

Back home by the Rhine three months later. And now came the problem of deciding what was to be written next. Browning had formed another friendship with a young Frenchman, agent of the Bourbons, Count Amédée de Ripert-Monclar[3] who suggested Paracelsus for subject, and the Browning library contained several books about that strange and fascinating character. But the poet, a year earlier, in March, 1833, had begun working on *Sordello*, which he wrote and rewrote, spending seven years on it, longer than on any other poem except *The*

Ring and the Book. His Italian tutor, Cerutti, had written about Sordello and discussed his place in Dante's *Purgatorio*, and he also appeared in the ever-useful *Biographie Universelle*. De Vane has shown that Browning used in *Paracelsus* some of the ideas originally intended for *Sordello*. In both, his "stress lay on the incidents in the development of a soul: little else is worth study." This he said in the preface to *Sordello* and developed more fully when writing to Isa Blagden many years later in relation to Tennyson:

> We look at the object of art in poetry so differently! Here is an Idyll about a knight being untrue to his friend and yielding to the temptation of that friend's mistress after having engaged to assist him in his suit. I should judge the conflict in the knight's soul the proper subject to describe: Tennyson thinks he should describe the castle, and the effect of the moon on its towers, and anything *but* the soul.

Yet nobody saw better than Browning the interaction between the soul and the material creation which "wrought upon" it. Think for instance of the meeting between Karshish and Lazarus:[4]

> I crossed a ridge of short sharp broken hills
> Like an old lion's cheek teeth. Out there came
> A moon made like a face with certain spots
> Multiform, manifold and menacing:
> Then a wind rose behind me. So we met.

Browning told Julia Wedgwood[5] many years later that he wrote *Paracelsus* on recovery from a fever and sore throat. How much had intensity of creation caused the fever—with *Sordello* already slowly maturing, and the conception of *Paracelsus* to be so swiftly completed? Or perhaps Browning's fevered state actually contributed something. Later in another fever a long poem was born, of which *Artemis Prologuizes* is all that he wrote down. Again he felt impelled by fever to recite aloud the poetry of Donne. And once in a dream he rewrote a play of Shakespeare. An acquaintance tells of meeting the Brownings

C*

on their first return to England; the poet "in very lively mood" had entertained them "with quotations from a dream the previous night, in which he had rewritten *Richard the Third*. The tent scene, in particular, was one of the maddest mixtures of Shakespearean poetry and modern slang that could be imagined."

Browning always spoke of the soul as a force behind and directing the mind—conceiving the mind as that which goes step by reasoned step. Whether we speak of soul and mind or mind and brain, the one thing certain is that we know but little of their possibilities in our hours of unconsciousness—sleep, fever, or even mental aberration. "The night brings counsel" applies not only to a night spent in watching, but also to emergence from profoundest slumber. Browning was fascinated by Christopher Smart's *Song of David,* the only great poem he believed Smart ever wrote—with a door key on the walls of his asylum.

Another element in Browning's best work is easier to state. Indeed he has stated it himself. He is struggling with the limitations of ordinary human language. The poet is the seer on whom is laid the burden of becoming the sayer—he is indeed entrusted with a message. George Duckworth sees Browning as suffering whenever he approached the "white light" of complete expression, which, in a letter to Elizabeth Barrett, he contrasts with the "prismatic hues" into which he commonly broke it.[6] In his first three long poems we can surely see the struggle, and mind and body both suffered in their interaction.

In form *Paracelsus* lies between the confessional of *Pauline* and the theatrical on which Browning wasted so many years. It is the closest of his early works to the dramatic monologues of his best period. We see him feeling after this form in his Introduction to the first edition of *Paracelsus*, strangely enough subsequently withdrawn:

> I have endeavoured to write a poem, not a drama: the canons of the drama are well known, and I cannot but think that, inasmuch as they have immediate regard to stage representation, the peculiar advantages they hold out are really such only so long as the purpose for which they were at first instituted is kept in view. I do not very well understand what is called a Dramatic Poem, wherein all those

restrictions, only submitted to on account of compensating good in the original scheme are scrupulously retained, as though for some special fitness in themselves—and all new facilities placed at an author's disposal by the vehicle he selects, as pertinaciously rejected. It is certain, however, that a work like mine depends more immediately on the intelligence and sympathy of the reader for its success: indeed were my scenes stars, it must be his coöperating fancy which, supplying all chasms, shall connect the scattered lights into one constellation—a Lyre or a Crown.

Paracelsus was the name chosen—to indicate his superiority to Celsus—by Philippus Bombastus, "a remarkable physician, who has removed with miraculous art those dire diseases, leprosy, gout, dropsy and other incurable and contagious diseases of the body, and ordered his property to be sold and distributed to the poor." So said his epitaph. He discovered laudanum and other drugs and also, a century ahead of Harvey, the circulation of the blood. He was reputed to have the secret of transmuting metals and he certainly in his youth practiced astrology and various kinds of magic. Wandering from country to country, he visited England—and, said his enemies, stole the secrets of one Roger Bacon! Despite marvelous cures and immense generosity to the poor, his arrogance and bad temper made enemies for him on a vast scale.

"You shall follow me," he proclaimed, "you Avicenna, Galen, Rhasis, Montagnana, Mesues, you gentlemen of Paris, Montpellier, Germany, Cologne, Vienna, and whomsoever the Rhine and Danube nourish; you who inhabit the isles of the sea; you likewise, Dalmatians, Athenians; thou Arab, thou Greek, thou Jew: all shall follow me, and the monarchy shall be mine."

There is in Browning himself at this point something of Paracelsus, and of Cyrano de Bergerac. But underneath the panache a struggle is engaged; conviction of his own powers is having a hard job in overcoming insecurity. Still vividly remembered is the Mill attack on *Pauline*. On April 16, 1838, writing to Fox, who had given him an introduction to two publishers, Browning describes the "dolorous" accent of the first when mentioning poetry, the "better hope" with the second, yet he is "not over sanguine."

Scared at the thought of a fresh eye

> . . . discovering blemishes of all sorts . . . obscure passages, slipshod verses, and much that worse is,—yet on the whole I am not much afraid of the issue, and I would give something to be allowed to read it some morning to you—for every rap o' the knuckles I should get a clap o' the back, I know.

This time there is to be no anonymity:

> I really shall *need* your notice, on this account; I shall affix my name and stick my arms akimbo; there are a few precious bold bits here and there, and the drift and the scope are awfully radical—I am "off" for ever with the other side, but must by all means be "on" with yours—a position once gained, worthier works shall follow— therefore a certain writer [evidently Mill] . . . must be benignant or supercilious as he shall choose, but in no case an idle spectator . . .
> Excuse all this swagger, I know you will.[7]

The typical Renaissance passion for universal knowledge and some facts of his career are used by Browning in *Paracelsus*. But the character is chiefly his own conception—largely perhaps of himself. Aprile, the poet conjectured to be drawn from Shelley, is his creation. So are Festus and Michal, a husband and wife who love Paracelsus but fear the results of his arrogance and self-confidence as he leaves them for the wider world he is determined to conquer. It is through knowledge that this conquest is to be achieved, and in his ambition Paracelsus is typical of the high Renaissance in Europe. But he has forgotten that men must love as well as know until he meets Aprile, who talks of love in impassioned fashion until finally Paracelsus cries out:

> . . . We must never part.
> Are we not halves of one dissevered world,
> Whom this strange chance unites once more?
> Part? Never!

> Till thou, the lover, know; and I, the knower,
> Love—until both are saved. . . .

But part they must for Aprile is dying, and Paracelsus cries:

> Thy spirit, at least, Aprile! Let me love! . . .

> I have attained and now I may depart.

Attainment was not so easy and the next scene is again entitled "Paracelsus Aspires." Five years have passed and Festus, himself on his way to Wittenburg to see Luther, finds Paracelsus a professor at Basle. He pictures him breaking the shackles of an outworn science, Luther renewing religion. But Paracelsus ends the conversation by rejecting his friend's homage. He has had successes, wrought some startling cures, made some minor discoveries. But he has not succeeded in the vast aims of his youth; he is worn out before his time. For a while, he tells Festus, he had tried like Aprile to live for love alone; but found

> My nature cannot lose her first imprint;
> I still must hoard and heap and class all truths
> With one ulterior purpose: I must know!

He has sunk from a state in which the body "used to care / For its bright master's cares and quite subdue / Its proper cravings . . ." into one where the body is chiefly concerned with delights of its own. (Historically Paracelsus had become a heavy drinker, often spent the night in some tavern, and went to bed in his clothes.) Festus speaks to him of God's will, but he has not found that so easy to discover. His mood is one of misery though not quite despair: "Utter damnation is reserved for hell!" But when Festus reminds him "That there is yet another world to mend / All error and mischance . . ." it is the old Paracelsus who bursts out—the Paracelsus of the Renaissance at its best, before faith in God was lost, when a certain fresh wind of belief in this life was blowing strong:

> Another world!
> And why this world, this common world, to be
> A make-shift, a mere foil, how fair soever,
> To some fine life to come? Man must be fed

> With angels' food, forsooth; and some few traces
> Of a diviner nature which look out
> Through his corporeal baseness, warrant him
> In a supreme contempt of all provision
> For his inferior tastes—some straggling marks
> Which constitute his essence, just as truly
> As here and there a gem would constitute
> The rock, their barren bed, one diamond.
> But were it so—were man all mind—he gains
> A station little enviable. From God,
> Down to the lowest spirit ministrant,
> Intelligence exists which casts our mind
> Into immeasurable shade. No, no:
> Love, hope, fear, faith—these make humanity;
> These are its sign and note and character,
> And these I have lost! . . .

Yet Paracelsus will aspire again.

The next scene shows him, dubbed charlatan and deceiver, cast out from his post at Basle, meeting Festus with an air of conviction that he will build upon the ruins. But for this close friend the "horrible despondency" of their last meeting was less alarming than to ". . . hear these incoherent words and see / This flushed cheek and intensely-sparkling eye."

Half crazed in this fourth scene, Paracelsus is dying in the sixth. In his delirium he speaks to the dead Aprile, to Festus, and supremely to God:

> Thou art good,
> And I should be content. Yet—yet first show
> I have done wrong in daring! Rather give
> The supernatural consciousness of strength
> which fed my youth! . . .
> Lost, lost! Thus things are ordered here!
>   God's creatures,
> And yet he takes no pride in us!—None, none!
> Truly there needs another life to come!
> If this be all— . . .

How very full
Of wormwood 'tis, that just at altar service,
The rapt hymn rising with the rolling smoke,
When glory dawns and all is at the best,
The sacred fire may flicker and glow faint
And die for want of a wood-piler's help!

He gathers together the forces of this failing body which has of old
heaped its wood on the soul's sacred flame, asks for his gown, the chain
for his neck, his sword Azoth, and stands for the last time as though to
deliver a lecture. His death cell becomes: "A shrine, for here God
speaks to men through me."

A treasure of the Berg collection is a copy of the first edition of
Paracelsus, corrected and altered by Browning at Pisa just after his
marriage. Many lines are added, many greatly altered, and a few passages are cut out altogether. One change is puzzling. In the original
version, Aprile says, "God is the perfect poet / Who in his person acts
his own creations." Browning altered the second line to read "Who in
creation acts his own conceptions." It is followed by six lines which
Browning inserted in the second edition, but later deleted:

Shall man refuse to be aught less than God?
Man's weakness is his glory—for the strength
Which raises him to heaven and near God's self
Came spite of it. God's strength his glory is,
For thence came with our weakness sympathy
Which brought God down to earth, a man like us.

These lines show already present in Browning's thinking the idea of
the Incarnation, imaginatively seen in *Pauline*, later to become a key
theme. Why did he decide to withdraw them from a later edition
of *Paracelsus*, leaving only a hierarchy of being which culminates in a
prophet through whom God speaks to man? Ten years later we find a
similar hesitation: the version of "Saul" he published in 1845 con-
sisted of the first nine stanzas only. David's vision of Christ was not included. We must wait for *Christmas Eve and Easter Day* (1850) and
Men and Women (1855), with "Saul," now completed, for Browning's

utterance of the faith, written into and then withdrawn from *Paracelsus,*
that God became man. Yet even with the omission the poem is incarna-
tional:

> So glorious is our nature, so august
> Man's inborn uninstructed impulses,
> His naked spirit so majestical! . . .
>   savage creatures seek
> Their loves in wood and plain—and God renews
> His ancient rapture. Thus he dwells in all,
> From life's minute beginnings, up at last
> To man—the consummation of this scheme
> Of being, the completion of this sphere
> Of life . . .

A passage deals with the assembling in man of all the scattered elements, hints and fragments in creation, meant by God

> To be united in some wondrous whole, . . .
> But the new glory mixes with the heaven
> And earth; man, once descried, imprints for ever
> His presence on all lifeless things: the winds
> Are henceforth voices, . . .
> The herded pines commune and have deep thoughts,
> A secret they assemble to discuss
> When the sun drops behind their trunks which glare
> Like grates of hell: the peerless cup afloat
> Of the lake-lily is an urn, some nymph
> Swims bearing high above her head: no bird
> Whistles unseen . . .

Not by Browning, certainly, but one cannot at all imagine the historical Paracelsus walking godlike through creation, seeing it all as good
because beautiful, because strange; seeing "enterprise" in the moon or a
shape in the forest "with small puckered mouth and mocking eyes."
This is not Paracelsus but Browning. Paracelsus would have been
looking for material for his cures, or trying to turn rocks into gold. Ambitious for himself and for his fellows, he saw God

... glorified in man,
And to man's glory vowed I soul and limb.
Yet constituted thus, and thus endowed,
I failed: I gazed on power till I grew blind.

In this blindness even the love which he had been slowly learning was ill directed. He

... saw no good in man,
To overbalance all the wear and waste
Of faculties, displayed in vain, but born
To prosper in some better sphere: and why?
In my own heart love had not been made wise
To trace love's faint beginnings in mankind,
To know even hate is but a mask of love's,
To see a good in evil, and a hope
In ill-success; to sympathize, be proud
Of their half-reasons, faint aspirings, dim
Struggles for truth ...
Their error upward tending all though weak,
Like plants in mines which never saw the sun,
But dream of him, and guess where he may be,
And do their best to climb and get to him.
All this I knew not, and I failed. ...
Meanwhile, I have done well, though not all well.
As yet men cannot do without contempt;
'Tis for their good, and therefore fit awhile
That they reject the weak, and scorn the false,
Rather than praise the strong and true, in me:
But after, they will know me. If I stoop
Into a dark tremendous sea of cloud,
It is but for a time; I press God's lamp
Close to my breast; its splendour, soon or late,
Will pierce the gloom, I shall emerge one day.

Paracelsus like *Pauline* was a financial failure, but contrary to all that Browning said in his later life, it was in every other respect a remarkable success. The earliest notices were somewhat feeble; but none of them justifies his statement that until the appearance of Forster's article in the *Examiner,* the poem was laughed at and denounced. As it appeared in mid-August and Forster's review on September 6, there would have been little time for any devastating effect from earlier notices. The *Spectator,* the *Atlas* and the *Athenaeum* had been hurried and cautious. The words "dreamy" and "obscure" were used and the *Metropolitan Magazine* had called it "a poem ambitiously unpopular." But there was nothing worse.

Forster wrote three columns full of copious quotation and praise: "It is some time since we have read a work of more unequivocal power. . . . We conclude that its author is a young man . . . we may safely predict for him a brilliant career." In a later long article in *The New Monthly Magazine* he spoke yet more strongly: "Without the slightest hesitation we name Mr. Robert Browning at once with Shelley, Coleridge, Wordsworth."

As Dr. Lounsbury points out, the praise grew stronger as time went on—for time was needed that all the greatness of the poem could sink into the reader's mind, all the ideas in it be assimilated. Of all the reviewers only Fox was a friend of the still so youthful poet.

No one reading contemporary biography can doubt that this acclaim in the periodicals expressed and increased a real wave of enthusiasm in the intellectual world. Browning at twenty-three had arrived. Even those who had not read *Paracelsus* realized that they ought to, while those who had were looking forward with eagerness to its successor. But few except intellectuals care to buy books, nor have most intellectuals got money to buy them with. A system of borrowing from libraries and among friends did not go far toward paying the expenses of publication, and Browning's father was out of pocket.

The chief immediate effects of *Paracelsus* were to make Browning a desired guest in many houses and to start him on his career as a playwright. And, whatever he may have said later, he realized enough of what the poem had done for him to put under his name on future works "By the author of *Paracelsus.*"

5 Browning and Macready

The medium of poetry is words, *the medium of drama is people moving about on a stage and using words.*

EZRA POUND

Η IS INTRODUCTION to William Macready is one of the milestones in Browning's life. The friendship led to others and also distracted him into the writing of a series of plays neither good nor successful. The inevitable quarrel with which their relations ended drove him back into poetry, but perhaps the plays prepared him for the dramatic monologue—a form which was to become distinctively his.

Macready kept a diary, written with rare frankness about himself—and (less uncommonly) about others: "My greatest enemy" he wrote "—*the stumbling block of my life*—has been *passion,* and its consequent evil, *precipitation.*" His pages are full of "this St. Vitus's dance of the mind," but also of bitter repentance, prayerful resolve, despairing self-pity: "I could curse the fate that threw me into a sphere of life with violent passions, where these passions are so *cruelly* acted on."

Macready was educated at Rugby till the age of sixteen, when the failure of his father as manager of a provincial theater threw him into a debtors' prison, and young William had to take charge of the theater and company until his release. With prospects of the university and a legal career thus destroyed, Macready appeared at Birmingham in the character of Romeo, announced only as "A young gentleman, being his first appearance on any stage." So great was his success that henceforward, under his own name, he played the leading parts in town after town for six years. He then got an engagement at Covent Garden and was, at twenty-three, recognized as "an actor of the first rank."

Convinced that he "must strain every nerve of thought or triumph is hopeless," he would study each character, trying to get the key to Macbeth, Othello, Lear, yet *I cannot reach in execution the standard of my own conception.*"

He tells of "rising thoughts over the madness of King Lear . . . that possession of my mind which is necessary to success"; and when acting the part he wept—"Tears . . . not those of a woman or a driveller, they really stained a 'man's cheeks.' "

The performance of a character was, Macready said, his "day"; he could do nothing else. Four different plays might be acted in a week, and he had to insist on a rehearsal when the management suddenly changed the play. He firmly refused to act, at royal command, the part of Joseph Surface, being, he said, "out of the character." "The King [William IV] cares for neither the play, nor the actors, nor their act and I see no reason why I should inconvenience myself for him." For Queen Victoria he acted often, though grumbling when she (aged after all only eighteen!) chose the Pantomime or *Rob Roy* in preference to Shakespeare.

Despite hours of immense triumph ("when wearied of shouting they turned the applause to a stamping of feet, which sounded like thunder; it was grand and awful"), Macready was never reconciled to his profession. An actor stood low in the fashionable world; he could not for instance attend a levee at Court. ("My pariah profession brings lavish expression of public praise but excludes from distinctions which all my compeers enjoy.") When letters came addressed "Mr." instead of "Esq.," he returned them or put them unread into the fire. He often suspected insult ("He advanced with one finger; I met him with one finger"). He got himself a coat of arms. Above all he rendered himself desperately unpopular with his fellow players by dissociating himself from them; despising the profession to which both he and they belonged, he acted as from an imagined height above them. However absurd this was socially, it was often warranted by bad acting which affected him acutely and sometimes ruined his own effects. "My experience of the professors of my art confirms me in my opinion of their vileness, their utter unworthiness." "I wish they were all tied in a sack together! they worry my heart out." Actors were "ignorant and conceited vermin."

So it would seem were most of the human race. An Irish audience made "blackguard noises"; indeed the "Dublin ruffians" were the worst specimens of human nature. The *Times* was a "base and profligate paper," its newsmen "dirty scribblers."

"Did the fiendish host whose name was legion . . . survive their leap and transmigrate through the bodies of certain reviewers?" Scott's son-in-law, J. W. Lockhart, one of these—a "hireling defamer," "a malignant trader in circumstances pointed to stab and draw by slow droppings the life-blood of a man's heart—is of the base the basest."

Macready was a proclaimed republican. Enthusiasm for the Queen was "the worship which the base wretches of this world are transferring from their God to a girl of eighteen whom they choose to call a Queen." "The self-praised aristocracy of England" are "gold-besotted, prurient, frivolous, and heartless wretches! The cellars and garrets of Manchester, and the dens and pig-holes of Ireland are echoing the moans of agony, as the boxes of these *things* at the opera-house are shaking with their applause of—what?" "What" was the opera, for which he had a supreme disdain; but he did not dislike the presence and applause of aristocrats at his own performances.

Despite his vanity and snobbery, Macready emerges from the diaries as an attractive personality. He was utterly devoted to his wife and children, and his chief concern in gaining success was to gain with it enough money to secure their future. When, with the awful inevitableness of that "scientific" age, first one daughter and then another died young, when his eldest son was stricken with an obscure disease, his grief is touching, and his total devotion to each small sufferer: ". . . went up to look at my dear dead child . . . I could only see visions of the little bright-eyed creature, entering from her walks, sitting at the table, laughing in her wild way on the stairs. . . . My boy once a wonder of beauty and intelligence will soon be laid by the side of his sweet sister."

No one knew better than he how false were certain of his habitual assumptions: "As I sat at dinner . . . the servant in livery attending on me . . . I thought how difficult it must be, and it is, for men to draw back their *naked selves*—their ideas of man, as God made him—from the disguise of pomp and circumstance with which they have invested him. Oh God . . . teach me the duties of charity, of kind consideration, of compassionate allowance."

Macready noted in his diary on September 6, 1835, that he had been reading extracts from *Paracelsus*—"of great merit." Lady Pollock relates how, learning she had not read the poem, he exclaimed, "Oh good God" —and adjured her to "hand over the babies to the nurse, and read *Paracelsus*."

Two months later he was still reading "beautiful and touching extracts" and was "very much pleased" to meet Browning at William Fox's house. "His face is full of intelligence, my time passed most agreeably. . . . I took Mr. Browning on, and requested to be allowed to improve my acquaintance with him. He expressed himself warmly . . . wished to send me his book."

And on December 7: "Read *Paracelsus,* a work of great daring, starred with poetry of thought, feeling and diction, but occasionally obscure; the writer can scarcely fail to be a leading spirit of his time." Finishing the poem on the following day, Macready felt again the fault of obscurity but also "the profoundest and the grandest thoughts and most musically uttered. The writer is one, I think, destined for great things."

On a first visit to Macready's home at Elstree, Browning was "very popular with the whole party; his simple and enthusiastic manner engaged attention and won opinions from all present; he looks and speaks more like a youthful poet than any man I ever saw." It was New Year's Eve and "we poured out a libation as a farewell to the Old Year and a welcome to the New."

Forster was present, the future biographer of Dickens, who had, with both Browning and Macready, a lifelong friendship broken by many quarrels but always mended again. "Browning," Macready remarked, "is his present *all-in-all*."

The poet was as enthusiastic over Macready's acting as the actor was

over Browning's poetry; he came often into his room after the play and
"seemed much delighted." On February 15, "Forster walked to chambers and took tea with me, reading to me passages from a poem by
Browning"; and on the next day they both called and began to talk
over the plot of a tragedy that Browning might write. "He said that I had
bit him by my performance of Othello, and I told him I hoped I should
make the blood come."

Browning was more and more winning a place in Macready's affections. Despite his "enthusiastic" manner, the actor felt his presence to
be more soothing than that of Forster and other friends. "My nerves and
spirit," one entry runs, "were quite quelled by them all, and I rejoiced
at seeing them leave me—except Browning, whose gentle manners
always make his presence acceptable." And of "a note from Browning"
after his acting of Ion he writes: "It was a tribute which remunerated
me from the annoyances and cares of years: it was one of the very
highest, may I not say the highest, honours I have through life received."

Ion, famous in its day but now forgotten, was the work of Serjeant
Talfourd, at whose house a supper party was held to celebrate the
success of the play. The actor proposed the health of the dramatist, who
ended his speech of thanks by returning the compliment "with much of
eulogy . . . it became then, a succession of personal toasts. . . . I was very
happily placed between Wordsworth and Landor with Browning
opposite."

Both Mrs. Orr and Dr. Hall Griffin relate how at this supper Wordsworth joined in drinking a toast proposed by Talfourd to the "Poets of
England"—and associated by him with the author of *Paracelsus*. Wordsworth, Griffin adds, "leaned across the table and remarked 'I am proud
to drink to your health, Mr. Browning.' "

No authority is given for this story, which had gone unquestioned
until Mrs. Miller's entertaining reconstruction (in the *Twentieth
Century*, 1953, CLIV, p. 53) of "This Happy Evening." Crabbe Robinson's diary, which she quotes, shows that he and Wordsworth left
the party together before Macready's reply to the toast of himself—and
could not therefore have been present for this later one. (Henry Crabbe
Robinson traveled all over Europe with Wordsworth and was one of his

closest friends. He left thirty-five volumes of diary besides notebooks innumerable.)

Mrs. Miller's account of both play and supper suggests that the event was for most of the participants very far from the "Happy Evening" proclaimed by Macready.

Miss Mitford was there and Macready spoke to her, "observing in badinage that the present occasion should stimulate her to write a play; she quickly said, 'Will you act in it?' I was silent." Another guest, felt by Macready to have inflicted on him "a deep and assassin-like wound," in *Blackwood's Magazine* said, "Aye, hold him to that"; whereat, says Macready, "I could not repress the expression of indignant contempt which found its way to my face." And as they left the house, he said to Browning, "Write a play, Browning, and keep me from going to America."

Was it this incident that awakened in Miss Mitford the implacable dislike of Browning displayed in her letters? Whether she overheard the remark or not, she was probably exasperated by the atmosphere of mutual admiration which surrounded—and excluded—her; Macready for Talfourd and Browning, Browning for Talfourd and Macready, Talfourd for them both, and Forster and Fox for all three of them. There were, too, Macready's wife and sister, and their neighbor, Euphrasia Fanny Haworth, who drove home with the Macreadys, "talking of nothing but the evening's events—this happy evening. We reached home about two and went to bed with the birds singing their morning song in our tired ears. Thank God."

This entry was made on May 30. On the twenty-eighth, Browning had written of "The admiration I have for your genius . . . you comprehend me as you comprehend Macbeth or Ion,— . . . I will give my whole heart and soul to the writing a Tragedy . . . should I be unequal to the task, the excitement and extreme effort will have been their own reward:—should I succeed, my way of life will be very certain, and my name pronounced along with yours."

At Elstree, Browning made friends with the Macready family and their friends. "The Pied Piper of Hamelin" was written for and inscribed to "W. M. the younger"—and this meant Willie Macready.

Browning wrote it for the boy to illustrate during an illness—and followed it by "The Cardinal and the Dog."

But at this moment, for Macready and Browning alike, the question was all-absorbing: What should the poet write to fit the actor's creative powers? Browning chose Strafford, Lord Deputy in Ireland under Charles I; he was beheaded by the king's enemies, the king signing the bill of attainder.

When the play arrived—not absolutely completed but the missing parts sketched in—Macready wrote: "I was greatly pleased with it . . . Browning called in some anxiety . . . was very much pleased, agreeing in my objections and promising to do everything needful." This was on November 20, and two days later "Forster called with Browning's m.s." November 23: "Began *very attentively* to read over the tragedy of Strafford, in which I find more ground for objection than I had anticipated. I had been too much carried away by the truth of character to observe the meanness of plot, and occasional obscurity." A little later Browning brought in the missing scenes, but Macready felt it "still is not up to the high-water mark."

Anyone who has been a publisher's reader will sympathize with Macready's changes of mood, and it must be even harder to picture the effect of a play that is to be acted than of a book that is to be read. And, too, how widely opinions differ. William Rossetti in 1886 witnessed a "mediocre" performance of *Strafford*, found "not a dull minute," found his "eyes dim from unshed tears," saw in Pym a "marble passion of patriotism," thought the play would become "a fine established stage piece."[1]

In between readings, Macready was acting an inferior play, after which one evening "Browning, with all his kind heart, called and sat a few minutes."

Macready was reading other manuscripts of marked inferiority: "utter trash . . . I cannot longer afford the time. Read some scenes in *Strafford*, which restore one to the world of sense and feeling once again." Yet on the following day his doubts are back. "I am by no means sanguine, I lament to say, on its success."

They put off the play for a while and Browning worked on it, bringing it back on March 29. "He looked very unwell, jaded and thought-sick."

These had been trying months for them both, but the owner of the theater, Mr. Osbaldiston, shown the play, "caught at it with avidity," made Browning a good offer in terms of the times—and made him "very happy." Forster, the indefatigable, was determined to persuade Longmans to publish it, Browning intended to dedicate it to Macready, which he did "with all affectionate admiration."

But the rehearsals went ill: ". . . it dragged its slow length along . . . *I fear it will not do.*" At one point Forster became enraged and the other two sympathetically agreed as to what a difficult temper he had (a matter in which both, but especially Macready, might claim to judge). "There was a *scene*," writes Macready—but he feels that Browning behaved well. He "assented to all the proposed alterations." But then he failed utterly to carry them out: "It was too bad to trifle in this way." After another attempt, however, Browning told his friend that he "had been oppressed and incapable of carrying his intentions into action. He *wished to withdraw it.*"

With cruel kindness Macready "counseled him against any precipitate step—warned him of the consequences and called Fox into counsel." "It was fixed to be done. Heaven speed us all."

It was Macready's first and immense mistake and within a week he was repenting it—wanting Helen Faucit, who thought her part too poor, to refuse to act; longing for "a *fair* occasion to withdraw it"; expecting "it will be damned—grievously hissed at the end"—and yet most strangely feeling that friendship obliged him to go forward to disaster. So the play went on, not running into the total disaster he had predicted, but certainly no success. Macready's and Miss Faucit's excellent acting saved it despite itself and an otherwise miserable cast. On the opening day, May 1, 1837, Longmans did publish it—the first of Browning's works to be brought out at the publisher's expense.

All this *Paracelsus* had won for him; but Browning, who was modest about his great poetry, tended to overrate all his bad plays. He was, Macready says, enraged with Forster for a review which was as favorable as his friend could honestly make it. There were five performances only and everyone seems to have emerged with frayed temper.[2] We begin to hear less of the soothing effect on Macready of Browning's presence. He had, said the actor, a "sickly and fretful over-estimate of his work," but the experience did not carry its true lesson to either man. Browning went on writing plays; Macready went on reading them— and eventually he produced another.

Obviously, Browning later doubted the value of *Strafford*, for he omitted it from his collected works; it has been suggested that this was because Elizabeth did not care for it; it was finally restored.

The Browning-Macready friendship still flourished. It is hardly likely that every meeting was recorded, but in January, 1838, Browning dined at Elstree and "we spent a cheerful afternoon"; in August he was in Macready's room—with Dickens, Forster and Horne—and a few weeks later was again dining. In December he was invited to listen to the reading of a play. On Christmas Eve, Browning, Forster, and Dickens arrived, rather to Macready's dismay, to watch a rehearsal of the Pantomime.

On August 24, 1839, Browning called. "His object, if he exactly knew it, was to learn from me whether, if he wrote a really good play, it would have a secure chance of acceptance. I told him certainly." On September 5, however: "Read Browning's play on Victor, King of Sardinia—it turned out to be a *great mistake*. I called Browning into my room and most explicitly told him so." But to a Macready depressed about his own acting, Browning still brought comfort. He "came into my room and said all that sympathy and friendly feeling could suggest."

No less than Browning had the actor-manager confidently expected a huge success for the promised "more popular" successor to *Paracelsus*. It would redeem the failure of *Strafford* and prepare a public for his next act-worthy play. But soon, trying desperately to read *Sordello*, Macready sadly concluded: "it is *not* readable." And when offered another play on July 31, he wrote: "Reading Browning's play, and with the deepest concern I yield to the belief that he will *never write again* —to any purpose. I fear his intellect is not quite clear. I do not know how to write to Browning."

Browning saved him a letter by calling: ". . . he talked of his play and *Sordello,* and I most honestly told him my opinion . . . most anxious as I am, that he should justify the expectations formed of him, . . . he could not do so by placing himself in opposition to the world."

Yet Macready did not merely consent to read again what he called a "mystical strange and heavy play," but actually *argued* Browning into leaving it with him. An entry on August 27 runs: "Browning came before I had finished my bath, and really *wearied* me . . . with his self-opinionated persuasions upon his *Return of the Druses.* I fear he is forever gone . . ." Yet "Browning accompanied me to the theatre, *at last consenting* [italics mine] to leave the MS with me for a second perusal."

Browning could never have been sure of avoiding Macready's bath hour, for the actor often got up late and bathed at all hours; sometimes after an afternoon walk. But extraordinarily wearing for an author was the fact that Macready could never make a firm decision. One would think that by now both men would have had enough. But no. *The Druses* had returned in September, and *A Blot in the 'Scutcheon* must have reached Macready before the end of the year, with the optimistic observation from Browning: " 'The luck of the third adventure' is proverbial. I have written a spick-and-span new Tragedy (a sort of compromise between my own notion and yours—as I understand it at least). . . . There is *action* in it, drabbing, stabbing, et autres gentillesses—who knows but the Gods may make me good even yet?"

The next mention of *A Blot* is on September 29, 1841, when Macready writes: "Forster *importuned me* after dinner to read Browning's tragedy, which I did." But the decision so vital for Browning was to be delayed more than a full year longer. Forster as well as Macready felt uncertain, and it was decided to call on Dickens for an opinion, which he supplied only in November, 1842.

Though Browning was getting impatient, his letter in April, '42, was a moderate one. He had begun the series of *Bells and Pomegranates,* had postponed publishing his play in this series, but now "I have nothing by me at all fit to be substituted for the work in your hands."

Still he had to wait. Macready had, at the end of 1841, moved from Covent Garden to Drury Lane. Lounsbury has shown that Browning's memory later confused two seasons. But Macready's folly seems to have lain in not mentioning Dickens, who still held the manuscript, and a letter of October 13 shows the unhappy author denied admission by Macready's dresser when he sent up his card after a performance. He writes with restraint and dignity, assuming a mistake, but it was on the actor's part clearly a stalling for time, which ended with a letter from Dickens:

> Browning's play has thrown me into a perfect passion of sorrow. . . . It is full of genius, natural and great thoughts, profound and yet simple and beautiful in its vigour. . . . Mildred's recurrence to that 'I was so young—I had no mother.' I know no love like it, no passion like it, no moulding of a splendid thing after its conception, like it. And I swear it is a tragedy that MUST be played: and must be played, moreover, by Macready. . . . And if you tell Browning that I have seen it, tell him that I believe from my soul there is no man living (and not many dead) who could produce such a work.

The mind staggers on reading such a judgment after reading the play, which takes us back a century or so behind Dickens' own date, perhaps to make the feudal atmosphere a trifle more plausible. A landowner, Lord Mertoun, calls on another, Lord Tresham, to ask for his very young sister's hand in marriage. Tresham delightedly agrees. But then he hears from a faithful and ancient retainer that a stranger, wrapped in a concealing cloak, is entering at night his sister's bedroom. He confronts the intruder (cloaked as before) attacks and stabs him— and then discovers he is Mildred's acknowledged suitor, Mertoun. Mertoun dies and Mildred promptly dies also (of grief), in her brother's arms. But Tresham has already taken poison, so three corpses lie upon the scene, and no amount of Greek Chorus work from another character, or suggestions of a derivation from *Romeo and Juliet,* can reconcile one to such a tissue of absurdities.

The play went on—marked from the first for disaster, chiefly because of its own intrinsic demerits, but also because Macready had taken it without really believing in it. Badly read to the cast by the prompter, it awakened laughter instead of tears. (And although Macready cut out at least one repetition of the lament Dickens found so moving, we are reminded of Oscar Wilde: "A man would need a heart of stone to read of the death of little Nell without bursting into laughter.") Macready refused to act and gave the part to Phelps. Phelps got ill, Macready learned the part and decided at the last minute to play it. But Phelps recovered and told Macready he would play if he " 'died for it' so that my time had been lost." Going down to the theater to give writer and actor the benefit of his study especially one idea which "I thought particularly valuable . . . Browning . . . in the worst taste, manner and spirit . . . expressed himself perfectly satisfied with the manner in which Mr. Phelps executed Lord Tresham. I had no more to say. I could only think Mr. Browning a very disagreeable and offensively mannered person. Voilà tout!"

Thus far Macready—but did he in fact, as Arnould wrote to Domett, even at this eleventh hour "hint" that he would himself act the part? Arnould writes vividly:

> Macready then again appears, hints that he has studied the character, will act the first night. Upon this our Robert does not fall prone at his feet and worship him for his condescending goodness— not that at all does our Robert do, but quite other than that—with laconic brevity he positively declines taking the part from Phelps, dispenses with Macready's aid &c., and all this in face of a whole green-room. You imagine the fury and whirlwind of our managerial wrath—silent fury, a compressed whirlwind, volcano fires burning white in our pent heart. We say nothing, of course, but we do our spiteful uttermost; we give no orders—we provide paltry machinery —we issue mandates to all our dependent pen-wielders—to all tribes of men who rejoice in suppers and distinguished society. Under penalty of our managerial frown they are to be up and doing in their dirty work.[3]

It certainly seems a little surprising that a man should *desire* failure for a play he was producing. Yet there is a confirmation of it in Elizabeth Barrett's correspondence with Miss Mitford to whom she writes on February 16, 1843: "Yes, Mr. Macready from all that I can understand, behaved execrably to Mr. Browning: would and would not act his play

—and at last acted it *for damnation* . . . but, not-withstanding every possible disadvantage, the poetry triumphed . . . Mr. Kenyon, who was
present, bears witness to the emotion of the full house . . . to the living
tears and compelled attention."

Manager and actor were certainly at war in Macready—and what
bad-tempered man is swayed only by his financial interests? In those
days of very brief runs, he may have thought it best, even as manager,
to let the play die, as his actor's pride demanded, and put on something
of which his managerial judgment approved. It lasted only three days.
Later revivals in London and Washington were more successful, but
even for nineteenth-century sentiment it was too cloying, while more
surprisingly Thomas Woolner reports "a shower of hisses and puri-
tanical anathemas."

One wonders whether the discussions about " 'young Robert' entering upon affairs connected with the stage" were being at this date
carried on (tactlessly perhaps) by aunts and uncles, including the
Masons. For Cyrus waxes indignant at Browning for bestowing no
tickets on the family. Going at his own expense, he gleefully describes
the " 'Scutcheon' rope ladder grotesquely managed . . . young lover
swinging and singing—one line ending 'drop' wailed in a suggestive
manner" and "received with titters."

Browning's two friends, Kenyon and Domett, speak of applause
and tears, but the fact was damning that the play was acted in Macready's theater yet not by him. And while many applauded and some
wept, there is no doubt that some also laughed, spelling death for a
tragedy.

Cyrus Mason's comment on the whole story was that toward Macready young Robert had shown a temper inherited from his grandfather.

There are a few more entries about Browning in Macready's
journal. He had at a chance meeting in March, 1843, accosted Macready and then hastened away "as if he had not meant to do so." He has
now become one of "these wretched insects about one." And in June,
1846, at a party Macready saw *Browning*—who did not speak to me—
the *puppy!*"

But life goes on, and one tends to sympathize with Browning's destructive instincts when imagining the utterance of past rage or acid criticism laid up for the future biographer.

Affectionate feeling swamped all past bitterness when, in 1852, Browning heard of the death of Macready's wife. In a letter,[4] written at a time of strain, bringing back keenly the grief of Browning's mother's death, there was no room now for other than good memories of those seven wearing years:

> My dear Macready,
>
> Pray forgive me for writing if it pains or troubles you, as it may, perhaps. How can I help telling you—tho' in but a poor word or two—that I dare think I can sympathise with you—even in my infinitely removed degree—dare think I comprehend your loss, having been taught by a loss of my own. Those were happy days when I lived in such affectionate intimacy with your family: and if some few of the idler hopes of that time came to nothing, at least all the best and dearest memories of a friendship I prized so much remain fresh in my heart as ever—else it would be too sad *now*. May God comfort you in this calamity. I will only say that I am, dear Macready,
>
> Most affectionately yours
Robert Browning

6 Sordello into Suspense

Victorian half-wits claimed that this poem was obscure.

EZRA POUND[1]

MACREADY had left Browning a legacy from the many visits to Elstree and the years of frustration as a playwright—a friendship with Euphrasia Fanny Haworth. It was never more than a friendship, but it was Fanny he thought of when several years later, Elizabeth Barrett was told that "Mr. Browning is to be married immediately to Miss Campbell." Denying even acquaintance—"I never in my life saw, to my knowledge, a woman of that name," he went on, "it must be a simple falsehood and not gossip or distortion of fact . . . I told you of the one instance where such distortion *might* take place—(Miss Haworth to avoid mistake)."

The surviving letters to Miss Haworth give a picture of a pleasant interchange, making visits to Elstree still very much worth while. In the Pfortzheimer Library, New York, is a copy of *Strafford* gilt-edged and bound in white silk, subscribed "Miss Haworth from the author." The first letter is of 1838 and begins abruptly: "Do look at a Fuchsia in full bloom and notice the clear little honey-drop depending from every flower . . . a bee's breakfast. . . . Taste and be Titania." He had himself such a love for flowers and leaves as to "satiate myself with their scent,— bite them to bits," and every scene had its own flowers which brought it back. "Snowdrops and Tilsit in Prussia go together; cowslips and Windsor Park . . . You will see *Sordello* in a trice, if the fagging fit

D

holds." And therein she will find herself as " 'Eyebright'—meaning a simple and sad sort of translation of 'Euphrasia.' "

Only just back from Italy, he is full of the story of a "ship floating keel uppermost," discovered when righted to be a pirate full of "tobacco and cigars, good lord such heaps of them, and then bale after bale of prints and chintz, don't you call it . . ." But also were revealed the dead bodies of the sailors, floating horribly disfigured. A sketch showed Fanny how the vessels lay when the captain, fearing plague, cut the ship adrift and she went reeling off "like a mutilated creature . . . into the most gorgeous and lavish sunset in the world." But she asks for his news—he has been to Trieste, Venice, Bassano, "delicious Asolo"—and the rest . . . "Shall you come to town, anywhere near town soon? . . . I shall be vexed if you don't write soon. . . ."

The fagging fit did indeed hold—and one wonders whether, *Sordello* being already in proof, a letter from Caroline Fox to Fanny Haworth may still have contributed to seal its fate with Browning's public. For she reported how John Sterling, Carlyle's friend and admirer, had been repelled by the "Verbosity" of *Paracelsus*. "Doth not Mr. Browning know that Wordsworth will devote a fortnight to the discovery of a single word that is the one fit for his sonnet?" It was probably sheer coincidence, but in those days a great deal could be done on proofs, and Dowden notices despairingly how in *Sordello* words insignificant but essential have been omitted, thus "jamming together" those "that gleam and sparkle. . . . The mind is at once dazzled and fatigued."

Yet William Rossetti states that Browning sent *Sordello* to a friend before it was published, "saying that this time the public should not accuse him at any rate of being unintelligible," while a letter to Fanny Haworth explains in prose far more obscure than the verse itself what he had intended to say in the lines addressed to her. He goes on to defend himself for not behaving like the translator who put in brackets ten words of explanation to five of translation. He really imagined, comments Dowden, "that his shorthand was Roman type of unusual clearness." But he was grateful to Fanny. "You say roses and lilies and lilac-bunches and lemon flowers about it while everybody else pelts

cabbage stump after potato paring—nay, not everybody—for Carlyle . . .
but I won't tell you what Milnes told me Carlyle told him the other
day."[2]

On the surface life was going on much as before, but while Fanny
Haworth was writing verse in honor of Browning's poetry, Eliza Flower
was disillusioned with the boy whom she had so warmly encouraged in
his early teens: ". . . he has twisted the old-young shoot off by the neck,"
she wrote to a friend. And in another letter: "If he had not got the
habit of talking of head and heart as two independent existences, one
would say he was born without a heart." Mind was developing in
Browning at a faster rate than heart. It is interesting to find him wanting
a "subject of the most wild and passionate love" and asking Fanny
Haworth for her opinion on what a complete self-forgetting devotion
may mean, and whether it would be best depicted in a man or a woman!
But there is a boyish touch when, hoping soon to see her, he feels sure
he will do something "snubworthy."

Browning was still a frequent visitor at the new establishment in
Bayswater where Fox, having settled an annuity on his wife, was
living with his daughter "Tottie," his son Florance, Sarah Flower, now
Mrs. Adams, and her husband—and Eliza Flower. But the two letters
quoted in the last chapter seem to show Sarah as now the closer friend.
Through her he sends messages to "Mr. Fox and Miss Flower," begging her to be "profuse in compliments" to the latter. She is herself
with equal formality "Mrs. Adams," but there is a jestingly familiar
note as he declares how proud his father will be to show her the Bank,
where he hopes she will "see somethink," and how he has been ill and,
longing to see her when his strength returns, yet feels " 'tis as good men
hope to get to heaven—only I really wish to go."[3]

The most vivid glimpse we get of Browning's visits to that household comes from "Tottie," later known as Mrs. Bridell-Fox. She remembered with special vividness (though she got the year wrong) Browning coming in one day saying that it was his birthday and would she
mind if he played the piano till the others came home. The bells of a
neighboring church broke out just then in a merry peal—to greet, she
fancied, the young poet. Like Macready she was impressed with his

appearance "slim and dark and very handsome."[4] Sarah Flower felt he would look "unexceptionally poetical if Nature had not played him an ugly trick in giving him an ugly nose."

Mrs. Bridell-Fox remembered, too, how on his return from Italy in 1839 he had graphically described and pictured the scenes—smoking a sheet of letter paper over a candle to help dark cloud effects. All through his life there is noticeable this eager pouring out of all the exciting, interesting, beautiful things the world had to show, but of the man himself one's surmises must be built chiefly on the poetry, and even then: "my deep of life I know/ Is unavailing e'en to poorly show."

It was unfortunate that *Pippa Passes*, a comprehensible poem, should have contained a line to do Browning more harm than anything else he ever wrote: "God's in his heaven,/ All's right with the world." For this utterance of the little silk spinner is a direct contradiction of Browning's chief Christian philosophy expressed by Chesterton so as to startle us into attention—a hope founded not only on the incompleteness of man but on the incompleteness of God. God, he is saying to us again and again in his religious poetry, would have shown less love than man had he not with divine jealousy become man to suffer for man.

Browning has been praised or berated for discovering hidden good in evil men, but he knew too well how much evil can lurk beneath good, how perilous is life for us all—and thereby how exciting:

> . . . any nose
> May ravage with impunity a rose:
> Rifle a musk-pod and 'twill ache like yours!
> I'd tell you that same pungency ensures
> An after-gust, but that were overbold.
> Who would has heard Sordello's story told.

But had he?

Tennyson remarked that he understood only two lines of *Sordello,* the first and the last: "Who will may hear Sordello's story told," and "Who would has heard Sordello's story told"—and that those two lines were lies. Jane Welsh Carlyle said she had read it through without discovering whether Sordello was a man, a city, or a book. Douglas Jerrold, recovering from an illness, thrust the book into his wife's hands and as he saw bewilderment growing in her face gave a deep sigh of relief; after all he had *not,* as he feared, become so mentally deranged as to be unable to read the English language. And a friend to whom Charles Gavan-Duffy lent it "sent it back with an inquiry, whether by any chance it might be the sacred book of the Irvingite Church, written in their unknown tongue."

Harriet Martineau had been kept awake for the first time in her life by *Paracelsus* and had formed unbounded expectations of *Sordello.* Browning had talked it over with her and she, too, had given him bad advice. "Denies himself preface and notes," she wrote in her journal, "he must choose between being historian or poet. . . . I advised him to let the poem tell its own tale." But when it appeared, "I was so wholly unable to understand it that I supposed myself ill."

Browning was a frequent visitor to Miss Martineau and his talk she found "absolutely clear and purpose-like. He was full of good sense and fine feeling amidst occasional irritability, full also of fun and harmless satire, with some little affectations which were as droll as anything could be."

Lowell, urged to read Browning, "shocked" Moncure Conway "by echoing the commonplaces about the poet's obscurity. 'I own' he said, 'a copy of Sordello and anybody may have it who will put his hand upon his heart and say he understands it.' "

One notes even today signs of impatience against its admirers in those who have decided that the poem is unintelligible: "It will remain," says Lounsbury, "a colossal derelict upon the sea of literature, inflicting damage upon the strongest intellects that graze it even slightly, and hopelessly wrecking the frailer mental craft that come into full collision with it."

As the stories multiplied it became the fashion to abuse *Sordello;* it is not a habit of the intelligentsia to stand out against the fashion of their own age, bold though they may be against fashions already well and truly buried. D. G. Rossetti, however, insisted on its acceptance by the pre-Raphaelite brotherhood, and himself read long extracts from it to all who would listen. And a little later Swinburne would learn the entire poem by heart.

Among Browning's own friends "Orion" Horne (so called after a successful epic he had written) had a mitigating word to say. "What pure diamonds of the first water," he wrote to Fox, "are to be found in this confused setting! His genius is equal to his perversity. . . . The poem wants a second volume of unreadable notes to make it quite perfect. What a waste of genius."

Tennyson's criticism was perhaps the most just and explains a good deal of the general exasperation. Sordello's thoughts are often magnificently rendered—and quite intelligibly for anyone who cares to concentrate on thought—but the story is the unintelligible thing. It is concerned with the wars of Guelphs and Ghibellines in Italy and for the modern reader, English or American, some slight historical introduction, some few notes, would be almost indispensable. But if it were concerned with the Wars of the Roses or the American Civil War, Browning's way of handling it would still be hopelessly confusing.

Sordello was a troubadour, who left thirty-five poems in Provençal which Browning must have studied. The first version of *Sordello* was devoted to his life as poet—his childhood at Goito, "Sordello in his drowsy paradise"—his contest with other troubadours, above all "the history of a soul": Sordello's adolescence, in the court and castle where he lived, his strivings to discover what a poet means, what he stands for in the world, how to communicate.

Browning's Italian tutor, Cerutti, had edited Danielo Bartoli's *De Simboli Trasportati e Morale,* which Browning took with him to Italy in 1838 as a model of style. Bartoli draws attention to Dante's treatment of Sordello in the fifth, sixth, and seventh cantos of the *Purgatorio;* Browning rereading this in 1845 told Elizabeth Barrett that Sordello was "one of the burdened contorted souls" described there. Failing on earth, they yet see a light from heaven and pass to God, "which is just my Sordello's story." The *Biographie Universelle,* which would give enough historical background for this first version, tells us that Sordello was born at Mantua about 1189, was warrior as well as troubadour and as such made his fame, that he was probably of the Visconti family, but that his parentage was uncertain, and that he met a violent death.

For some reason Browning laid *Sordello* aside to write *Paracelsus* and only after completing this returned halfheartedly to the earlier poem. I say halfheartedly because of the innumerable distractions in the two years that followed. He wrote *Strafford* and fought his first round with Macready. He dined, danced, and otherwise diverted himself, intending to complete *Sordello* after the production of *Strafford* (on the published version of which he had advertised it). But before he could do so a rival version was announced by a Mrs. Busk, telling the same story in the same kind of verse.

Browning now made a fresh start deciding to develop the warrior more and to increase the romantic element in the poem. The real Sordello had loved and been loved by Cunizza (already five times married) of the Ezzelino family, but Browning changed her into her younger half sister, Palma. Apparently when the Busk poem actually appeared, he found that it too dwelt on the warrior Sordello, after whom a square in the city of Mantua is still named, and that her poem, too, dwelt on the love theme. There must be yet more thinking, yet another start.

And there was certainly a great deal of reading done, perhaps too much for the poem—Giambatista Verci's three volume *Storia degli Ecelini*, Antonio Muratori's collection of Italian historical documents, and so on.

The uncertainty about Sordello's parentage gave Browning an opening for making him the son of the great Ghibelline leader Salinguerra. His own visit to Italy (where in Venice he witnessed scenes of great poverty), combined with his historical researches both for this poem and for *Strafford* and the liberalism first inspired by Shelley,—to create a Sordello, aware from youth of mankind's: "petty enjoyments and huge miseries."

Sordello's love for Palma, the ambitions opened by the discovery of his parentage, which would make him successor to the rule of northern Italy, war in his soul against the belief he has formed that mankind will be served, peace will be restored, only by the triumph of the Pope's party, the Guelphs, that they are the party of the people. The story, insofar as it has been told, ends with Sordello's death, brought about by the intensity of his internal struggle. But the historical Sordello lived into old age.

The poem gives the impression that Browning did not so much rewrite at each fresh start as shove new elements in among the old. And in the third book we find the author suddenly, bewilderingly "on a ruined palace-step/ At Venice," asking, "why should I break off, nor sit/ Longer upon my step, exhaust the fit/ England gave birth to?" Only after several pages of his own reflections does Book II end with the promise, again unfulfilled, "And you *shall* hear Sordello's story told." [Italics mine.]

If you read *Sordello* for ideas and descriptions, it will exhilarate you; if you read it for the story, it will have you, like Douglas Jerrold, questioning your sanity. W. S. Landor said of Browning, "I only wish he would atticise a little. Few of the Athenians had such a quarry on their property, but they constructed better roads for the conveyance of the material." Who was there to quarry for Browning or to cart the buried treasure and display it?

Chesterton (and many others following him) have attributed Browning's obscurity to two things: his knowledge of matters where the average reader has no knowledge, and his almost insane haste to get his story told. Both these elements appear all the time in the external story of *Sordello*. Republishing the poem in 1863, he added a note: "I wrote it twenty-five years ago for only a few, counting even in these on somewhat more care about its subject than they really had." Acknowledging "many" faults of expresssion, he yet clearly felt that more industry and enthusiasm would have made better readers. Brought up in a library, he expected a knowledge of words and allusions unreasonable even with educated readers in that era of high education. In the latest edition of his complete poetical works footnotes have been added from which—to take a few instances at random—one learns that a pavis is a shield, a carroch a car of state, orpine is stone crop, a valvassor is a vassal, the Miramoline signifies *Emir al Maromenim, i.e.,* Prince of the Faithful, filamot is the color of a dead leaf, a manganel is an instrument for throwing stones, knops are buds, almug is sandalwood, a pompion is a mellon, byssus is a fine cloth, a basnet a light helmet, an angelot is a lute, a platan is a plane tree, colibri are humming birds, and so on, and so on. I suppose one ought to know that Tagliafer was a minstrel knight of William the Conqueror and Eglamor a troubadour, but I didn't. Then there is the Bible and Aeschylus and Don Quixote and various Provençal terms, to say nothing of an occasional botanical one (St. Bruno's lily, the *Authericum liliastrum*).

For the enjoyment of *Sordello* I would suggest reading it through once or twice, marking the passages that most impress you, and then rereading those passages. As you go from mark to mark, you will find, I think, that you are learning much of the poetic process in Browning's mind and of the further shaping of his own convictions.

This was what he wanted us to understand—"the development of a soul: little else is worth study." But a spiritual soul involves intellect, and Sordello's intellect, as interpreted by Browning, brings with it obscurity of another kind. When he spoke of the "incidents" in that development, his critics saw them only in the tangled story of an Italian republic, but for Browning they lay as much—perhaps more— in the scenes in which young Sordello's boyhood passed, when "Virtue took form, nor vice refused a shape; / Here heaven opened, there was hell agape."

The discovery of himself as poet was for Browning the supreme event:

> He loosed that fancy from its bonds of rhyme,
> (Like Perseus when he loosed his naked love)
> Faltering; so distinct and far above
> Himself, those fancies! . . .
>   Then how he loved that art!
> The calling, making him a man apart
> From men . . .
>   Since verse, the gift,
> Was his, and men, the whole of them, must shift
> Without it, e'en content themselves with wealth
> And pomp and power, snatching a life by stealth.

D*

But it was not easy, and here we reach the *necessary* obscurity of this very great poem. He was discussing, untrained as he was, some of the deepest problems that the greatest philosophers have discussed, which cannot of their nature be made easy for anybody. "Out of that aching brain, a very stone, / Song must be struck." It was a song whose essence sought language fiercely but often in vain:

> He left imagining, to try the stuff
> That held the imaged thing, and, let it writhe
> Never so fiercely, scarce allowed a tithe
> To reach the light—his Language.

To Domett he wrote of "the misery I made [Sordello] feel at 'inadequate vehicles' of feeling—of which this letter-writing always seemed to me the worst and is now got down to something absolutely horrible."

Venice, the mountains, devastated Ferrara, troubadours in contest, Guelphs and Ghibellines. All this "the harness of his workmanship" made easy to depict, but

> Piece after piece that armour broke away,
> Because perceptions whole, like that he sought
> To clothe, reject so pure a work of thought
> As language: thought may take perception's place
> But hardly co-exist in any case,
> Being its mere presentment—of the whole
> By parts, the simultaneous and the sole
> By the successive and the many.

But what could not be explained syllogistically might perhaps be shown.

> They climb; life's view is not at once disclosed
> To creatures caught up, on the summit left,
> Heaven plain above them, yet of wings bereft.

The dramatic monologue was Browning's true form, not the long narrative poem. Yet he did flash upon the screen the horrors of Ferrara besieged: "howe'er the battle went / The conqueror would but have a corpse to kiss",—the misery of this internecine strife:

> ". . . proved alike, men weighed with men
> And deed with deed, blaze, blood, with blood and blaze, . . .
> The Guelph the Ghibellin may be to curse—
> I have done nothing, but both sides do worse
> Than nothing . . ."

Sordello was seeking "A cause, intact, distinct from these, ordained /
For me, its true discoverer." And we find him struggling with one of the
unresolved problems of Browning's youthful ambition—the desire to
choose everything.

> God has conceded two sights to a man—
> One, of men's whole work, time's completed plan,
> The other, of the minute's work, man's first
> Step to the plan's completeness! . . .
> Read the black writing—that collective man
> Outstrips the individual . . .

Man and men, time and eternity, matter and spirit, finite and infinite, man and God, these are the concepts with which he is wrestling.
He discovers that whether his ambition be to shine or to serve, he can
only pray:

> Let the employer match the thing employed,
> Fit to the finite his infinity, . . .
>   A sphere is but a sphere;
> Small, Great, are merely terms we bandy here;
> Since to the spirit's absoluteness all
> Are like.

Browning seems, while realizing the union of matter and spirit in
man, to have thought not only of God but of spirit itself as infinite. Yet
he marvelously depicts the soul's effort to get from the body more than
it can give, to pour in her own endlessness, "supply the power it lacked
/ From her infinity . . ."

> And the result is, the poor body soon
> Sinks under what was meant a wondrous boon,
> Leaving its bright accomplice all aghast.

Browning has seen a philosophic concept totally unfamiliar to his age, which Newman was hinting at in his illative sense—that of Animus and Anima. Animus all thinkers recognize, making its choices, working out its problems; but deep beneath, deeper even than the subconscious of psychology, lies Anima where God the Creator is still continually creating the being He brought out of nothingness, and it is at this depth that the great decisions of life are made. So Sordello

> . . . cast
> Himself quite through mere secondary states
> Of his soul's essence, little loves and hates,
> Into the mid deep yearnings overlaid
> By these . . .

Sordello dies of the struggle: only a very young man could so readily see in death the solution of the problems Browning sets. This death is also an overcoming:

> A triumph lingering in the wide eyes,
> Wider than some spent swimmer's if he spies
> Help from above in his extreme despair . . .

Yet, characteristically enough, the poet then takes us through an absolutely headlong summary of the history that followed Sordello's death and casts on his hero the doubts he may well have been feeling about himself:

> All he was anxious to appear, but scarce
> Solicitous to be. A sorry farce
> Such life is after all!

Was there nothing more to be said for Sordello, did he not live "for some one better thing? this way." Turning back to "sparkling Asolo," Browning sees a child "barefoot and rosy" climbing the hill.

> Up and up goes he, singing all the while
> Some unintelligible words to beat
> The lark, God's poet, swooning at his feet . . .

This boy, this lark, were the true picture of

> ... the complete Sordello, Man and Bard,
> John's cloud-girt angel, this foot on the land,
> That on the sea, with, open in his hand,
> A bitter-sweetling of a book.

But you must read *Sordello*. No brief quotation can convey the greatness of a poem which because of its great faults, fell like a stone into a sea of scorn.

"A great fuss," said a leading barrister of the hour to Holman Hunt, "had been made about one Browning, but it had all ended in smoke."

Almost fifty years later Gosse relates how Browning talked "with complete frankness" of "the long-drawn desolateness of his early and middle life as a literary man," of how "a blight had fallen upon his very admirers."

No wonder the reception of *Sordello* became a sore spot, though it was slowly that he realized the almost irreparable damage done to his reputation. Lounsbury does not exaggerate in attributing to it the determination not even to read him that began with this poem and lasted for more than a quarter century. Had *Pippa Passes* only preceded it, the fame won by *Paracelsus* might have been strengthened enough to be proof against the really immense disillusion that set in. None would review a book they believed impossible to understand.

Elizabeth Barrett had it in her heart, she said, to covet the authorship of *Pippa Passes* above all Browning's other poems. It is the story of the one day's holiday of a little silk spinner of "delicious Asolo," whose passing by influences for good people unaware of her existence. Originally the scenes were entitled Morning, Noon, Evening, and Night. The idea had occurred to Browning earlier, yet the poem stems from *Sordello,* both in its descriptions of what he had seen in Asolo and in Pippa's likeness to and contrast with the Provençal poet himself. Sordello is struggling self-consciously to help mankind; Pippa does it far more deeply in her total unconsciousness. Both are depicted as poor, and both are discovered in the end to be the children of wealthy parents. But this, which seems to fit perfectly in *Sordello,* is surely, as Chesterton notes, an artistic blemish in *Pippa Passes*. Her anonymity is of the poem's essence. Her songs and her disembodied voice are all that is known of her to those whose lives she changes.

Like Micawber prospering in Australia or Tennyson's Enoch Arden posthumously comforted by a costly funeral, Pippa's social elevation belongs to the period, as does Elizabeth's coveting of the authorship. But even the people helped by Pippa to face the evil in themselves would not have sung as she did: "God's in his heaven, / All's right with the world!"

It was after *Sordello* that the publisher suggested bringing out the next poem in a small cheap edition as the first of a series. This series Browning entitled *Bells and Pomegranates*—and into it went *Pippa Passes*.

More than forty years later, forwarding to Professor Norton the letter he received from Carlyle after having sent him *Sordello* and *Pippa*, Browning wrote: "The goodness and sympathy which began so long ago continued unabated to the end of the writer's life. I returned them with just as enduring affectionate gratitude. It was not I who ventured to make the acquaintance nor ask the correspondence of Carlyle: his love was altogether a free gift, and how much it has enriched my life, I shall hardly attempt to say . . ."

Carlyle wrote, in care of Browning's publisher:

Chelsea, June 21, 1841.

My dear Sir—Many months ago you were kind enough to send me your *Sordello;* and now this day I have been looking into your *Pippa Passes*, for which also I am your debtor. If I have made no answer hitherto, it was surely not for want of interest in you, for want of estimation of you: both Pieces have given rise to many reflexions in me, not without friendly hopes and anxieties in due measure. Alas, it is so seldom that any word one can speak is not worse than a word still unspoken;—seldom that one man, by his speaking or his silence, can, in great vital interests, help another at all!—

Unless I very greatly mistake, judging from these two works, you seem to possess a rare spiritual gift, poetical, pictorial, intellectual, by whatever name we may prefer calling it; to unfold which into articulate clearness is naturally the problem of all problems for you. This noble endowment, it seems to me farther, you are *not* at present on the best way for unfolding;—and if the world had loudly called itself content with these two Poems, my surmise is, the world could have rendered you no fataller disservice than that same! Believe me I speak with sincerity; and if I had not loved you well, I would not have spoken at all.

A long battle, I could guess, lies before you, full of toil and pain, and all sorts of real *fighting*: a man attains to nothing here below without that. Is it not verily the highest prize you fight for? Fight on; that is to say, follow truly, with steadfast singleness of purpose, with valiant humbleness and openness of heart, what best light *you* can attain to; following truly so, better and ever better light will rise on you. The light we ourselves gain, by our very errors if not otherwise, is the only precious light. Victory, what I call victory, if well fought for, is sure to you.

But spoken to a poet the suggestion that followed must have been dismaying:

If your own choice happened to point that way, I for one should hail it as a good omen that your next work were written in prose! Not that I deny you poetic faculty; far, very far from that. But unless poetic faculty mean a higher-power of common understanding, I know not what it means. One must first make a *true* intellectual representation of a thing, before any poetic interest that is true will supervene. All *cartoons* are geometrical withal; and cannot be made till we have fully learnt to make mere *diagrams* well. It is this that I mean by prose;—which hint of mine, most probably inapplicable at present, may perhaps at some future day come usefully to mind.

But enough of this: why have I written all this? Because I esteem yours no common case; and think such a man is not to be treated in the common way.

And so persist in God's name, as you best see and can; and understand always that my true prayer for you is, Good Speed in the name of God!

I would have called for you last year when I had a horse, and some twice rode thro' your suburb; but stupidly I had forgotten your address;—and you, you never came again hither!

Believe me, Yours most truly,

                                        T. CARLYLE

Discussing *Sordello* a few years later with Gavan Duffy, Carlyle asked, "Was there any good reason why the problems of poetry should be made more abstruse and perplexing than the problems of mathematics?"

But the friendship prospered. Carlyle wrote from Scotland July 29, 1841, to

. . . apprise you straightway that your loyalminded welcome little note finds me . . . here—on the Scotch shore of the Solway Firth; . . .

I have fled hither for a few weeks of utter solitude, donothing-ism and sea-bathing; such as promised to prove salutary for me in the mood I was getting into. London in the long-run would surely drive one mad, if it did not kill one first. Yearly it becomes more apparent to me that, as man "was not made to be alone," so he was made to be occasionally altogether alone,—or else a foolish sounding-board of a man, no *voice* in him, but only distracted and distracting multiplicities of echoes and hearsays; a very miserable and very foolish kind of object! . . .

The spirit you profess is of the best and truest: perhaps one man only, yourself only, could do much more for you than I who can do nothing, but only say with all my heart, Good Speed! Doubt it not at all, you will prosper exactly according to your *true* quantity of effort, —and I take it you already understand that among the "*true* quantities of effort" there are many, very many which the "public," reading or other, can simply know nothing of whatever, and must consider as falsities and idlenesses, if it did. But the everlasting Heart of Nature does know them, as I say; and will truly respond to them, if not today or to-morrow, then some day after to-morrow and for many and all coming days. Courage!

A first view of Browning in "a green coat" had displeased Carlyle. We know that his early tastes were a little flamboyant: this, he has explained, was a riding coat—and he could and did ride over to Chelsea. Carlyle writes, on December 1, 1841:

> The sight of your card instead of yourself, the other day when I came down stairs, was a real vexation to me. The orders here are rigorous. "Hermetically sealed till 2 o'clock!" But had you chanced to ask for my Wife, she would have guessed that you formed an exception, and would have brought me down. We must try it another way. For example: The evenings at present, when not rainy, are bright with moonlight. We are to be at home on Friday night, and alone: could you not be induced to come and join us? Tea is at six or half-past six.—If you say nothing, let us take silence for yes, and expect you!
>
> Or if another night than Friday will suit you better, propose another; and from me in like manner, let no answer mean yes and welcome. At any rate contrive to see me.

Very soon Carlyle's inveterate habit of making his friends work for him asserted itself, and Browning was commissioned to seek out a "Mr. X," descendant of Oliver Cromwell and "some kind of a fool," in an endeavor to get some material. Later in Florence far more arduous tasks would be set him and this one was sweetened by a further invitation; he had been "absent without leave" and was to call on the Carlyle's forthwith.

Carlyle said years later to Moncure Daniel Conway:

> I remember Browning as a fine young man . . . I liked him better than any young man about here. He had simple speech and manners and ideas of his own. A good talk I recall with him, when I walked with him to the top of a hill which had a fine prospect. When he published "Paracelsus" I did not make much out of it: it

seemed to me to have something "sensational" as they say about it; but that and his other works proved a strong man.[5]

These were the years when Mill and Carlyle were intimate, and Mill told Caroline Fox that he thought the Carlyles a very happy pair, although she would in conversation invent stories about him and you could see him "panting for the opportunity to stuff in a negation." Browning, Mill, Macready, and the rest all attended Carlyle's lectures; but Mrs. Carlyle told her he was unhappy as he delivered them, wondering all the time whether people felt they were getting their guinea's worth. "It is so difficult for him," she complained, "to try to unite the characters of the prophet and the mountebank"—which sounded several degrees worse than his own comparison—prophet and actor! "Carlyle is lecturing with éclat—", wrote Browning, "the Macreadys go, and the Bishop of Salisbury, and the three Miss Styles that began German last week."

Jane must have been an awkward wife to her exceedingly difficult husband—and awkward to some of his friends. But at that time she, too, accepted the young poet. "I dined with dear Carlyle and his wife," writes Browning to Fanny Haworth "(catch me calling people dear in a hurry except in letter beginnings!) yesterday. I don't know any people like them."

Browning was a useful and agreeable guest even for those who had given him up as a poet (Kenyon admired his "inexhaustible knowledge and general reasonableness," but thought his poetry "muddy and metaphysical"). The breakfast party was for men the great opportunity for good talk, and to breakfast with Mr. Kenyon he often walked with that swift step with which, a later friend declared, he passed not between but through the vehicles in his path.

Cyrus Mason viewed his cousin's habitual headlong pace as an element in his arrogance. "Are you mad?" he cried out once, almost run down by Browning rushing by on horseback. And " 'young Robert' recognised me for he dropped his whip, without deigning to speak, wheeled the horse again towards the city and galloped away." Cyrus could never, he said, read of the good news brought to Aix without picturing that furious gallop.

At the breakfast parties, over coffee and tea and substantial viands, old friendships were strengthened and many new ones made. And the Browning family was on the move—an affair far more serious than it would be deemed today.

Browning writes in an undated letter to Laman Blanchard of having "just got up from a very sick bed, indeed, where a fortnight's brain-and-liver fever has reduced me to the shade of a shade." The family were now at Hatcham and the letter is conjecturally dated late 1841. Browning begs his friend to "conquer the interminable Kent Road," pass the turnpike at New Cross, and finally " 'descry a house resembling a goose pie'; only a crooked, hasty and rash goose-pie. We have a garden and trees, and little green hills of a sort to go out on." At present he can hardly crawl—but in a week or two "Will you come?" It seems to be especially after this illness that Browning's head so often troubled him. He speaks of it to Domett, and to Christopher Dowson he writes in '44: "I have a head that aches oftener than of old to take care of."

But not long after the brain fever he writes to Fanny Haworth in the best of spirits: "Thank you, dear friend of mine—if I can I'll call at this week's end." He is drawing again and enjoying it. Had he ever told her he was in childhood "a young wonder (as are eleven out of the dozen of us) at drawing?" He had called on Forster who "pressed me into committing verse on the instant, not the minute." And on the instant, for a Venetian scene by the painter Maclise, he poured out for a catalogue what would later go into "In a Gondola"

> I send my heart up to thee, all my heart
>   In this my singing.
> For the stars help me, and the sea bears part;
>   The very night is clinging
> Closer to Venice' streets to leave one space
>   Above me, whence thy face
> May light my joyous heart to thee its dwelling place.

"Singing and stars and night and Venice streets in depths of shade and space are 'properties' do you please to see . . ."

"In marked contrast," writes Mrs. Miller, "to the life—'so pure, so energetic, so simple, so laborious, so loftily enthusiastic'—that the young man led under his parent's roof at Camberwell or at New Cross, is the manner of his existence in London during those years in which, night after night, in the wake of Macready, he was to be found haunting the stage-doors and dressing-rooms of Covent Garden, the Haymarket, or Drury Lane."

As with Dowden, talking of *Pauline*, I can only cry "instance, instance!" For the struggle to understand an actor, write plays, and produce them is a very different thing from hanging around stage doors.

Actually the phrase quoted "so pure, so energetic . . ." is from Arnould, written to Domett, and does not, as Mrs. Miller thinks, belong to past years but to *this very period* with which she contrasts it. The two men were constantly together, the young barrister attending the rehearsals and the performance of his friend's play.

Arnould and Domett talked often of Browning in their letters: ". . . he is a fine friend," says Arnould; "he has an energy of kindness about him which never slumbers." Through him Arnould had "obtained an entrance into Periodical Literature" long promised by less zealous acquaintance. So, not at rehearsals only but at friends' houses, Arnould might meet men like Fox, Forster, Talfourd, Horne, and Landor. His letters to Domett in New Zealand usefully complement those with which Browning kept Domett informed of his own doings and feelings from 1842 until his marriage. Domett it was who inspired "Waring" and was recalled in "The Guardian Angel."

A long letter in May, 1842, seems to show Browning half doubting whether he, too, should not leave the country where he felt at times so stifled. It was probably a mood; he was still enjoying breakfast parties at Mr. Kenyon's, his arguments—perhaps even his rows—with Forster, and above all the opportunity, when it came, of sitting at the feet of Carlyle. But he was uneasy, often unhappy. A poet must crave an audience—to say nothing of the money question. The decision he had

Robert Browning, 1837. Pencil drawing by Comte Amedee de Ripert Monclar

Apr. Yes; I see now—God is the PERFECT POET,

Who in ~~his person~~ acts his own ~~creatures~~.
creation ... *conceptions.*

Shall man refuse to be aught less than God? &c

Had you but told me this at first!? . . . Hush! hush!

Par. Live! for my sake, because of my great sin,

To help my brain, oppress'd by these wild words

And their deep import.   Live! 'tis not too late:

I have a quiet home for us, and friends.

Michal shall smile on you . . . Hear you? Lean thus,

And breathe my breath : I shall not lose one word

Of all your speech—~~one~~ *no* little word, Aprile.

Apr. No, no . . . Crown *me?* I am not one of you!

'Tis he, the king, you seek.   I am not one . . .

Par. ~~Thy~~ *Give me* spirit, at least, ~~Aprile.~~ *Let* me love *too*!

I HAVE ATTAIN'D, AND NOW I MAY DEPART.

Shall man refuse to be aught less than God?
Man's weakness is his glory—for the strength
which rises him to heaven and near God's self
came spite of it—God's strength his glory is,
for these came with our weakness sympathy
which brought God down to earth, a man like us.
Had you &c.

Left　　A page from the first edition of *Paracelsus*
corrected and altered by Browning

Above　　Edward, Henrietta and Elizabeth Barrett

Robert Browning,
1854. Painted in
Rome by W. Fisher

Elizabeth Barrett
Browning, 1858
From an engraving
after a photograph
by Macaire

made was not irrevocable. Perhaps that magic word "Colonies" attracted him, and he felt that Domett had something he was missing.

> I shall never read over what I send you—reflect on it, care about it, or fear that you will not burn it when I ask you. So do with me. And tell me all about yourself, . . . how you are, where you are, what you do and mean to do—and to do in our way, for live properly you cannot without writing . . . the little I, or anybody, can do as it is, comes of them *going to New Zealand*—partial retirement and stopping the ears against the noise outside; but all is next to useless—for there is a creeping, magnetic, assimilating influence nothing can block out. When I block it out I shall do something. Don't you feel already older (in the wise sense of the word) and farther off, as one "having a purchase" against us? . . . At present, I don't know if I stand on head or heels; what men require I don't know—and of what they are in possession know nearly as little.

Letters came and went with a slowness we can today hardly imagine:

> You do not [writes Browning on October 9, '43]—that is, did not six months ago—write to me; . . . People read my works a little more, they say, and I have some real works here, in hand; but now that I could find it in my heart to labour earnestly, I doubt if I shall ever find it in my *head,* which sings and whirls and stops me even now at this minute—an *evening* minute by the way.

Sadly enough, between these two letters had appeared—and had sunk without a ripple in the world of contemporary literature—Browning's *Dramatic Lyrics.* In this volume he showed both the immense range of his genius—from "The Pied Piper of Hamelin" to "Soliloquy of the Spanish Cloister," and his musical power in lyric poetry—"Rudel to the Lady of Tripoli," "In a Gondola." But one poem alone should at least have stirred a rare excitement, a first dramatic monologue, never I think surpassed: "My Last Duchess."

None of this did the critics discover. John Forster praised the volume (in *The Examiner*), and it is hardly surprising that to the remark "Mr.

Browning is a genuine poet," he should have added, "and only needs to have less misgivings on the subject himself."

These must indeed have been dark years—a sense of "toiling in immeasurable sand," as play after play failed or was rejected—and now his lyrics too had fallen flat. To Domett, Browning had written that May:

> Carlyle came here a few weeks ago—walked about the place, and talked very wisely and beautifully. . . .
>
> So glides this foolish life away week by week! I have a desk full of scrawls at which I look and work a little. I want to publish a few more numbers of my "Bells"—and must also make up my mind to finish a play I wrote lately for Charles Kean, if he will have it. They take to criticizing me a little more in the reviews—and God send I be not too proud of their abuse . . . the proper old drivelling virulence with which God's Elect have in all ages been regaled.[6]

Shouting, surely to keep his spirits up. Browning was at the cross-roads with no clear view of what to do next. He had made a considerable circle of friends, but the Macready row had cooled off some of them and he seemed to be cast for the part of the very promising young man who has failed to keep his promises. Depressed he might be, but he fought back at fortune, and we soon hear of a fresh attempt, in the letters of an admirer he had unknowingly won.

"I must tell you," wrote Elizabeth Barrett to Miss Mitford, "that Mr. Browning is said to have written two plays—one for Charles Kean and the public, the other for himself and *Bells and Pomegranates*. I am sorry." She was, alas, undemocratic enough to grudge him to "the Great Unwashed who can't read aright. . . . Yet after all, he is a true, soul piercing poet."

Her informant was probably Kenyon who had got as near the truth as reports commonly go. Browning had criticized Kean fiercely enough when working for his great rival, but nothing could cure him of writing plays, so *Colombe's Birthday* was finished and read to Kean and his wife who agreed to play it—but not for a year or more. Unlike Macready, Kean was a "slow study" and when he had finished his existing engagements, would need at least two months to learn the part. Meanwhile, he said, the play must *not* be published.

Another instalment was due for *Bells and Pomegranates,* and Browning surprisingly told Christopher Dowson that he felt he would lose his hold on his existing group of hearers (whom at other times one finds him treating as inexistent; his feelings seem to have gone up and down according to letters received or lacking, friends just met and suchlike impalpables). Anyhow he decided after taking advice that "for the sake of two or three hundred pounds" it was not worth waiting; into *Bells and Pomegranates* the play should go. "I sent it to press yesterday and merely put the right of *the acting* at his disposal." All this seems plain midsummer madness (though the letter was written on March 10) until one remembers the past history with Macready. "After Easter next year . . ." How long after? What fresh postponements might be hidden in the word "after"? Could an actor really, Browning asked, need two months to learn a part? He might perhaps force Kean into quick production by invoking his publishers, as he had earlier saved a play from mutilation by Macready.

If such was his train of thought, it proved erroneous. *Colombe's Birthday* went unacted until many years later. But "the good fortune" which Browning had told Dowson "seems slowly but not mistakeably settling in upon me just now" failed, as ever, to materialize. Even Forster, the one admirer of *Dramatic Lyrics,* ended his review of *Colombe's Birthday* in *The Examiner:* "As far as he has gone we abominate his taste as much as we admire his genius."

It is not surprising that estrangement should follow such blunt speech from a friend. During an earlier row we find Forster begging in a letter to Fox for Eliza Flower's opinion on his own behavior: "Her 'Roman-nosed grandeur' is the only thing that mars my self-approving recollections of the foolish quarrel." Wanting to be "quite clear in conscience," he still felt Browning should make the first move, but it would be worse to lose "a friendship on which I place no indifferent value."[7]

Eliza, laughing at Forster, may still have felt the irritation Browning provoked in her while he was Paracelsus. He seems throughout to have

enjoyed his frequent visits to her and to Fox, whom he described to
Fanny Haworth as his "literary father." But much of this pleasure, too,
was ending, for Eliza's health was causing intense anxiety. Browning
in his last letter to her—dated only "Monday," but placed by Mrs. Orr
in 1845—writes:

> Of your health I shall not trust myself to speak: you must know
> what is unspoken. I should have been most happy to see you if but
> for a minute—and if next Wednesday, I might take your hand for
> a moment—
> But you would concede that, if it were right, remembering what
> is now a very old friendship.

It was in Pisa in 1846 that he heard of Eliza's death and wrote to
Hengist Horne of "her strange, beautiful memory."

The friendship with Forster continued despite many a quarrel, but
Browning was passing through a stage of immense difficulty as poet and
as a man. Everything seemed crumbling except a social life about which
his feelings were fascinatingly ambivalent. He had not yet—did he
ever?—seized the clue to a mystery that would affect him for good or
for evil all his life through. Just now he was bewildered; lonely yet
spoiled by his family, surrounded by friends and acquaintances, a socialite (if the word had then been known) who would dance from ten
to six and come home in broad daylight, a dilettante who had staged
two unsuccessful plays and done odd jobs for other writers, a spoiled
poet about whom a great fuss had once been made. But that had been
almost a decade ago.

7 Elizabeth Barrett

I have a sad heart and a merry mind.

ELIZABETH BARRETT BROWNING

ELIZABETH BARRETT BARRETT was the eldest of the eleven children (one died in infancy) of Edward Barrett Moulton Barrett. Only in England could such names be borne, in both senses of the word, but the Barretts were colonial English having large estates in Jamaica, owning many slaves until emancipation. Edward Barrett had settled in England, leaving a younger brother Sam to manage the plantation. He had bought an estate of four hundred acres in Herefordshire. There he built a "Turkish house" described by Elizabeth as "crowded with minarets and domes," and "crowned with metal spires and crescents." In *Aurora Leigh* she writes of the "sweet familiar nature" surrounding her, of trees and flowers and sun and moon, but says nothing of the large family that we meet in her early letters, undated notes mostly, and in a handwriting gradually forming.

"My dear old gentleman," she writes to her father, "say inexorable monarch of Hope End, can no entreaties mortal or immortal prevail upon you to command the crested chariot to be linked to the four high mettled steeds to bear us to Kinnersley?" But to her mother, addressed as "Dear old Lady" goes a note "Do you not think dearest Mama it would be a good way to write a nice funny letter to him, he is in a very good humour?"[1]

Edward Moulton Barrett was in those years a benevolent tyrant, and letters written to Uncle Sam in Jamaica tell of his encouragement of the family games and works. The children opened a soup kitchen for the poor, selling the soup at a penny a quart, and Elizabeth writes, "Papa has made us a handsome present of a quarter of an ox." They had put their own pocket money into the scheme, but I have found no record of how it prospered or how long it lasted.

Life was richly full. There were compositions to be written and judged by her mother—"a note by John to the schoolroom" is begged for that she may know the verdict at once. There was an immensity of reading—Corneille's *Télémaque*, Racine, the poet Southey whom she loved "contrary to all the others" excepting "Bum" (their aunt). One note to Mama asks that she may omit her music to "alter my poetry, get flowers, write my verses."

The flowers may well have been a useful excuse, for in such a household it was probably the only thing asked of a girl that could possibly be called a domestic task. No beds had to be made, no dusting done, still less sweeping. Commonly a housekeeper would even take over from the mistress of the house the onerous tasks of overseeing the cook and her provisioning, the maids and their work. "Henrietta always 'managed' everything in the house," Elizabeth would later tell Browning, "even before I was ill because she liked it and I didn't, and I waived my right to the sceptre of dinner ordering."

It was her poetry that mattered to Elizabeth. At the age of six she had been dubbed by her father Poet Laureate of Hope End, and every birthday, every "occasion," called for its appropriate verses. Then, too, she had organized a family theater. "Madame," she writes, "We have the honour to announce to you the representation of a new tragedy this evening."

In an appendix to *Letters of the Brownings to George Barrett* is one from Elizabeth to her grandmother written at the age of ten (dated July 27, 1816), describing the delights of Hope End. "Nature here displays all her art." The grapes that are ripening, the ivy that this same Nature "fastens up to some majestic tree without the aid of nails or the active gardener. . . . We have played at a new game lately, we have each been Queen or King of some country or island, for example I and Arabella are the empresses of the Hyères, Bro [her name for Edward, the oldest of her brothers] and Henrietta are the emperor and empress of Italy, Storm is the Prince of Rome, and Sam is Emperor of Oberon. . . . we sometimes have Battles, the other day Henrietta and I fought. I conquered, took her prisoner and tied her to the leg of the table."

An undated letter from Mrs. Moulton reads like a reply to this one —except for the fact that George is referred to as perhaps running about—which means that it must have been written at least a year later. Mock battles can turn into serious ones, and the grandmother feels that Elizabeth is getting "too BIG to attempt fighting with Bro. He might give you an *unlucky* Blow on your Neck which might be serious to you. He is strong and powerful."

All brothers and sisters fight when they are little; most grow out of it quickly, and Elizabeth early became too busy to do much fighting. Soup kitchens and dramas alike demanded organizing; every year there was a new brother or sister to be guided and brought on. Eldest sisters do become a little tyrannical, being encouraged in this by harassed parents or nurses who leave them in charge of "the little ones."

Elizabeth, in an Autobiography written by her at the age of fourteen, has either really forgotten or consciously pushed away the memory of early quarrels. She frankly proclaims her determination to be the undisputed ruler with "no UPSTART to usurp my authority," but goes on to state that "my dearest Bro' though my constant companion and beloved participator in all my pleasures never allowed the rage for power to injure the endearing sweetness of his temper."

Describing the Autobiography as "glimpses into my own life and literary character," she declares that "no human eye" may ever see this writing, prompted "by no excessive vanity, but perhaps SELF LOVE.

"At four I first mounted Pegasus. . . . At eleven I wished to be considered an authoress. . . . At twelve I enjoyed a literary life in all its pleasures. Metaphysics were my delight."

She does not mention here the first event that must have shaken her, as any ambitious girl of that period would be shaken: the discovery that a higher education was offered to her brother and not to herself. But she won her point when allowed to share Bro's tutor and learn Greek with him. Was an early message in Latin part of an exercise?

"*Puero eruditissimo et elegantissimo Bro a manu stultissimo Sam de puella impudentissima.*" By her thirteenth birthday, she had, she boasts, learned "to throw away ambition," and great self-command now conceals "a turmoil of conflicting passions."

Were these passions, this turmoil, aroused when the time came for Bro to leave home for a public school? She does not record it, and we may as readily imagine either intense concealed bitterness, or long loving talks with her mother and the realization that she still reigned at home. There were other compensations: judging by the letters she wrote in French, she had good teaching in that language and it was she, not her brother, who traveled with her parents to France. Only the year before she had written her longest and most ambitious poem *The Battle of Marathon*—and now at the age of fourteen she saw herself in print. For her father, full of pride and delight, had fifty copies of the poem printed and bound.

Elizabeth prays for Bro's happiness and safety, his protection from temptation. "If I ever loved a human being I love this dear Brother— the partner of my pleasures, of my literary toils. If to save him from anxiety, from mental vexation, any effort of mine could suffice, Heaven knows my heart that I would unhesitatingly buy his happiness with my own misery."

Exclamation marks liberally bespatter this record of the "tragic comedy" of a life "chequered by my own feelings, not by external causes, and like Rosalind I have 'laughed and wept in the same breath. . . .' My destiny lies in the hands of God."

As partner of her "literary toils" Bro was presently replaced by an older man Hugh Boyd, a neighbor and classical scholar. They were mutually dependent, for Boyd was blind and Elizabeth read aloud to him by the hour, while he guided her reading of the classics and introduced her to the Greek poets of Christianity.

One element in Elizabeth's childhood reading goes unmentioned in her Autobiography. There was at Hope End a large library and Elizabeth's father had indicated one side where the books were all hers, the other where she must not read them. Obediently she avoided *Tom*

Jones, but devoured Tom Paine and Voltaire. As a very little girl she had filled her pinafore with sticks and gone out to burn a sacrificial fire to Minerva. But growing doubtful of her goddesses she fell "into a vague sort of general scepticism" and would follow the childhood's prayers she still recited with one she had found in an old book: "Oh, God, if there be a God, save my soul if I have a soul." In adult life Elizabeth became intensely religious; her poems show an awareness of God's presence; heaven was a reality to her; she could bear her narrow life, showing cheerfulness always to her family. She would not ever be guilty "Of taking vainly in a plaintive mood/The holy name of Grief—holy herein/That by the grief of One came all our good."

An intense personal devotion to Our Lord is present throughout her verse. Like Browning she was brought up a Nonconformist; she hated ritualism with a greater violence than he, loved and read the Bible and apparently even enjoyed the extempore prayers uttered by the strange father almost better known to the world in general than she is.

Between her childhood and her letters to Browning had come events that changed the precocious, gay child into the famous "poetess," recluse, and invalid.

The story of an injury when saddling her pony is today, probably correctly, dismissed as apocryphal, although one undated letter seems to confirm it. "Dr. Baron comes to examine my back accurately and with particular care. . . . I trust in God it will prove not to be the spine the restraint attending such a disease would indeed be irksome." But the accident she does not mention, then or ever. There are at the University of Illinois three letters from doctors about her illness, all published in *Letters of the Brownings to George Barrett.* These were expounded to the editor, Paul Landis, by the late Dr. D. J. Davis (Dean Emeritus of the University's Medical School) as a diagnosis of "general tuberculosis from girlhood."

The letters depict first a severe pain in the head, then in the side and back ("The suffering is agony," says Dr. Coker), paroxysms, and night frights. She was treated by bleeding, and "Opium at one time relieved the spasms." Having another patient with similar symptoms, who proved to be suffering from spinal trouble, Dr. Coker suggested treating

Elizabeth for this, although "the positive proofs are wanting of the existence of a diseased spine."

The doctors were in fact baffled, as so often in that century, by *the*
disease of the era, tuberculosis. Blood-spitting and high fever followed,
as we see from her letters to George. All three Barrett sisters probably
had some slight beginnings of the disease, but with Arabel and Henrietta it had apparently cleared up. If Dr. Davis' view is correct, it would
seem that in Elizabeth the disease had only been arrested and was in
middle age the cause of her death.

The commonly held idea that in going to bed, and thus escaping
social and family obligations, Elizabeth was almost magnificently ma-
lingering may have been started by her brother George: ". . . it isn't
altogether as agreeable," she wrote to him from Torquay, "to be here
half in the dark as you might possibly fancy." But the theory was
strengthened and became common coin as a result of a vicious attack on
Elizabeth made by Arabella Moulton Barrett (daughter of her brother
"Stormie") as late as 1938. Infuriated by the play *The Barretts of Wimpole Street,* she defended her grandfather by savaging her aunt.

Jeannette Marks in *The Family of the Barrett* tells us of her discovery that opium in some form was at that date used as a common
"household remedy" in Jamaica. One cannot tell whether the children's
nurse was a Jamaican and had begun to give it to Elizabeth in childhood.
But, as we have seen, doctors had prescribed it when she was only
fifteen. Certainly she was using it at Torquay, for, in a letter to George
she writes of longing for solitude "in a forest of chestnuts and cedars, in
an hourly succession of poetical paragraphs and morphine draughts. . . .
Not that I do such a thing." And he is to be very careful "not to say a
word of the morphine when you write."

Does this mean that her father did not know about the drug? Yet he
might have disapproved, even had it been given by doctor's orders.

By the time she was corresponding with Browning she could not, her
physicians told her, manage without a minimum of sixty drops of
laudanum a day. Morphine was another form used. Little or nothing
has been said of this by most of her biographers, from what Miss Marks
calls "an unthinking alliance to shield her 'reputation' . . . from some

of the cruel untruths spoken of opium dependents." During her lifetime she was protected by her social position, "belonging," as Miss Mitford rather quaintly put it, to "that best class in the whole world . . . the affluent and cultivated gentry of England." A foolish "protection," Miss Marks feels, and she notes how striking in Elizabeth is the development, against odds, of "mental power, strength of character and fearless plain speaking."

Poets are half drugged by their awakening powers. Is it fancy to see also some more literal drug in Elizabeth's early verse: the storm on the Malvern Hills later described so vividly in prose to Robert Browning, the gaze "Into the deep Eleusis of my heart/To learn its secret things"? The great thunderstorm had brought deaths with it, and in her dream Elizabeth sees in the lightning's flash "a white and corpse-like heap . . . The man was my familiar."

The "familiar" is, say the dictionaries, "a supernatural spirit often embodied in an animal" and again "a demon or evil spirit supposed to attend at call." It would almost seem that Socrates' daimon had been transformed into a demon: "I knew that face," cries Elizabeth. "His who did hate me—his whom I did hate."

But there is something more deeply personal in it, closer than the demonic familiar. The poem might have depicted a struggle between that dark supernatural spirit and some bright angel—but no—the struggle was in "mine heart. For there had battled in her solitudes,/Contrary spirits." Sometimes the dark seems the real "I," sometimes the bright—either might long to do the other to death, yet shudder if in a dream he found the corpse at his feet.

Elizabeth would ask Browning, "Did you ever feel afraid of your own soul. . . ?" She saw the double personality reconciled only when "Cymon bears/dares to look at Psyche *by the force of woe*." And in a vision of the "Divine Agony" of Christ comes reconciliation.

None of it was very clear during that night of storm, but there remained with Elizabeth a terror of thunder and lightning which her father deemed disgraceful for anyone who could read or write. And whenever it began there was, too, the opium.

Elizabeth's mother had died in 1828, the family fortunes had declined with the abolition of slavery in Jamaica, Hope End had been sold, a greatly altered father had moved them all, first to a smaller house in Devonshire, then to London. Her beloved Uncle Sam had died, also one of her brothers, another Sam. The doctors had decreed that London was no place for her to live.

She tells the story in a letter to Browning of how, sent back to an aunt at Torquay, she had been accompanied by Bro, "whom I loved best in the world beyond comparison and rivalship." The tears she shed at the thought of losing him moved her aunt to write and ask if he might stay. And the father giving permission, said "that he considered it to be *very wrong in me to exact such a thing.*" These words were "burnt into me as with fire." For Bro stayed—and then one day he went out sailing and did not return.

"For three days we waited. . . . And the sun shone as it shines today, and there was no more wind than now . . . and other boats came back one by one. Remember how you wrote in your "Gismond"

> What says the body when they spring
> Some monstrous torture-engine's whole
> Strength on it? No more says the soul,

and you never wrote anything which *lived* with me more than that. It is such a dreadful truth. But you knew it for truth, I hope, by your genius, and not by such proof as mine—I who could not speak or shed a tear, but lay for weeks and months, half unconscious, with a wandering mind, and too near to God under the crushing of His hand, to pray at all. I expiated all my weak tears before, by not being able to shed then one tear—and yet they were forbearing—and no voice said 'You have done this . . .' I do not reproach myself with such acrid thoughts as I had once—I *know* that I would have died ten times over for *him.*"[2]

With immense courage she insisted after this blow on returning to London to spare her father further separations. The journey was made in a huge carriage fitted with a water bed.

All the surrounding circumstances show that despite the loss of their slaves the family was still a wealthy one and that the interests which called Mr. Barrett daily into the city were important.

But Elizabeth, although extravagant, seems to have been indifferent to wealth; its loss would have meant little to her. What had shattered her was the loss of a much-loved mother; a happy home; the two Sams, uncle and brother; and now the dearest "in all the world." Whatever the origin of her illness, she had been heavily shaken psychologically. Nor was other medical treatment of that date helpful: the doctor who took her inkstand out of the room, deeming poetry a kind of disease; the medicines used "when my pulse was above a hundred and forty with fever . . . digitalis to make me weak—and, when I could not move without fainting (with weakness) quinine to make me feverish again. Yet, and they could tell from the stethoscope, how very little was really wrong in me . . . if it were not on a vital organ—and how I should certainly live . . . if I didn't die sooner."

That was down in Devonshire, but the treatment after her return to London, with its probable effect on both body and mind, is equally inconceivable: an airless room, ivy with some difficulty trained against the windows, flowers dying in the atmosphere, dust rising from the carpet. The room was thoroughly cleaned only once a year when the family migrated to the country. One hardly finds this credible, but Elizabeth describes the dust, the swift death of the flowers, the exclusion of all air through the winter, the painting of her window and the effort to keep alive the ivy—designed like the painting to recall the nature she could no longer live with.

Into this room between eleven and twelve each night came Edward Moulton Barrett to pray over his afflicted daughter, whose reliance on him was surely a chief reason for his love: she at least, the "purest woman" he knew—and the most dependent—would never even threaten him with a love affair, as two of his children already had. For that brilliant play *The Barretts of Wimpole Street* does not give a true picture of this abnormal man. Of the special unhealthiness depicted in the play there is no historical trace: not incest but tyranny, and a strange fear of sex, set up a barrier against marriage, not for Elizabeth

E

only but for the whole family. Two sisters and one brother married in
the father's lifetime—and no one of them was forgiven. Before Bro
died he had wanted to marry, and Elizabeth had tried in vain to help by
making over her small fortune to him. It mattered not whether parental
permission was asked or not. Henrietta asked and was refused, Elizabeth did not. Both had to escape from the house and marry secretly;
both were women arrived at or nearing the age of forty.

It was a daily tyranny under which they lived. None could invite
his own friends to dinner. All except Elizabeth, inheriting a little from
her uncle, were wholly dependent on their father. It was some relief
from the tension of his presence that he was out at business from morning to late afternoon, not near enough to Wimpole Street to get home
before six or seven. But Elizabeth describes the heavy silence while he
held forth on the rights of parents, the duties of children, and related
topics. She tells how, when Henrietta was first discovered to be in
love, "her knees were made to ring upon the floor" and she was carried
out of the room "in strong hysterics," while Elizabeth herself fainted
away from horror at the scene.

That had been many years ago, and as the letters go on we see poor
Henrietta plucking up heart to fall in love once more. We see the three
sisters in closest possible intimacy; the brothers visiting Elizabeth singly
or in a body; Stormie carrying her up and down stairs as she grew
stronger and able to leave her room; all of them full of gaiety when, the
parental pressure lifted a little, they gathered every Sunday in Elizabeth's room. It was a tyranny limited by a large degree of self-regarding
occupation, and an eye consequently blind for long periods but hide-
ously keen once his attention was drawn. "I have," Elizabeth wrote, "a
great deal of liberty, to have so many chains; we all have in this house:
and though the liberty has melancholy motives, it saves some daily
torment, and I do not complain of it for one."

Elizabeth lived in one large room, shared at night by her sister
Arabel. Whether or not her pet dog slept there, he was always with her
in the daytime. Her family visited her there; meals were brought up;

and Wilson, her personal maid, waited on her, brushed and arranged the glorious dark hair, helped her to dress and even, when she was well enough to go out, put on her boots (probably high, and buttoned with the assistance of a long silver button hook such as I once possessed—a relic, I believe, of my grandmother).

Alone for many hours Elizabeth read incessantly, following politics, but absorbed above all in current literature. She loved novels, having a special passion for George Sand (who like herself had in childhood worshiped the gods of Greece). But besides reading she wrote—both poetry and letters.

The Seraphim and other Poems had appeared in 1838, she had become a contributor to *Blackwood's Magazine* and *The Athenaeum,* and was already a more popular poet than Browning when, in 1844, she published two volumes of poems which had a vast success in the literary and sub-literary worlds of both England and America.

Receiving an immense mail, she answered nearly all of it, and her regular correspondents increased. She wrote, of course, to her brother George when he was on circuit; to Mrs. Jameson, author of *Sacred and Legendary Art,* who was also among her visitors; to old friends, Mrs. Martin and Hugh Boyd; and to a number of notable people she had never seen (and most of whom she was quite determined not to see). There was Miss Martineau, there was Haydon the painter, there was Chorley a now-forgotten writer whom Miss Mitford energetically and unsuccessfully urged her to admit.

And there was Richard Hengist ("Orion") Horne who in the autumn of 1843 asked two poets, both known to him but not to each other, Elizabeth Barrett and Robert Browning, to help him in supplying mottoes descriptive of the writers dealt with in his forthcoming book, *The New Spirit of the Age.* For Elizabeth Browning chose Shelley's lines:

> I'll sail on the flood of the tempest dark,
> With the calm within and the light around!
> —And then when the gloom is deep and stark,
> Look from thy dull earth, slumber-bound,—
> My moon-like flight thou may'st mark

The linking is fascinating between the poet so enthroned in Browning's heart and imagination and that other whom he would later call "my moon of poets." And she, already joined with him in public estimation for her obscurity, is at once attracted and alarmed. "The sin of sphinxine literature I admit," she wrote to a Mr. Westwood in April, 1845. "Do you know that I have been told that *I* have written things harder to interpret than Browning himself? Only I cannot, cannot believe it—he is so very hard. . . . Tell me honestly. . . . He cuts his language into bits—and one has to join them together, as young children do their dissected maps. . . . The depth and power of the significance (when it is apprehended) glorifies the puzzle."

Browning's circle is therefore small, "very strait and narrow. He will not die because the principle of life is in him—but he will not live the warm summer life which is permitted to many of very inferior faculty, because he does not come out into the sun."

We can watch an encounter beginning to dawn, very remotely, unseen and unguessed in its first distant prospect, through reading more of Elizabeth Barrett's letters—above all those to Miss Mitford. The author of *Our Village* was described by Jane Austen as having been the silliest, prettiest, most husband-hunting of young ladies and having turned in maturity into a very stiff and proper specimen of single-blessedness. She took care of a selfish old father to whom she sacrificed all her time and money, lived away from London for his sake, but had a fair amount of social life and carried on a voluminous correspondence with many friends, including Elizabeth Barrett. There was much kindness in this: the beloved little dog Flush was her gift, named after her own dog; she sent books and periodicals and, whenever she came to London, paid long visits, first to Devonshire Place, later to Wimpole Street.

Elizabeth Barrett and Miss Mitford had long been exchanging literary and other gossip when Elizabeth wrote of *Paracelsus*: "I am a little discontented even *there* and would wish for more harmony and rather more clearness"; yet "There is a palpable power—a height and depth of thought—and suddenly repressed gushings of tenderness which suggest to us a depth beyond . . . the author is a Poet in the holy sense."

But hearing of *Strafford,* she could not "even guess how he will be quite wide awake enough, from the peculiar mystic dreaminess, to write a historical tragedy."

Elizabeth's cousin, "dear Mr. Kenyon," is in and out of these letters: he sends her a copy of *Pippa Passes* ahead of Miss Mitford; they fear for his health (Wordsworth spoke of him as of "too full a habit"). They comment on his overwhelming social engagements ("he lives in such an unnatural whirlwind or whirlpool or both"); they even scheme, not perhaps very seriously, at finding him—already twice widowed—another wife.

Elizabeth had read *Pippa Passes* three times when she wrote to Miss Mitford of the "noble and beautiful things everywhere to be broken up and looked at," of the "great tragic scene . . . which pants again with its own power." Browning, she feels, is at once affected by Landor and immensely original, but she misses music in his writing "and that struck me with a hard hand, while I was in my admiration over his *Paracelsus.*"

The letters get more and more preoccupied with this new poet whose reception by the critics displeased her greatly—"that light, half jocose, pitifully jocose, downward accent of critical rallying. I would not dare speak so of Mr. Browning in a whisper."

This was written in January, 1842, and Browning was by then deep in the tunnel of critical opinion that was to remain so dark and stretch so far. And, whether it was from personal feelings, or merely because Miss Mitford was receptive to atmosphere, she had begun to lend her voice to attacks by some of those who had warmly welcomed him when *Paracelsus* had made him fashionable. Elizabeth writes on April 1, 1842: "Poor Mr. Browning! Was that extreme irritability of nerves supposed to be occasioned by the disappointment, or the exercise of an overwrought faculty?" Miss Mitford wished him to turn to some less exciting occupation: "In the first place *could* he so turn? . . . dare we ask silence from such a poet?" Like a prophet "he has a word to speak from Nature and God and he must speak it."

She still believes her friend to share her admiration for the poet, but by October she has begun to doubt: ". . . you speak more severely of Mr.

Browning than I can say 'Amen' to. Amen would stick in my throat even supposing it to rise so high." Browning is great in "my eyes, not blinded by friendship." But does Miss Mitford know that "Mr. Browning is a great favorite (I mean as a man) of Mr. Kenyon's," who speaks "warmly of his high cultivation and attainments, and singular humility of bearing. I should like to hear you praise him a little more indeed." But more criticisms follow, and the point is reached when Elizabeth, after praising Browning's "concentrated passion . . . burning through the metallic fissures of language," and promising to send her friend his latest works, goes on, "And yet you half frighten me from sending you Mr. Browning's poetry. Promise not to say again that it was a pity he missed being . . . an attorney . . . an engineer . . . a merchant's clerk . . . what trade was it?"

Nevertheless she does admit his failure as a playwright. "He appears to me capable of most dramatic effluences and passionate insights"; but still, as Miss Mitford would say, "acting a play of Mr. Browning's is like reading a riddle-book right through without stopping to guess the answers! Something like . . . perhaps, yet after all, he is a true soul-piercing poet."[3]

Mr. Kenyon was hoping and planning to bring about a meeting between them, but in January, 1845, a poem of Elizabeth's and a letter of Browning's made his intervention unnecessary.

8 Robert and Elizabeth

She was the smallest lady alive,
Made in a piece of nature's madness . . .

"THE FLIGHT OF THE DUCHESS"

"EMOTION recollected in tranquility" was Wordsworth's defini-
tion of poetry. With this Santayana agrees. Love in what he calls the
"contemplative" poets, "ceased to be a passion" and was transmuted
into reflection. But Browning's, he declares indignantly, is "the poetry
of barbarism." He writes not about, but passionately within, experience
—more especially the experience of love. His love is "lava hot from the
crater, in no way moulded, melted or refined." And again: ". . . we are
in the presence of a barbaric genius . . . of a volcanic eruption." But the
best criticism of today is beginning to say with Robert Langbaum that
when Santayana deprecates the " 'fierce paroxysm' which for Browning
is heaven . . . one has only to be a romanticist to reply 'You are quite
right about Browning, and that is why I admire him.' "

Edwin Muir had already noted that Browning "wrote unlike the
romantic poets, as a practised lover, and his subject was neither happy
nor unhappy love, but love as an experience."

Paolo and Francesca, Abelard and Heloise, Petrarch and Laura—
and Robert and Elizabeth: this last and most improbable of love stories
has long been linked with the others, but to talk of it today is felt to be
plunging into a "bath of inspirational treacle"—a phrase used by Hoxie
Fairchild (with occasional justice) of nineteenth-century enthusiasm
for Browning.[1] This reference is specifically to praise of his religious

poetry, but Dr. Fairchild appears to have an unbounded contempt for the man himself, centered especially on the unreality of his love poetry. We are told of his "cold sluggishness of temper" and "factitious ardour. . . . His robustious poetry contrasts embarrassingly with his sedentary, unadventurous, nineteenth-century bourgeois life. . . . Mrs. Miller has made out a strong case for the thesis that what he always sought in Elizabeth and in other women before and after her, was not a mate but a mother. . . . What recent studies have taught us about this man's life and character renders the aggressive virility of his love-gospel a little embarrassing."

"A most amusing essay," says a Michael Innes character, "might be written on the quite peculiar sense of evidence that the professional English scholars have developed," and surely this is an outstanding example. For speculation is not evidence and speculation is the only new element that has been produced in support of what Dr. Fairchild correctly calls a "thesis"—but treats as proven. "There is," as Hilaire Belloc says, "great psychological value in a strong affirmation."

That Browning has been idealized is true; but in trying to understand him no such shock awaits one as I, at least, felt when I met the real Abelard. Getting closer to Petrarch, if Gilson's *Choir of Muses* is reliable, also destroys a certain amount of glamour, for even the best poets are human. Browning, far nearer to us in time, has had the spotlight turned upon him in full measure; and whatever his other weaknesses, it has shown none in a relationship which began even before the writing of the first letter of his two years' correspondence with Elizabeth Barrett.

At Wellesley College, in the box in which he placed them, these letters lie, and on them he has noted each day the hours and minutes spent with her. Only one is missing—his first vehement expression of a love which swept aside apparently insuperable obstacles, above all Elizabeth's own fears and scruples—her age, her ill health, her physical dependence, the sacrifice he would be making of a possible brilliant future. Men do not take for a mother-figure the risks that Browning took when he repudiated the mere continuation of a friendship and insisted on the consummation of his love.

The letters of two years, the poetry of a lifetime expressed this love
—to say nothing of four miscarriages and a baby! The evidence of
scores of visitors to the Casa Guidi and the correspondence of both
poets with their friends and relatives, add, if it be needed, a great weight
of uncontradicted testimony—not to the absurd and unattractive idea
of two people in perpetual peaceful agreement, but of two personalities
each with strengths and weaknesses, each giving and each receiving in
a union at once physical, intellectual, spiritual.

Both had their difficult hours, and Elizabeth writes to Mrs. Jameson
(in a letter lost in the sinking of the *Titanic* of which only the catalogue
quotation has survived): "You must learn Robert—he is made of
moods—chequered like a chess-board; and the colour goes for too much
—till you learn to treat it as a game. He was very tired that evening."

There were vast problems for Browning in the health, the nerves,
the drug addiction of the woman he so loved. There are elements in him
one would wish changed especially in later years, expressed in his own
feeling that he must "wash his hands clean" to be fit to rejoin his love.
But the story of that love is fact and, as so often, it is the cynical and
destructive view which is fancy.

But how to tell with any freshness a story told so often . . .

Two green-covered volumes lay on Browning's table "at arm's
length," to be reached for "when my head aches or wanders or strikes
work . . . and round I turn, and . . . read read read."

To their author he wrote, on January 10, 1845, "I love your verses
with all my heart, dear Miss Barrett, . . . into me has it gone, and part of
me has it become, this great living poetry of yours . . . the fresh strange
music, the affluent language, the exquisite pathos and true new brave
thought. . . . I do, as I say, love these books with all my heart—and I
love you too."

Once he had come near to seeing her, brought by Mr. Kenyon, but
there was some "bar to admission, and the half-opened door shut, and
I went home my thousands of miles, and the sight was never to be?"

Elizabeth answers the half-question: ". . . what I lost by one chance

E*

I may recover by some future one. Winters shut me up as they do dormouse's eyes; in the spring, *we shall see . . .*"

Meanwhile there could be letters. And Browning marveled at the way he went "on and on to you"—he, who feels letter writing the worst of burdens and commonly comes down " 'flop' upon the sweet haven of page one, line last. . . . You will never more, I hope, talk of 'the honour of my acquaintance,' but I will joyfully wait for the delight of your friendship, and the spring . . ."

It must have been hard to fuse in one picture the poet and mystic Elizabeth had discovered in *Paracelsus* and the smart young man of London society. Browning, while often decrying the social world, dined out frequently, went on to balls and parties, dancing the polka and the "Cellarius" until six in the morning. This cannot at all have helped his exceedingly troublesome head and it all seemed to Elizabeth "a strange husk of a world!"

She was six years older than he, a fact of which she was continuously aware, as also of her ignorance of a world of which both he and she a little exaggerated his experience. He had, of course, traveled—to Russia and to Italy, through Europe—and had met many people of whom Elizabeth had only heard, whose works she had devoured, in whose personalities she took an immense interest.

In the intellectual field they were almost uncannily well matched, quoting to each other Greek, Latin, Italian, French, the English classics and the literature of their own time. Both were keen observers of nature, but while Browning wrote as spring approached of what he saw in his mother's garden, the flowers he brought her were all that Elizabeth could now observe. She had for many years, moved only from bed to sofa: ". . . the brightest place in the house," she felt, "is the leaning out of the window." And he replied: "And pray you not to 'lean out of the window' when my own foot is only on the stair; do wait a little for

Yours ever

R.B.

To her old friend, Hugh Boyd, Elizabeth was writing: "I am getting deeper and deeper into correspondence with Robert Browning, poet and mystic; and we are growing to be the truest of friends."[2]

They were united, she told Browning, in a popular report "that we love the darkness and use a sphinxine idiom in our talk." But if they were to collaborate, "I should not like it a bit the less for the grand supply of jests it would administer to the critical Board of Trade, about visible darkness, multiplied by two, mounting into palpable obscure." She had once planned a play in collaboration with "Orion" Horne about "a man haunted by his own soul; . . . (making her a separate personal Psyche, a dreadful, beautiful Psyche)—the man being haunted and terrified through all the turns of life by her. Did you ever feel afraid of your own soul, as I have done?"

Browning perhaps could have shared this theme with her, but certainly not Horne. Poor man! He was perpetually praying for admission to the shrine, threatening to bring his guitar and play to her sisters, leaving the door open that she too might hear and her heart be softened toward him. One wonders what would have happened had he encountered Mr. Barrett on the doorstep—no man certainly to share the vision of a haunting Psyche.

For Browning the physical and mental strain of writing was heavy; for Elizabeth writing represented all that she was missing in her lonely room: "I seem to live while I write—it is life for me. Why what is to live? Not to eat and drink and breathe—but to feel the life in you down all the fibres of being, passionately and joyfully."

On May 3 Browning writes: "If you do not continue to improve in health . . . I shall not see you—not—not—not—what 'knots' to untie. Surely the wind that sets my chestnut-tree dancing, all its baby-cone-blossoms, green now, rocking like fairy castles on a hill in an earthquake —that is South West surely! God bless you, and me in that."

Elizabeth grows as concerned about Browning's headaches as he about her health, but intimate as they are becoming, her fears continue as to that face-to-face meeting for which he so longs. It is mid-May before she is willing to agree that spring has come. And even then she warns: "There is nothing to see in me; nor to hear in me. . . . If my poetry is worth anything to any eye, it is the flower of me . . . it has all my colours; the rest of me is nothing but a root, fit for the ground and the dark."

How deep that "I love you too" went in Browning's first letter we cannot be sure; possibly he had fallen in love through reading Elizabeth's poetry, almost certainly he had before, on May 21, he called for the first time. He was thirty-three, she thirty-nine. The gap in age was probably painfully perceptible. At thirty, says Miss Mitford, Elizabeth would have passed for a mere child; she had masses of dark brown hair and beautiful eyes. She was so tiny that her brothers could easily carry her up and down stairs. But illness and grief had greatly changed her; her eyes remained beautiful, but in the careworn face of a middle-aged woman.

The lady of the poems and the letters had been as remote as she of Tripoli for Rudel the troubadour. Browning had felt "thousands and thousands of miles away," while she often wondered later at the chance (so it seemed) whereby she had chosen among the many strangers who asked—indeed vociferously demanded—to be admitted into that lonely room, just this one. "When I wrote that letter to let you come the first time, do you know, the tears ran down my cheeks . . . I could not tell why: partly it might be mere nervousness. And then, I was vexed with you for wishing to come as other people did, and vexed with myself for not being able to refuse you as I did them."

Nine years after Browning's death his son told the world how the only letters that had passed between Robert and Elizabeth (for after marriage they were never again separated) were kept "in a certain inlaid box . . . letter by letter, each in its consecutive order and numbered on the envelope by his own hand."

"There they are," Pen reported him as saying, "do with them as you please when I am dead and gone."[3]

Controversy raged: Were these letters too sacred for publication, or was Leslie Stephen right when he found his scruples "vanquished by the remarkable revelation of beautiful character. . . . These letters demonstrate to the dullest that the intensity of passion which makes the poet was equally present in the man."[4]

Few correspondences exist yielding more sheer delight to the addict, at a second, third, tenth reading. Yet whether it was wise to publish them in their entirety is another question. The Sphinxine element can be irritating—and misleading. Elizabeth herself asks for an explanation of some of Browning's "Sordelloisms," and if these were unclear to her what do they become to us? It is a peculiarly—perhaps uniquely— tantalizing correspondence: letters written daily between meetings lasting two or three hours twice a week, which go unrecorded except in an occasional cryptic allusion.

Two plain enough letters follow the first encounter. Browning hopes he may come again, that he did not stay too long, that he did not talk too loud. "I am proud and happy in your friendship." And she: "Indeed there was nothing wrong—how could there be. And there was everything right—as how should there not be?" Each feels the other's friendship to be "honour" as well as "happiness," and Elizabeth says: ". . . it is hard for you to understand with all your psychology . . . what my mental position is after the peculiar experience I have suffered." While he feels wholly at her feet, she sees him from "the height of your brilliant happy sphere" entering her dim world.

With every deep love each feels the superiority of the other, each desires to kneel—and these two were already in love, however little Elizabeth realized her own state. Browning knew his better. He received her letter on Thursday and wrote the same day a declaration of his devotion.

"I myself am supremely passionate," he told Elizabeth months later. No doubt she knew it from this letter, which badly frightened her. Whatever stirrings there were in the depths, she certainly wanted the surface of her life unruffled by passion, and she was keenly aware of her physical state: bed to sofa, sofa to bed. She begs him to let the "intemperate things" he has said "die out *between you and me alone,* like a misprint between you and the printer." His friendship she values, but should he repeat this outburst, "*I must not . . . I will not see you again*— and you will justify me later in your heart. So for my sake you will not say it—I think you will not—and spare me the sadness of having to break through an intercourse just as it is promising pleasure to me; to me who have so many sadnesses and so few pleasures." She cannot, owing to relatives arriving, see him as planned this week, but will he come the following Tuesday?

I wish we had this alarming letter of Browning's. He, too, was badly frightened, and for all his famed psychology, he acted with such incredible stupidity that only Elizabeth's heart, already more than half his, saved them from catastrophe. For he now declared that he had meant nothing by his declaration—and we can guess at the vehemence of the lost letter from the simile with which he explains it away: ". . . for every poor speck of a Vesuvius or a Stromboli in my microcosm there are huge layers of ice and pits of black cold water—and I make the most of my two or three fire-eyes, because I know, by experience, alas, how these tend to extinction—and the ice grows and grows." He speaks dramatically in his poetry, so no wonder if he "*bungle* notably" in private life, but he hopes she will not think him "very brutal if I tell you I could almost smile at your misapprehension of what I meant to write."

In a long and involved explanation which explains nothing, he goes on: "I am but a very poor creature compared to you and entitled by my wants to look up to you." Perhaps his "over-boisterous gratitude" for the pleasure of seeing her has wrought this mischief, but he will be "too much punished" if she will not let him come again. May he have back the erring letter "if you have not inflicted proper and summary justice on it?"

Elizabeth's answer shows a woman, bewildered and hurt certainly ("I assure you I never made such a mistake. . . . No, never in my life before"), but willing to take refuge in the general attitude toward Browning's poetry and carry it over into this curious prose of his: "I have observed before in my own mind, that a good deal of what is called obscurity in you, arises from a habit of very subtle association . . . till the reader grows confused as I did . . . I was certainly innocent of the knowledge of the 'ice and cold water' you introduce me to, and am only just shaking my head, as Flush would, after a first wholesome plunge." She has had the almost supernatural strength of mind not to have reread what he had written: "however (to speak of the letter critically, and as the dramatic composition it is) it is to be admitted to be very beautiful,

and well worthy of the rest of its kin in the portfolio . . . 'Lays of the
Poets' or otherwise . . . I venture to advise you to burn it at once. . . .
And we will shuffle the cards and take patience, and begin the game
again if you please—and I shall bear in mind that you are a dramatic
poet . . ."

Any woman, or I at least, cannot but delight in the contrast between
the appalling clumsiness of the "man of the world" and the exquisite
riposte from the cloistered recluse who had esteemed his worldly knowledge so highly. But poor Browning had really thought that the postpon-
ing of his visit for a week was but the beginning, that he was to lose
altogether what already he valued above all else. It was perhaps when
another meeting was secure that he wrote "The Lost Mistress:"

> Tomorrow we meet the same then, dearest?
> May I take your hand in mine?
> Mere friends are we,—well, friends the merest
> Keep much that I resign . . .
>
> Yet I will but say what mere friends say,
> Or only a thought stronger;
> I will hold your hand but as long as all may,
> Or so very little longer!

Shuffle the cards as they might, they were not quite at ease. "And
now," he wrote, " 'exit, prompt side, nearest door, Luria'—and enter
R.B.—next Wednesday—as boldly as he suspects most people do just
after they have been soundly frightened"; and she: ". . . we have both
been a little unlucky, there's no denying, in overcoming the embarrass-
ments of a first acquaintance." Each has to say several *"quite quite"* last
words, and Elizabeth begs him in one letter to "make out these readings
of me as a *dixit Casaubonus;* and don't throw me down as a corrupt
text" . . . and again: ". . . determine to read me no more backwards with
your Hebrew, putting in your own vowel points without my leave!
Shall it be so?"

Their heads came to the assistance of their hearts. Soon he was helping her over her translation of *Prometheus,* and she was suggesting alterations in his new poems. Browning took criticism gladly from anyone

willing and fit to give it, and most surprisingly underrated the lyrics which revealed his greatest powers. "Now I will write you the verses," he says, "some easy ones out of a paper-full meant to go between poem and poem in my next number, and break the shock of collision."

And again: "You may like some of my smaller things, which stop interstices, better than what you have seen; I shall wonder to know."

Dramatic Romances and Lyrics was to be the next in the *Bells and Pomegranates* series and the correspondence about this title is a perfect example of a problem Elizabeth took very seriously: how to make the general public read his poetry. "Do tell me," she writes on October 17, 1845, "what you mean precisely by your 'Bells and Pomegranates' title." "The Rabbis," he answered, "make Bells and Pomegranates symbolical of Pleasure and Profit, the gay and the grave, the Poetry and the Prose, Singing and Sermonizing—such a mixture of effects as in the original hour (that is quarter of an hour) of confidence and creation, I meant the whole should prove at last."

He promised a note with the next volume, but in the following March Elizabeth is again urging him: "I persist in thinking that you ought not to be too disdainful to explain your meaning. . . . Mr. Kenyon and I may fairly represent the average intelligence of your readers . . . why should you be too proud to teach such persons as only desire to be taught?"

His lyrics, too, she has to defend against their author! "Am I not to thank you for all the pleasure and pride in these poems? While you stand by and try to talk them down perhaps." But could he not indicate that "Saul" is a fragment? ". . . people can't be expected to understand the difference between incompleteness and defect unless you make a sign."

Then, too, he would throw shorter poems onto the page without any heading except a number. "Your spring-song is full of beauty as you know very well—and 'that's the wise thrush' so characteristic of you (and of the thrush too). Would it not be well if you were to stoop to the vulgarism of prefixing some word of introduction as others do, you know . . . a title . . . a name? . . . Some of the very most beautiful of your lyrics have suffered just from your disdain of the usual tactics of writers in this one respect."

Was there already growing in Browning a mustard seed of resentment against misunderstanding, which blocked him from trying to remove it in a quiet and reasonable fashion and would thirty years later burst out in *Pacchiarotto*?

It has been conjectured that by "The Flight of the Duchess" he hoped to forward more subtly the courtship his rash letter had so deeply compromised: ". . . love is the only good in the world. / Henceforth be loved as heart can love, / Or brain devise," and "If any two creatures grew into one, / They would do more than the world has done: / Though each apart were never so weak." If the poem was a love letter, he may have been disappointed to receive from Elizabeth, seventy-three suggested emendations, even though they were softened by the remark: "You are not to think that I have not a proper respect and admiration for all these new live rhymes." He accepted all but four of the changes.[5]

Emerson has said: "The greatest genius is the most indebted man" and, in relation to Elizabeth, Browning positively clamored to be indebted: ". . . when I try to build a great building, I shall want you to come with me and judge it and counsel me before the scaffolding is taken down, and while you have to make your way over hods and mortar and heaps of lime, and trembling tubs of size, and those thin broad whitewashing brushes I always had a desire to take up and bespatter with."

He seems not to have recognized that he was moving just then into his two great forms, the lyric and the dramatic monologue, but he reiterates a conviction that his best work is in the future, and that he is making a fresh start. Also we can perhaps trace the origin of certain poems. In a letter of June 30, Elizabeth says: "Miss Martineau is practising mesmerism and miracles on all sides she says, and counts on Archbishop Whately as a new adherent." And the next day Browning says of an old friend: "His poor brains are whirling with mesmerism in which he believes, as in all other unbelief." And Elizabeth: "But belief in mesmerism is not the same thing as general unbelief—to do it justice —now is it? It may be super-belief as well." But to Boyd she had written that she shrank "from these temptations as from Lord Bacon's stew of infant children for the purposes of witchcraft." She would as time went on fall to the temptation, but Browning's view is the same in his poem "Mesmerism" as in "Mr. Sludge, The Medium," written so long after it. He hates more than he disbelieves.

Another question arising in the Letters concerned the still-accepted custom of dueling, fiercely attacked by Elizabeth, defended by Browning. And I think we can see in "Before" and "After" the line the musings took, which brought him over to her view. For "Before" is a defense of the duel, with the absolute assumption that the innocent man will be a martyr, the guilty will be punished enough by living on:

> Better sin the whole sin, sure that God observes;
> Then go live his life out! Life will try his nerves,
> When the sky, which noticed all, makes no disclosure,
> And the earth keeps up her terrible composure.

As for the other:

> Ah "forgive" you bid him? While God's champion lives,
> Wrong shall be resisted: dead, why, he forgives.

How great is the drama of "After" when the "hero" has in fact killed the "villain," the "saint" destroyed the "sinner":

> Take the cloak from his face, and at first
> Let the corpse do its worst!
>
> How he lies in his rights of a man!
> Death has done all death can.
> And, absorbed in the new life he leads,
> He recks not, he heeds
> Nor his wrong nor my vengeance; both strike
> On his senses alike,
> And are lost in the solemn and strange
> Surprise of the change.
>
> Ha! what avails death to erase
> His offence, my disgrace?

> I would we were boys as of old
>   In the field, by the fold:
> His outrage, God's patience, man's scorn
>   Were so easily borne!

> I stand here now, he lies in his place:
>   Cover the face!

They gossip in their letters as well as arguing and making love. Wordsworth had been to court in a bag wig and a borrowed court suit; bowing low he had fallen on his knees; but Elizabeth cannot agree he was wrong to become Poet Laureate; he does honor to the office, which will be the fitter for Browning to hold later. An American admirer has sent her a letter addressed Elizabeth Barrett, Poetess, London, which the Post Office has miraculously delivered. A "stray gentleman from Philadelphia" is "to perform a pilgrimage to visit the Holy Land" and herself.... And Edgar Allan Poe has dedicated a book to her. Browning is to realize, if he hears Mr. Chorley has been at Wimpole Street, that this is Miss Mitford's doing. Elizabeth has said she will not see him, that Miss Mitford must entertain him in the drawing room if he comes.

It was a tremendous problem: half literary London and all literary visiting Americans wanted to see the "poetess" of the age, as she was so generally considered and so barbarously described. Miss Mitford showed the mistaken kindness of staying five hours with a hostess who had no polite way of cutting the visit short. Almost the only other regular visitor, besides the family—of which one letter mentions forty visiting London at one time and bearing down on Wimpole Street—was Mrs. Jameson, whose books had a great influence in opening the eyes of the English world to the value of Renaissance and medieval art. Elizabeth believed women by and large were inferior to men intellectually, though by no means morally. Women's minds are "of quicker movement, but less power and depth," but Browning is never to tell Miss Martineau or Mrs. Jameson that she has said so. One exception she makes—George Sand, "a colossal nature in every way ... magnanimous and loving the truth." But he did not admire George Sand:

Consuelo "wearies me—oh, wearies," he complains. But he confesses that, unlike his "dear Romance lover," he does not enjoy romances.

Browning had begun to work steadily at raising Elizabeth from her deathbed of seven years. She must move about, leave her room, go out into the noisy house and the noisier street. In a letter postmarked June 10 she writes: "I went downstairs—or rather was carried—and am not the worse." And on the fourteenth she is "better altogether." The same day he answers: "I thank God you are better: do pray make fresh endeavours to profit by this partial respite of the weather!"

By July 8: "I have really been out; and am really alive after it— which is more surprising still—alive enough I mean to write even *so* to-night."

Browning is "happy and thankful." Indeed, she is to be sure to go out again, even if it means he shall miss his visit; he will be "as glad as if I saw you or more—*reasoned* gladness, you know." Yet already he was noting down each half hour spent in her company and once, when the question arose between Friday and Saturday, he had replied, "Friday is the best day because nearest, but Saturday is next best—it is next year, you know."

The word friend was worked hard. There is no question of first names, but they were only briefly "Mr. Browning" and "Miss Barrett." And soon "friend" alone is not enough: she is "My own dear friend," "dearest friend," "my dear first and last friend; my friend." He is "the most grateful of your friends." But he is annoyed at *her* gratitude. "I *do not* seek your friendship to do you good—any good—only to do myself good—though I would, God knows, do that too."

One chief good besides the undeniable improvement in health was the opening of her heart as never before since her brother's death. At first, "so used to discern the correcting and ministering angels by the same footsteps," she had hesitated: "Have I not been ground down to browns and blacks . . . if some natures have to be refined by the sun and some by the furnace . . . both means are to be recognised as good . . . though furnace fire leaves scorched streaks upon the fruit. . . ."

"I am like Marianna in the moated grange and sit listening too often to the mouse in the wainscot."

It came as a shock to Browning when Elizabeth told him some weeks before his first visit that sleep came to her only "in a red hood of poppies." She had called him "Paracelsus" and in his studies for that poem he had probably learned far more than she ever knew about the dangers of the drug. He began at once to combat its use—at the least to implore a cutting down. And in November she emphasizes doctor's orders as though in defense against a criticism, spoken or unspoken. She took it, not for her " 'spirits,' in the usual sense, you must not think such a thing." Her doctor one day, arriving early, had while she was "talking quite cheerfully" ordered it before the right hour "just for the need he observed in the pulse." It was designed "to give the right com-posure and balance to the nervous system."

The doctors had, it seems, combined with West Indian tradition to turn her into an addict—the word was probably not used at that date—and she had one quality, curiously incompatible with drug addiction—an obstinate truthfulness. Browning's eyes were wide open when his love leaped a barrier which his optimism determined to sweep away. Miss Marks believes that Elizabeth's strong feeling of unworthiness, of the harm she would do him by marrying him, was partly based on an obscure realization of an incurable addiction. The subject recurs in the Letters, and in February, 1846, Browning writes: "All the kind explain-ing about the opium makes me happier. 'Slowly and gradually' what may *not* be done? Then see the bright weather while I write—lilacs, hawthorn, plum-trees all in bud; elders in leaf, rose-bushes with great red shoots; thrushes, whitethroats, hedge sparrows in full song—there can, let us hope, be nothing worse in store than a sharp wind, a week of it perhaps—and then come what shall come."

This "week," thinks Miss Marks, suggests a reference to the so-called withdrawal agony, but more important perhaps was the picture of a spring that "bursting out all over" carried its message of hope into the stuffy prison of an airless room.

Half afraid to confess what in England at that date was little more respectable than to confess to Catholicism—Elizabeth tells Browning that she is a Nonconformist, and people send her " 'New Testaments' to learn from, with very kind intentions." But she hates "all that rending of the garment of Christ, which Christians are so apt to make the daily week-day of this Christianity so called" and thinks "there is only one Church in heaven and earth, with one divine High Priest to it." Despite the woeful narrowness among dissenters, she has found in a Congregational Chapel a simplicity she likes. They stand, she feels, "on a higher ground" than "those do who call themselves 'Churchmen.' "

Browning is amused. "Can it be you, my own you past putting away, *you* are a schismatic and frequenter of Independent Dissenting Chapels? And you confess this to *me*—whose father and mother went this morning to the very Independent Chapel where they took me, all those years back, to be baptised." Will she be encouraged to bring up any other points of difference "for so sure as you begin proving that there is a gulf fixed between us, so sure shall I end by proving that . . . Anne Radcliffe avert it! . . . that you are just my sister: not that I am much frightened, but there are such surprises in novels!"

Bodily exercise tired Elizabeth far more than mental, of which she was capable of a great deal. But doctors could be "tryingly stupid," telling one "not to think or feel, just as they tell one not to walk out in the dew. . . ." Her present adviser Dr. Chambers was, however, taking more seriously her physical condition and her present improvement— and talking less than former pundits about her nervous system and its "excitability," which one of them had pronounced almost unique in his experience.

Up to now Moulton Barrett had been justified by medical opinion in treating Elizabeth as a total invalid, unable to leave her room, far less to walk, drive, travel. But now Dr. Chambers pronounced that another English winter was the worst possible hazard to her health, that this year she positively must go to a warmer climate. To Miss Mitford she wrote of the medical opinion that, had she gone years ago, "I should be well now, that one lung is very slightly affected but the nervous system *absolutely shattered*."[6] In July, Malta—or Alexandria—was talked of, she heard, between her father and aunt, but, says Elizabeth,

"I suppose *I* should not be much consulted." "Sometimes," she told Browning, "I have haste to be done with it all," feeling "weary unto death with the uses of this life."

"Alexandria!" says Browning. "Well, and may I not as easily ask leave to come 'tomorrow at the Muezzin' as next Wednesday at three?"

Alexandria, Malta, Pisa. He would meet her anywhere, but would she be allowed to go? August had come and still there was silence.

Browning could bear no more. Not vehemently this time, but ardently, he wrote: "When you bade me, that time, be silent . . . dare I say you did not know . . . the power I had over myself, that I could sit and speak and listen as I have done since. Let me say now—*this only once*—that I loved you from my soul and gave you my life, so much of it as you would take,—and all that is *done,* not to be altered . . . you would not need that I tell you—(*tell* you!)—what would be supreme happiness to me in the event—however distant."

"Your life!" she answered, "if you gave it to me and I put my whole heart into it: what should I put but anxiety, and more sadness than you were born to? What could I give you that it would not be ungenerous to give?"

The doctor came again and said, "All the good" of her health "he *used* not to say." So "the Pisa case is strengthened all round by his opinion."

The "Pisa case" rested on that city's repute early in the century as a resort for English consumptives. But Elizabeth's doctor and other friends appear not to have known that it had been the presence of Dr. Vacca of the University of Pisa, not the climate, which had drawn them thither, and that with his death the special reason for going there had disappeared.

George declared there would be anger if she went, but anger also if she did not, and it would all settle down later. But there was the "dead silence of Papa," and then, when she spoke to him herself, he would not answer.

Her eyes, she told Browning, were "swelled with annotations and reflections." She could not travel alone. "I doubt about Arabel and Stormie . . . and it seems I *ought* not to mix them up in a business of this kind." George—so often away on circuit and anyhow privileged —need not fear what the "disobedient" Stormie and Arabel would have to face on their return. She asks Browning's advice and some of what he had been feeling so long bursts out:

> You have said to me more than once that you wished I might never know certain feelings you had been forced to endure . . . and I truly wish *you* may never feel what I have to bear in looking on, quite powerless, and silent, while you are subjected to this treatment which I refuse to characterize—so blind is it *for* blindness. . . . I wholly sympathize, however it go against me, with the highest, wariest, pride and love for you, and the proper jealousy and vigilance they entail—but now, and here, the jewel is not being over guarded, but ruined, cast away . . . all common sense interferes—all rationality against absolute no-reason at all. And you ask whether you ought to obey this no-reason? I will tell you: all passive obedience and implicit submission of will and intellect is by far too easy, if well considered, to be the course prescribed by God to Man in this life of probation—for they *evade* probation altogether, though foolish people think otherwise. Chop off your legs, you will never go astray; stifle your reason altogether and you will find it is difficult to reason ill. . . . The partial indulgence, the proper exercise of one's faculties, there is the difficulty and problem for solution, set by that Providence which might have made the laws of Religion as indubitable as those of vitality, and revealed the articles of belief as certainly as that condition, for instance, by which we breathe so many times in a minute to support life. But there is no reward proposed for the feat of breathing, and a great one for that of believing . . . all our life is some form of religion, and all our action some belief, and there is but one law, however modified, for the greater and the less.
>
> . . . you are in what I should wonder at as the veriest slavery— and I who *could* free you from it, I am here scarcely daring to write . . . what *shall not* be again written or spoken, if you so will. . . . Now while I *dream*, let me once dream! I would marry you now and thus—I would come when you let me, and go when you bade me—I

would be no more than one of your brothers—'*no more*'—that is, instead of getting tomorrow for Saturday, I should get Saturday as well—two hours for one—when your head ached I should be *here*. I deliberately choose the realization of that dream (—of sitting simply by you for an hour every day) rather than any other, excluding you, I am able to form for this world, or any world I know. . . .

Elizabeth replied:

. . . to receive such a proof of attachment from *you*, not only overpowers every present evil, but seems to me a full and abundant amends for the merely personal sufferings of my whole life. When I had read that letter last night I *did* think so. I looked round and round for the small bitternesses which for several days had been bitter to me, and I could not find one of them. The tear-marks went away in the moisture of new, happy tears.

. . . Henceforward I am yours for everything but to do you harm . . . it rests with God and with you—only in the meanwhile you are most absolutely free . . . "unentangled" (as they call it) by the breadth of a thread—and if I did not know that you considered yourself so, I would not see you any more, let the effort cost me what it might. You force me to feel . . . but you cannot force me to *think* contrary to my first thought . . . that it were better for you to forget me at once in one relation.

And Browning:

. . . *My own*, now! For there it is—oh, do not fear I am "entangled"—my crown is loose on my head, not nailed there—my pearl lies in my hand—I may return it to the sea, if I will!

9 One Winter and Then . . .

"If we love in the other world as we do in this I shall love thee to eternity."

CERUTTI'S ITALIAN GRAMMAR

"TELL ME I am not wrong," Elizabeth wrote, after a final pronouncement by her father, "in taking up my chain again. . . . The bitterest 'fact' of all is that I had believed Papa to have loved me more . . . but . . . I never would *un*know anything . . . even were it the taste of the apples by the Dead Sea . . ."

Browning, too, was feeling the strain. His headaches became more frequent and more intense: sometimes bad pain, sometimes what he calls "bewildering." He had nightmares—he who commonly never dreamed—and they were invariably "of one sort. I stand by (powerless to interpose by a word even) and see the infliction of tyranny on the unresisting man or beast—and I wake just in time not to die. . . ." But he wrote, "Be sure my own dearest love, that this is for the best . . . and you will, I know, knowing you—*will* be well this one winter if you can, and then . . ."

And she: "I *will not* be beaten down if the will can do anything. . . . My cage is not worse but better since you brought the green groundsell to it—and to dash oneself against the wires of it will not open the door. We shall see . . . and God will oversee. . . And let us both be busy and cheerful."

In that golden autumn which occasionally follows an English summer, Browning must have the news that Elizabeth is "well and walking, and working for my sake towards *the time*."

And a few days later: "Try, try dearest, every method, take every measure. . . . Why, we shall see Italy together."

His whole mind was now set on this great "consummation" to her sad life and to his own life "of wonders—absolute wonders, with God's hand over all. . . . And this last and best of all would not have begun so, and gone on so, to break off abruptly even here, in this world for the little time. . . . There is life before us."

But he must beat down Elizabeth's self-doubting, her depression, her recurrent conviction that she could only damage this other life. "I who sat here alone but yesterday, so weary of my own being that to take an interest in my very poems I had to lift them up by an effort and separate them from myself." Grateful even to Flush for staying near her, grateful to her family for not making her feel a burden, she was a burden to herself, "shut up too long face to face with my own spirit." Evil seemed to her so "dreadfully natural"; she was a Cassandra, was born under the star of Wormwood.

"My best, dear, dear one," he writes, "may you be better, less *depressed*. . . . Now, *walk*, move . . . *anima mia dolce*. Shall I not know one day how far your mouth will be from mine as we walk?"

Why will she persist, he asks, almost despairingly, in thinking of him simply as full of "fidelity to a given word and noble constancy. . . . I love you because I love you. . . . Let me have my way, live my life, love my love." And in another letter: "You say, 'I am a man and may change' —I answer yes—but, while I hold my senses, only change 'for the *presumable* better . . . not for the *experienced worst*." After seeing her, he can say about marriage as Voltaire did about God—if it did not exist "I should infallibly *invent* it." Her friendship, once so important, now seems nothing. "I am wedded to you now. . . . So take me and make me what you can and will. . . ."

In the first month of 1846 Elizabeth could tell him she had "walked down-stairs into the drawing-room —walked, mind. Before, I was carried by one of my brothers." This was real "glory," and her sleep too was improving, owing probably to the increase of movement and the fresh air breathed in through summer and autumn. She was as she had promised, cutting down the morphine with increasing success.

And after all he did "confidently expect *the* end." He had told Elizabeth that he always got what he wanted. They were busy and fundamentally they were happy that winter. She continued to read and criticize, growing more and more enthusiastic over " 'St. Praxed,' 'Pictor Ignotus,' 'Night and Morning'—and the 'Earth's Immortalities.' "

Earlier she had written: "The *Duchess* appears to me more than ever a new-minted golden coin—the rhythm of it answering to your own description, 'Speech half asleep or song half awake?' You have right of trove to these novel effects of rhythm. Now if people do not cry out about these poems what are we to think of the world?"

The world, alas, remained blind and deaf. Browning's poetry was newer, more startlingly original to the nineteenth century than T. S. Eliot's to the twentieth. But the twentieth is readier to welcome the new, the startling. There were one or two good reviews, but the only real enthusiasm came from Landor in a poem he sent from Italy, four lines of which especially were to become more and more appropriate:

> Since Chaucer was alive and hale,
> No man has walkt along our road with step
> So active, so inquiring eye, or tongue,
> So varied in discourse.

"Those noble verses," Browning said happily in a letter to Mr. Kenyon, who had with equal delight sent a copy to Elizabeth. It meant more than a court decoration: "I may be allowed to wear my 'order' at my button hole on gala days, therefore, and where should I go when dressed like the man whom the King delighteth to honour, if not to Miss Barrett? I sent her a copy directly; but am none the less grateful to you for your good office."[1]

As for Elizabeth, she found herself beginning to take pleasure only in those visitors who talked with appreciation of Browning. Mrs. Jameson startled her into the secret delight of realizing that *she* was thought generous and magnanimous for admiring the work of a rival poet. Miss

Mitford disliked him, and Elizabeth confesses to shame in wearying utterly of so kind a friend. Mr. Kenyon, however, did admire fittingly, so his visits would have been a pleasure but for the eyes which looked piercingly at her with the often repeated question, "Has Browning been here lately?"

These visitors, like her relatives, were accustomed to thinking of visiting Elizabeth as a pure kindness and would often leave it uncertain on which day they were to be expected. As Browning's visits grew to twice a week, the unobtrusive arranging of them became more and more difficult. "Take away the doubt about Miss Mitford," one letter runs, "and Mr. Kenyon remains—and take away Mr. Kenyon and there is Mrs. Hedley," (an aunt). Inside the house only her sisters were in the secret; of the rest—brothers, servants—she could say that there were many suspectors, but no informers. But when Mr. Kenyon asked her abruptly if there was anything between Henrietta and Captain Surtees Cook, she knew what he really meant, and only reminded him that such feelings were not allowed in this house. She rejoiced when his spectacles were broken and the gaze which made her blush idiotically became less piercing: "Those detestable spectacles—like the Greek burning glasses, turned full on my face."

Browning grew restive over these fears and precautions. He would have liked openly to approach Mr. Barrett; it was hard for any man in a century as civilized as the nineteenth to believe in what Elizabeth told him the result would be. Her letters would be intercepted and she herself guarded so closely as to make further intercourse impossible. Browning must allow, too, for a physical state which made it impossible for her to stand up to the violent scenes that would ensue. Mentally, spiritually, she would not fail; but physically she easily might; they must leave the house secretly when the day came—none must know lest they suffer for the knowledge; a servant would be summarily dismissed and the heaviest displeasure would strike sister or brother.

A defense of Moulton Barrett was put up to Jeannette Marks by his grandson. It is embodied by her in her interesting book, *The Family of the Barrett*. He was, we are told, a most affectionate father and a man of kindest heart. He treated the slaves on his plantation generously.

None of them had revolted in the big insurrection and when they were turned into apprentices, he was among the few ex-owners who remained humane and just, not like many others managing to make their last state worse than their first.

His opposition to the marriages of Henrietta and Alfred (said Alfred's son) was entirely reasonable. There had been far too much intermarrying in the Barrett family already, and these marriages were both with second cousins. This, Miss Marks objected, did not apply to Elizabeth's marriage—but here the grandson agreed with his grandfather even more thoroughly: Browning's grandfather had kept a public house!

In the terribly snobbish England of those days, the father (however cultured) a bank clerk, certainly supplied another plausible excuse. But the opposition to marriage had not begun with either of these problems. Henrietta's previous attachment, Bro's desire to marry, had been frustrated with the same brutal finality. Surtees Cook was not far out when he enquired meekly of his future father-in-law whether children were to be regarded as slaves. In spirit the ex-slaveowner, the descendant of generations of slaveowners, remained just that. Kind he could be, affectionate he could be, but he must always be supreme. No affection, no tenderness could subsist where he had been defied.

At least, Browning urged, could they not confide in Mr. Kenyon who was, he fancied, pretty well aware of the situation already? He hated to keep so warm a friend in the dark. But no, said Elizabeth, above all Mr. Kenyon must not be told: "I beseech you to avoid by every legitimate means the doing *that* . . . oh DO NOT *ever speak* THAT *to him.*" Had Browning never heard Kenyon speak of his "organ of caution? . . . We should involve him in ever so many fears for us, and force him to have his share of the odium at last."

Elizabeth must have known that not only her health but the lack of finances would frighten their cautious old friend. She does comment: "A marriage without lawyers would be an abomination in his eyes. Moreover, to discover ourselves to him, and *not submit to his counsels,* would be a real offence." But he might forgive two poets if they "poetically rush into a foolishness."

They felt this problem of secrecy from different angles: she wanting to say a word to Mrs. Jameson, who kept urging her to accept her escort to Italy; he feeling treacherous to Kenyon. Then he fancied she did not want him to tell his parents; and when that was cleared up, he was distressed at her feeling that *he* should not bring his sister to see her and that *she* ought not to drive to Hatcham to see his father and mother. Each perceived so vividly one set of dangers which seemed to the other not so dangerous after all that only a profound love could have carried them through these months.

Would her health build up enough for the journey to be made before winter was upon them? Could they keep the secret as they made their plans, did such packing as was minimally necessary, and worked out traveling difficulties greater than a trip to Australia would offer today.

Flush was a minor problem; he had become jealous of Browning. He bit him twice, was smacked by the maid, Wilson, reproached by Elizabeth and told he would never be loved again. Whereupon he looked at her "with an expression of quite despair on his face." He must go with them; he *must* not bark when leaving the house. Wilson taken into confidence agreed to go with them. Elizabeth had hesitated: She was "an expensive servant—she has £16 a year!" He would, Browning answered, be "simply, exactly INSANE to move a step" without "Wilson or someone in her capacity." It was the sort of hesitation that awakened in him a half-comic, half-serious despair. "Yet you write of this to me *so*, my Ba!"

This is the first time I have written the name by which her family, and now her lover, called her—instead of the really beautiful Elizabeth. It signified, Mr. Kenyon said, that she was only half a ba-by—but it seems, alas, to have been pronounced as in Baa-lamb. Given to her by her brother in infancy, the name had stuck, as pet names will. So Browning did not, like Jane Austen's Darcy, call her, when he proposed, "Dearest, loveliest Elizabeth." He seems to have liked Ba, for Ba she remained to the end of the story.

One side event of this intense summer illustrated the problems of a secret engagement. Elizabeth had corresponded with the painter Haydon, a curious character who had gone up and come down like a rocket. He had a real talent for a likeness and has left sketches of Keats often reproduced; but he had ambitions of a more grandiose sort and was for a while paid big sums for vast historical cartoons. Success went to his head, he developed a delight in insulting other artists, and had made so many enemies that it was hard to tell how much his eclipse owed to this, how much to the fact that his pretentious canvasses had been greatly overrated.

He had married in the days of his prosperity and when his cartoons were rejected in a contest for the decoration of the new Houses of Parliament, his wife exclaimed, "Then we shall starve." Already several times imprisoned for debt, and overwhelmed with despair, he committed suicide.

Haydon, though he had never seen Elizabeth, had begged her to store for him some pictures and several trunks of papers, and now in his will came the request that she should edit them for publication. She had unwittingly brought it on herself by agreeing three years earlier to read part of his memoirs. Browning and Mr. Kenyon agreed that Haydon had hoped her ignorance of the world would result in the publication of his most treasured indiscretions! With skillful editing she felt a fascinating book was possible, but much of the manuscript was "fervid and coarse at once, with personal references blood-dyed at every page. . . ."

"And," commented Browning, "how horrible are all these posthumous revelations,—these passions of the now passionless, errors of the at length better instructed." It was indeed a "*dispiriting* bequest." But *how* dispiriting he realized only after a dinner at the house of Sergeant Talfourd, Haydon's executor. For that busy gossip, Miss Mitford, had forwarded to Talfourd some extracts from Elizabeth's letters when first the books and pictures had been dumped on her. Landseer, Forster, Babbage and others were present, and "the words, 'H.' it seems, has been in the habit of using Miss B's house etc.' (or to that effect) had so offensive an implication,—that I felt obliged to say simply, you had never seen Haydon and were altogether amazed and distressed." Browning said only enough, he wrote, "to remove the impression from the minds of the people present that you must have 'known' Haydon, as they call 'knowing.'" But in conversation, as we learn from a letter of Elizabeth's to her brother George, he told her that "somebody said that her house appeared the receptacle for his goods against his creditors"; others wondered how Miss Barrett should have come to know a man of his type. "Poor Haydon," comments Elizabeth, "did not lead the most prudent of lives it appears. See what a scrape I am in." As to Miss Mitford "none of the ridicule of what appears to have been a most ridiculous letter fell to the ground"—least of all her grandiloquent conclusion "*And so speaks our great poetess.*"

It all sounds quite bad enough, but Elizabeth adds: "Worse things were said or implied I do not doubt, than what [Mr. Browning] told me, he was *so* angry."

That evening, however, Browning managed to get Talfourd alone and he agreed to take over all responsibility; he knew George Barrett and promised to "arrange everything" with him "when I meet him on circuit."

They could breathe again, yet the letter to George is full of injunctions of caution—toward Talfourd, toward Papa, toward all the world. As to Haydon's papers, a brilliant three volumes was drawn from them seven years later, and called by Miss Mitford "the most melancholly, painful, fascinating book that I ever took up."[2]

But Elizabeth was left sad. Her help could not have filled the great abyss of Haydon's debts, yet she wished she had offered it. He was so nearly, she felt, a great man, but "Think what an agony life was to him, so constituted!—his own genius a clinging curse! the fire and the clay in him seething and quenching one another!—the man seeing maniacally in all men the assassins of his fame! ... struggling, stifling, breaking the hearts of the creatures dearest to him, in the conflict for which there was no victory."

This tragedy crossing the path of their love has an interesting relation to Browning's own life and character. "You have the opinion," he would write in 1867 in reply to a request for criticism, "of the most unpopular poet that ever was, and so will be sure not to mind too much the sour sayings of the likes of him."

Perhaps it is easier to bear failure before than after wealth and fame.

F

Browning may never have been tempted to extravagant living or to envy of his fellow craftsmen. But now and throughout his married life he showed a strength the greater for its possible appearance of a weakness. His letters are at first full of suggestions as to how he could earn enough money for the cheap living offered by Italy. He had finished for Forster a life of Strafford; he had once compiled a French primer to help his teacher, and the very papers which abused *Paracelsus* had praised it highly. He could, he believed, write a novel. Or again, he could perhaps get government employment. "How do you not know," objected Elizabeth, "that you may not be sent to Russia or somewhere impossible?"

He could write for a periodical, and this she thought more feasible, but "it is not a necessity, there is no sort of need of it in fact—and why should you be tormented 'in the multitude of the thoughts within you' utterly in vain?"

The decision to live on her small fortune in the simple way both liked may have been unwise, but was certainly courageous. Is it better for the poet to be free from the toils of earning that living which poetry seldom if ever brings? For Browning it probably was. Added to his headaches, to the intense concentration on his writing, the keen and constant observation that fed it, he was now in large part taking on himself the task of nurse and doctor. He had not known when he fell in love with Elizabeth that she had money of her own, but relief must have mingled with his natural feeling that a man ought not to be dependent on his wife. She was steady in her determination that he should remain solely and totally a poet. As for what the world would say, had he, she remarked, with justice, wanted money, he would have gone for thousands and not for her poor little hundreds. He could (she claimed with less plausibility) have married the millionairess Miss Burdett Coutts, or indeed any other woman in the world.

Then, too, they always went on hoping his poems would begin to sell. Fifteen hundred of Tennyson's latest volume had sold in a year, he heard, which in those days meant a very fair sum for the author. As to work "Did not Shakespeare do more than Cromwell?" she asked.

One day when all their problems pressed, Browning felt attracted to the *sortes Virgilianae*. Reaching blindly for a book, he came up with the unhelpful Italian Grammar of his old teacher Cerutti: "What could it prove but some assurance that you were in the Dative Case, or I, not in the ablative absolute?" He would have been thankful only to find such a word as "conjunction" or "possessive pronoun." But after all it *was* an Italian Grammar and a phrase stood out from the "Promiscuous Exercises" for translation at which he opened. *"If we love in the other world as we do in this, I shall love thee to eternity."*

"Do my eyes see double," says Elizabeth, "dazzled by the light of it? 'I shall love thee to eternity'—I *shall*."

It is often pointed out that Browning's own experiences were basis and inspiration for many of his poems, and he was now going through the greatest. While he told of triumph in "The Flight of the Duchess" and *The Ring and the Book,* he showed in "The Statue and the Bust" how close failure lay. This poem starts with love at first sight—the woman being already married. Compare the picture with that given of Elizabeth in "By the Fireside":

> Hair in heaps lay heavily
> Over a pale brow spirit-pure. . . .
> And vainly sought to dissemble her eyes
> Of the blackest black our eyes endure

Each night the man determines, each day she vows, that on the morrow they will break away:

> But next day passed, and next day yet,
> With still fresh cause to wait one day more
> Ere each leaped over the parapet. . . .
> So weeks grew months, years; gleam by gleam
> The glory dropped from their youth and love,
> And both perceived they had dreamed a dream;
>
> Which hovered as dreams do still above:
> But who can take a dream for a truth?

And again in "Youth and Art," young people too poor to marry:

> Each life unfulfilled, you see;
> It hangs still, patchy and scrappy:

We have not sighed deep, laughed free,
Starved, feasted, despaired,—been happy

It would have been so terribly easy to fail. In January, 1846, Browning had written: "I claim your promise's fulfillment—say at the summer's end . . . you will think of the main fact as *ordained,* granted by God, will you not, dearest?—So, not to be put in doubt *ever again*—then we can go on quietly thinking of after matters." But this hardly seemed possible for them; quiet was not the distinctive adjective for either. A small boy once pointed to the sun's path across a room and said, "Look, that's the sun's shadow." And so Elizabeth: "You have fallen like a great luminous blot on the whole leaf of the world . . . of life and time . . . and I can see nothing beyond you, nor wish to see it."

Yet each felt uncertain in turn as they tried to complete their plans in the best possible way. Various places in Italy were thought of, and discovered to be unfit because of bad water, malaria, or the prevalence of English tourists. Various ways of travel were discussed—boat or train had each its disadvantages. The hour of her departure must be precisely one in which her family would be all safely out—or at dinner. Nothing must be done that could involve her sisters or brothers in the parental wrath. Elizabeth was immensely concerned about this, was distressed at the thought that the word "elopement" might be used of their action, kept recurring to her fear of ruining Browning's life. And, inevitable though it was, she still suffered at the thought of deceiving and distressing her father.

Browning's problem was a far greater one than the Duke's, the young artists' or even Elizabeth's own. The Duke could snap his fingers at society's judgments; the young artists had youth and strength on their side, and no watching world to condemn. Chesterton was the first to note that the best shadowing of Browning himself lies in his picture of Caponsacchi in *The Ring and the Book.* Half Rome would condemn Pompilia and Caponsacchi alike, but the main problem for him was: should he leave Pompilia to die in Arezzo at the hands of her husband, or should he risk the pursuit which might, and indeed did, equally end in death.

For this mysterious illness of Elizabeth's might have killed her on the journey. And Browning may well have been asking himself in the words of his own "Clive" "How should I have borne me, please."[3] Only one doctor had recommended an earlier journey which had everything to make it easy—sister and brother with her and plenty of money for the best hotels and the easiest traveling. And now she was going under conditions which made important the difference between tickets costing £5 or so more or less, under an intense emotional strain, into a life of comparative poverty. To all this Browning with his vivid imagination was intensely alive. Yet he had already raised her from her bed; he trusted God for the rest.

That was a tremendous element in the decision. Deeper still was the plain fact that they were so much married already. When Browning (in November '45) added up the hours they had spent together and brought them out at two days, Elizabeth said, "So little! so dreadfully little! What shallow earth for a deep root."

But there was surely also strong passion, at any rate on Browning's side. When, thinking she might be too ill for fullness of marriage, he offered to marry her and be only as one of her brothers, one realizes (and I think she did) the magnitude of the offer. And when he writes that if she rises to receive him, he will be utterly overcome; when both feel that to meet in the presence of others will be an intolerable strain; when he writes: "I that stammer and answer haphazard with you— Have you not discovered by this time that I go on talking with my thoughts away?"—they do not allude merely to the keeping of a secret. Victorian prudery brooded even over the poetry, but human passion was there.

10 Married in Italy

In the great right of an excessive wrong ...

THE RING AND THE BOOK

BOTH WERE strained to breaking point. Browning got one of his customary disabling headaches; Elizabeth forgot her own health in anxiety for his. And then Flush was stolen by a gang which specialized in collecting ransom from distracted owners of stolen pets. Mr. Barrett forbade the brother, deputed by Elizabeth, to pay the ransom. The dog's death was threatened and Elizabeth, in desperation, herself went down to the dog stealers' haunts and interviewed the wife of the "intermediary" to whom the ransom was to be paid. For once Browning agreed in principle with his future father-in-law and wrote of the sin of encouraging this evil; but after all Flush was Flush ("a sort of dog," said Elizabeth, "to whom you couldn't reasonably refuse the franchise") and Browning would never (he said) have written thus but for the belief that Elizabeth had already got him back!

Flush was home, thin, thirsty and still terrified, on Sunday, September 7, 1846, but Browning was now in the doctor's hands and forbidden to go out until Wednesday—and on Wednesday came the parental decree that a house in the country was to be found and the Barrett family transferred to it without delay while Wimpole St. was cleaned, painted, renovated.

That day he had again been with Elizabeth and again pressing for instant action. "I will not add one word to those spoken yesterday [runs Thursday's letter] about the extreme perilousness of delay,"—and after receiving this fresh news: "I will go for a licence today and we can be married on Saturday. . . . We can leave from Dover &c., *after* that,—but otherwise impossible!"

With Wilson, on Saturday morning September 12, Elizabeth slipped out of the house and Robert and she were married at Marylebone Church at eleven. Elizabeth went on to Mr. Boyd, a visit to whom had been the cover used with her family. She sent Wilson home and lay down on the sofa to recover, her host being "happily engaged with a medical counsellor." And then came Cyprus wine and a light wedding breakfast of bread and butter, after which her sisters arrived. "And so, to complete the bravery, I went on with them in the carriage to Hampstead . . . as far as the heath,—and talked and looked."

The next day Mr. Kenyon "came with his spectacles, looking as if his eyes reached to their rim all the way round . . . '*When did you see Browning?*' . . . 'He was here on Friday' . . . Dearest he saw something but not all."

Chesterton has said and others have repeated that Browning would not come to Wimpole Street after the wedding because he scrupled to ask for his wife as Miss Barrett, but the Letters do not bear this out. On Sunday he writes "I confide in your judgment. . . . I will not ask to see you for instance—though of course a word brings me as usual to you." And on Monday she says, "It is best, I continue to think, that you should not come here. . . . I don't know how to put my feeling into words, but I do seem to feel that it would be better, and less offensive to those whom we offend." The decision to avoid another meeting before their departure was certainly hers.

Now they must write the letters and notices to be sent to their friends, and again she is terrified of his being too precipitate, especially concerning Mr. Kenyon. "Do let no letter or intimation be given till the very last. Remember that I shall be *killed*—it will be so infinitely worse than you can have an idea."

Both write to Mr. Kenyon and to Mrs. Jameson; they compose a notice of the wedding for the *Times*; Robert looks up departures of boats, gets them wrong, follows one letter with another and yet another to correct himself, fusses over the need to keep down the weight of their luggage (they might almost have been traveling by air), and she questions his impression that every pound will be charged for. Then, too, Elizabeth cannot take boxes or bags openly out of the house. Wilson contrives somehow to get the baggage sent ahead to Vauxhall station. The entire servants' hall must, of course, have been in the secret and enjoying it heartily. The postscript of the last letter Elizabeth ever wrote to Browning runs: "The boxes are *safely sent*. Wilson has been perfect to me. And *I* . . . calling her timid."

Finally Elizabeth must write the farewell to her family, and she chose her brother George as the channel of communication. This letter has survived—and very moving it is. A letter to her father is enclosed, but she begs George first to break the news to him gently—and himself to understand her letter. "Oh, love me George, while you are reading it. Love me—that I may find pardon in your heart for me after it is read." If she were to give up this prospect of life and happiness "there would be a victim without an expiation & a sacrifice without an object. My spirits would have festered on in this enforced prison & none of you all would have been the happier. . . . Also I should have wronged *another*. . . .

"If you have any affection for me George, dearest George, let me have word at Orleans."

And Browning's family? Father, mother and sister were all in the secret, bound up, as Cyrus Mason saw them, in an exclusive little enclave within the larger family; but, to that larger family, Mason witnessed a curious farewell. In the cottage at Hatch End their grandmother was sitting one afternoon, looking very pretty and well dressed, when

> . . . the door was suddenly opened and "young Robert" bounded into the room, his face ablaze with excitement. For a moment he stood admiring grandmother Browning; she sitting too astounded to speak; then for an instant the Poet regarded her approvingly, advanced, seized one of the old lady's hands in both of his and said cheerily, but not without a sort of catch in his voice:

'A monstrous mistake! According to the Book of Common Prayer a man is forbidden to marry his grandmother! The pity of it.'

He then stooped and reverently and impressively kissed the surprised and flattered old lady. I was astounded, for with him kissing was an unusual form of salutation.

Browning's entrance and exit struck Cyrus as "hysterical." Looking back, he saw it as the climax of preparation for the momentous flight, a farewell to the family conveyed by an impressive kiss to its oldest member.

Mrs. Jameson was astonished at seeing the Brownings in Paris, perhaps even before she had received their letters; she suggested that they should complete the journey to Pisa with her. She was taking her niece to Italy and she knew all there was to know of travel by diligence and rail, and of inexpensive yet adequate hotels.

" 'You wild dear creature,' " she cried as she embraced Elizabeth. " 'You dear abominable poets . . . ought to have a little prose. But he is a wise man and you are a wise woman, let the world say as it pleases. I shall dance for joy both in earth and in heaven my dear friends.' All this in interrupted interjections," writes Elizabeth to Arabel.

Mrs. Jameson, writing to her friend Lady Noel Byron, describes the arrival of "my poet" and "my poetess. . . . She is nervous, frightened, ashamed, agitated, happy, miserable." "The charming fugitive pair are a great interest and a great care . . . the deportment of both is perfect. . . . Both are *so* good."

At Orleans they would find letters from home and Elizabeth had written on the back of hers from Paris, "Do you think Arabel, dearest Papa will forgive me at last—answer."

"Love me," she had entreated her brother; and for her father's love her yearning was greater yet. But this great faculty, so strong in her and her sisters, seemed left out of the surviving men of her family. Her father, she had known, would not forgive: the only thing recorded of his letter is the accusation that Elizabeth had sold her soul (by which he probably meant her social position) for genius! But from her

F*

brothers she had expected some measure of affectionate understanding. "I thought it hard, I confess, that he [George] should have written to me so with a sword." Only her sisters sympathized—and that with all their hearts. To them she wrote of the "death warrant" she had more than half expected while she held the letters in her hand "not able to open one, and growing paler and colder every moment."

Only the kind letters would she show to Browning, whom she had sent away while she read. And there was comfort in the affectionate understanding of dear Mr. Kenyon. Never again would she fear those spectacles. "I know no two persons so worthy of each other. . . . It is a pleasant vision to me to think that, if I live, I may hereafter enjoy your joint society and affection . . . if the thing had been asked of me I should have advised it, albeit glad that I was not asked. . . ."

After all she could not but be happy, and Mrs. Jameson watched with delight "you and Mr. Browning together. If two persons were to be chosen from the ends of the earth for perfect union and fitness, there could not be a greater congruity."

To her also were shown only the kind letters, and she reports to Lady Noel that Elizabeth "is much comforted and certainly gaining strength in spite of the exertion and fatigue. As yet there is not a trace of animal spirits, though evidently a sense of deep happiness, gratitude and love. As to *him* his joy and delight, and his poetical fancies and antics, with every now and then the profoundest seriousness interrupting the brilliant current of his imagination make him altogether a most charming companion."

A little nervous as to the effect on her young niece of such an unconventional marriage, she reports once more that: "The deportment of both is in the best taste and Gerardine can only gain by what she sees and hears." But at Avignon, Elizabeth had to be lifted, fainting, from the carriage, bruised all over by the movement; the rest of the journey must be made by sea so that she could lie down. Still their guardian angel abounds in enthusiasm for the unselfish devotion of each and for a "mutual deportment . . . marked by a most graceful propriety without any appearance of gêne. Gerardine has profited every way."

At Vaucluse they honored the memory of Petrarch, and Browning enthroned Elizabeth on a high rock above the stream, in that glorious green shade shot through with sunlight, Flush barking furiously the while at the fate of his mistress.

The sea passage to Genoa took twenty-six hours, and it was even rougher on the boat to which they changed for Leghorn. The journey was completed by train and, at Pisa, Mrs. Jameson left them:

> With all the abundance of love and high principles, I have had now and then a tremor at my heart about their future. *He* is full of spirits and good humour and his turn for making the best of everything and his bright intelligence and his rare acquirements of every kind rendered him the very prince of travelling companions. *But* (always *buts!!*) he is in all the common things of this life the most impractical of men, the most uncalculating, rash, in short the worst *manager* I ever met with. She, in her present state, and from her long seclusion almost helpless. Now only conceive the menage that is likely to ensue and without FAULT on either side. For the present our first care is to get her into some comfortable lodgings.[1]

The "lodgings" were in the Collegio Ferdinando, a "huge pile" in the front of which they could count forty-seven windows and doors. It was a bitter winter in England, and Elizabeth wondered as the months passed whether this might shake the assurance of those who blamed her. In Pisa it was usually warm, but when it was not, Elizabeth kept "by the fire feeling very contented and very well." Not quite so well one day, she saw a doctor who discovered her to be over five months' pregnant. She writes to her sisters, furious at her own stupidity; all would have been well the doctor said, had he known in time. As it was, the miscarriage was quickly got over and she was able to write to Mrs. Martin: "I am wonderfully well and far better and stronger than before what you call the Pisan 'crisis.'"

On February 24, 1847, Browning was writing to his publisher Edward Moxon of a new edition of *Paracelsus*, *Pippa* and some "others," which would improve them not "by cutting them up and reconstructing them but by affording just the proper revision they ought to have had before they were printed at all." The Berg collection copy of

Paracelsus on which Browning worked, inscribed *To Frederick Locker from R. B. April 13, 1869,* contains a good deal of new material and many corrections, mostly augmenting the music of the verse. But the omissions are sometimes unfortunate, especially that of the Preface, where, without using the word, he made a plea for the technique of the dramatic monologue as contrasted with that of the drama. The letter to Moxon ends: "I say nothing of my wife's poems and their sale. She is, there and in all else, as high above me as I would have her."

They went on to Florence where they entertained Mrs. Jameson for a week. She arrived on Shakespeare's birthday, with a bottle of wine from Arezzo "to do it the due honours in company with 'two poets.' "[2]

In their first year in Florence they moved five times. But in April '48 they established themselves in an apartment and later an entire floor of the Casa Guidi. Robert at siesta time would settle Elizabeth in the deepest shadow to be found, "pours eau de cologne into my hands and on my forehead and fans me till my eyes shut of themselves." He persuades her in the evening to walk down the stairs into "a bath of cool air at the bottom of the house"—"last night we . . . got as far as the Baptistery where we sat down in the half-dark and talked of Dante." But by July the heat was overwhelming; they must go somewhere, Elizabeth finally setting her heart on Vallombrosa: "forty miles through the mountains of wild, roadless rock and forest." But only a monastery to receive them—and would women be received at all? To some sort of guesthouse, Elizabeth and Wilson were allowed to come, but after five days, were turned out by "that little holy abbot with the red face" who, she had feared on sight, would be "jealous of his sanctity and the approach of women." But the scenery had been glorious and Elizabeth had shown an almost incredible strength, dragged by oxen in a laundry basket along rough paths up the mountain. Returning to a slight respite in the weather, they decided to remain in Florence.

Looking across the sea from Italy to the room in Wimpole Street, Elizabeth felt that on the one side was life—on the other death. "I was buried," she wrote to Mrs. Martin, "and that was the whole. . . . A thoroughly morbid and desolate state it was, which I look back now to with a sort of horror with which one would look to one's graveclothes, if one had been clothed in them by mistake during a trance."

Mr. Kenyon had written: "I considered that you had *perilled your life* upon this undertaking, and reflecting upon your last position, I thought that *you had done well.*"

"You are not improved," Mrs. Jameson said, "you are transformed." And Elizabeth had to tell Robert that he really must not boast so much of how she had walked here or walked there, as if a wife with two legs was a marvelous phenomenon in nature.

Of those nearest to her "tomb," Elizabeth wrote, "my family had become so accustomed to the idea of my living on and on in that room, that while my heart was eating itself, their love for me was consoled, and at last the evil grew scarcely perceptible. It was no want of love in them, and quite natural in itself: we all get used to the thought of a tomb."

Love would surely have welcomed the throwing off of the grave clothes, the rising from the sepulcher, but Elizabeth's father and brothers were complaining bitterly that Browning was living on his wife's money; George was asserting that no one should marry with an income of less than £2,000 a year. The disproportion is almost too great, and perhaps an underlying consciousness of their own failure was stoking the flames of their wrath. After some years Elizabeth's brothers forgave her for choosing life over death; her father never did.

Miss Marks sees in Edward Moulton Barrett's original opposition to his daughter's going abroad a fear he did not choose to voice of the absence of her doctor and the craving for her drug. His sense of personal responsibility for his children was abnormal, and it had, as she points out, gone unchallenged all their lives. There had been occasional "hysterical scenes but never year after year any persistent, courageous, and independent development of their own lives." The daughter with feeble body and shattered nerves had now found the courage to break away, and in doing so set an example. True she had what the others had not, a little money of her own, but surely their health and strength would have outweighed this. It may have been sense of his own failure that sharpened the "sword" with which George wrote to his sister.

It was not he, but Henrietta, who had broken the news to Papa. He was standing on the staircase, a heavy book in hand, which he dropped—or threw. Henrietta, dodging the book, slipped and fell. One version has it that he knocked her down; but this is improbable. As Miss Marks says, "It is one thing to throw down a book. It is another to throw down your daughter." (But Occy [Octavius, brother number eight], remarked, "My old Dad was hasty, very hasty.") And "the records suggest," Miss Marks says, "that several scenes of hurricane violence followed one another," until he lapsed into the silence which buried henceforward any mention of Elizabeth's existence. Her letters were unopened, her name unspoken. The family seems to feel that he became not quite sane on the matter. "A monomania," said Mr. Kenyon.

And Miss Marks, visiting Jamaica, studied on the spot the story of a family, generous and liberal with the slaves they had owned for three hundred years, but bringing up each eldest son with a mentality that turned his own children into replicas of well-treated slaves. "Then a member of that group," she concludes, "handicapped nervously and physically, shattered the history of three hundred years and in flight broke through and surmounted Barrett backgrounds."

But Mr. Barrett, once a Jamaican slaveowner, remained "an English gentleman" and a trader, going to the city daily to arrange about cargoes of sugar and rum from Jamaica and to hear the news of his ships *Statira* and *David Lyon*. The Barretts were living in the world of what Dickens called Podsnappery. Mr. Barrett, like Mr. Podsnap, "got up at eight, shaved close at a quarter past, breakfasted at nine, went to the city at ten" and found in this world of convention a substitute for life.

An American song takes up the Dickens theme, picturing a similar though less grim world than that of nineteenth-century England. In this modern world there are "boxes on the hillside," of one color and another color, but

> They're all made out of ticky-tacky
> And they all look just the same.

In them men and women live: "lawyers and doctors and business executives," and they marry and have children

> And they're all made out of ticky-tacky
> And they all look just the same.

The children too grow up and marry, and we leave without regret
a society where

> They're all made out of ticky-tacky
> And they all look just the same.

I have heard Browning's poetry depreciated on the ground that the
later nineteenth century with its closed social life, its ingrown conform-
ity, the blindness of the successful to human suffering, *could not* produce a major poet. I wonder whether the world of Podsnappery, of
boxes made of ticky-tacky, ever can in any century. Browning had been
living wholly outside that world when he wrote *Pauline* and *Paracelsus,*
had never been fully immersed in it, when he escaped to Italy and
entered on the period of his greatest poetry, *Christmas-Eve and Easter-
Day, Men and Women,* and much of *Dramatis Personae.* Only *The
Ring and the Book* belongs at once to the time when he had returned to
England and to the highest peak of his genius—and, indeed, it was only
after it was published that English Society really caught and held him.

To Fanny Haworth, he wrote on June 29, 1847:

> I should not altogether wonder if I do something notable one
> of these days, all through a desperate virtue which determines out
> of gratitude—(not to man or the reading public, by any means!)—
> to do what I *do not* please: I could, with an unutterably easy heart,
> never write another line while I have my being—which would
> surely be very wrong considering how the lines fall to poets in the
> places of this world generally. So I mean to do my best whatever
> comes of it—

They were busy now just being happy, but with all the happiness
Browning was facing a huge responsibility. Perhaps as unpractical as
Mrs. Jameson thinks, he had to become, and he did become, very
practical in organizing their lives and caring for a physically sick and
mentally overstrung wife. They continued to cut down the morphine,
but could she ever entirely dispense with it? The facts must be faced

that she could *never* spend a winter in England, that she could never handle for herself the affairs of daily life. There must always be a Wilson. Soon there would be a baby if the doctors (whose bills had also to be met) were successful in bringing her through her second pregnancy.

The changes of abode in Florence had come about partly through Elizabeth's precipitate choice of rooms that proved uninhabitable. To her sisters she wrote with amazed gratitude of Browning's patience, but she thought less well of his determination to pay every bill the minute it became due. Incapable with money herself, Elizabeth had always been in debt, and she considered it, she said, "morbid and unpoetical" to fuss about one's bills. Browning replied that *he* was thinking of the butcher and the baker. Mr. Barrett had refused to have anything more to do with his daughter's affairs, but Mr. Kenyon faced his wrath and took over for her such business as could only be handled on the spot.

We have to imagine a world in which were no airmails, no telephones, no automobiles, and only very incomplete rail connections. The postal arrangements in Italy were startling. Browning would call at the post office for his letters, be handed the whole bundle and allowed to select his own. Many letters were lost; all came with incredible slowness. English newspapers they almost never received; a news sheet was available at Galignani's Club (for men only). "I say," Elizabeth wrote to Henrietta, " 'Bring me back news of a revolution' and generally he brings me back news of two." In a sense we can hardly realize today, it was an exile in which their lives were lived, with ups and downs like other lives, but always with a fundamental happiness.

There are letters to Arabel and Henrietta from Robert as well as from Elizabeth; it would be hard to say which of the pair expresses the greater adoration of the other. But Robert's letters are far less interesting; devotion almost wholly fills them, while she adds a lot in the way of daily news. From her we learn how Robert bought incredibly cheap antique furniture for the Casa Guidi, his only mistake being a superfluity of chests of drawers and not enough chairs. A dinner for three sent in from the trattoria with enough left over for supper cost less than two shillings; wine was a few pence the bottle; fruit cost almost nothing, and it was delightful to see the Florentine populace enjoying it. Indeed, unlike England, the poor had the same pleasures as the rich—food and displays and music. In dress the classes were indistinguishable. There was much merriment but little crime, almost no drunkenness. The love for Italy, which became almost a passion had seized her; and, for both her and Robert, Italy was not a mere museum, picture gallery, or panorama; it was a living nation.

Elizabeth's letters are full of delight over walks and talks and music, much of it made by Browning on a hired piano. With a "spring" sofa and chair, "I resume my habits of lolling with extraordinary pleasure." Carlyle had written of their marriage as a "union indicated by the finger of Heaven itself. . . . Courage, therefore; follow piously the Heavenly Omens, and fear not . . . unless I altogether mistake, here is a life partnership which, in all kinds of weather, has in it a capacity of being blessed . . . if joy be even absent for a season, may nobleness never!" Joy was certainly present now and Elizabeth wrote: "No human being ever comprehended human love so divinely."

Carlyle's at least was an exception to a general opinion expressed in Wordsworth's comment on the marriage. "Well, I hope they may understand each other—nobody else could." Barely established in Florence, Browning wrote, entreating Carlyle to come and visit them, ". . . let us have the happiness—the entire happiness of remembering that we got ready the Prophet's-Chamber in the wall, with bed and candlestick, according to Scripture precedent." Telling him, too, of the easy journeying in Italy, the cheapness of horses, carriages, lodgings, he goes on "if ever you are disposed to pass a winter here, we will go to any part you decide for, and be ready for you at any time." His feeling was "something beyond affection and far better than pride—that you have been and are what you are to me."

He had longed to tell Carlyle of all that had led up to the marriage. "My wife, in all probability, will become quite well and strong . . . from the accounts from England, and from the nature of the place in the country to which she was to have been removed . . . this winter would have ended the seven years' confinement without my intervention." They had found in her love and reverence for Carlyle "a common point of sympathy. . . . So that there was one way left for me to love her the more."

One day in the street Browning had run into an old acquaintance, "Father Prout," and several letters home are filled with exasperation at the Irish Jesuit, turned journalist and quite a lion in London, whose pen name this was. "A Roman Catholic Priest," Jane Brookfield described him, "who only officiates as a boon companion." His was, I suspect, an influence increasing in both Brownings a jaundiced view of the Catholic Church. They were half amused, half exasperated as, long past their normal bedtime, he sat and smoked and spat into the spittoon they had provided, and called Elizabeth "Ba" without invitation. Yet "the utmost kindness and warmheartedness" had characterized him, and he had earned Elizabeth's gratitude by mixing for a weak and feverish Robert "a potion of egg and port wine," calming his pulse in a fever and sending him to sleep.

They met a few old friends and made a few new. They kept their first anniversary on a great fiesta in Florence in honor of the granting by the Grand Duke of a constitution and a national guard, rejoicing with the people. Elizabeth commented: "Our poor English want educating into gladness . . . our religious teachers in England do not sanctify the relaxations of the people." The Florentines had gone first to the cathedral to sing *Te Deum* and then been happy in the streets.

"Italy was my university," Browning said later, and it had been so, long before he and she were established there. Perhaps it was the country "seen only in his soul" as Cerutti talked to him and he read Dante, Petrarch, and this and that old chronicle. It became an intense reality on his two visits—stirring in him "No simple and self-evident delights, / But mixed desires of unimagined range, / Contrasts or combinations new and strange."

In *Sordello* we see castles, minstrels, warriors, devastated battle scenes and sunsets, intensified color, light and darkness. "O'er the far forests, like a torch-flame turned / By the wind back upon its bearer's hand / In one long flare of crimson; as a brand, / The woods beneath

lay black. . . ." Breathlessness is one element in that "incomprehensible"
poem, and it is there still in *Pippa Passes*. As with his love poetry, all
Browning's writing is poetry of experience, "recollected" not "in tranquility," but with passion.

Sordello, Pippa Passes, King Victor and King Charles, "My Last
Duchess," "The Italian in England," "The Englishman in Italy," "St.
Praxed's Church," *Return of the Druses*—all these are situated in Italy,
all were written in England. And Browning's special outlook and bent
of mind become clearer and clearer as we read them. He said once that
he loved nature, but cared more for men. And he could not think fruit-
fully of men as "mankind." The characters (as Macready complained)
were always more important than the plot—or than the multitude.
This, which would be a weakness for a social reformer, was an immense
strength for a psychologically minded poet. He could not take "Italian"
freedom with the same simplicity as his wife. He was too conscious of
the medieval cities at war with one another (*e.g.*, Florence and Pisa in
The Druses); of the wars of Guelphs and Ghibellines, with their in-
cessant permutations and combinations; of complexity far greater than
she saw in the relations between Pope and Emperor.

In Elizabeth's poetry mankind and causes are more alive than any
individual; in *Aurora Leigh* not one of the characters lives; while
Browning could write more vividly of the man caught in the political
or social machine than of the masses oppressed by it. Luigi, hesitating
whether or not to assassinate a tyrant, is seen as the boy, almost child,
he is; Sebald, Ottima, are people; and so is the Italian in England looking back at Italy. But who cares for the "causes" in *Sordello*? And I cannot help fancying that it was chiefly through his wife's fervor that
Browning became enthusiastic about the Risorgimento.

In these early years above all he was chiefly watching people, and
although written a little later, "Up at a Villa—Down in the City" belongs to any year in which he was looking out of the window in any
Italian city. From the Casa Guidi windows Elizabeth listened to a child
singing "*O bella Liberta, O bella*" and went on to dream of the future.
But the fascinating present was more intensely vivid to Browning, looking and listening, as he conceives an "Italian person of quality" would,

to the sights and sounds beneath, or walking the lanes of the Tuscan countryside.

There are exquisite touches in the Villa stanzas, but the dominant note of the poem is the riotous high spirits of Mrs. Jameson's "prince of travelling companions."

Ere you open your eyes in the city, the blessed church-bells begin:
No sooner the bells leave off than the diligence rattles in:
You get the pick of the news, and it costs you never a pin.
By-and-by there's the travelling doctor gives pills, lets blood, draws teeth;
Or the Punchinello-trumpet breaks up the market beneath.
At the post-office such a scene-picture—the new play, piping hot!
And a notice how, only this morning, three liberal thieves were shot.
Above it, behold the Archbishop's most fatherly of rebukes,
And beneath, with his crown and his lion, some little new law of the
    Duke's! . . .
Noon strikes,—here sweeps the procession! our Lady borne smiling and
    smart
With a pink gauze gown all spangles, and seven swords stuck in her heart!
Bang-whang-whang goes the drum, *tootle-te-tootle* the fife;
No keeping one's haunches still: it's the greatest pleasure in life.

11 Italian Background

*. . . Pure hands, stretched simply to release
A bond slave, will not need a sword to draw
To be held dreadful . . .*

CASA GUIDI WINDOWS

ITALY, so long Browning's inspiration, had now become the world he lived in. Both he and Elizabeth were profoundly interested in the new nation struggling to emerge as their own *vita nuova* was growing into its fulness.

When Browning first went there, in 1838, the very name of Italy was rare except on the lips of patriots, poets, and antiquarians. "Since the fall of the Roman Empire," wrote one nineteenth-century historian, "(if even before it) there never has been a time when Italy could be called a nation any more than a stack of timber can be called a ship." Venice and Genoa, Milan and Florence, Pisa and above all Rome played their parts on the stage of medieval history, but by the eighteenth century the multitude of states had become insignificant petty princedoms. They were ruled over by Bourbon or Hapsburg princes, excepting Rome itself and the States of the Church, and Piedmont where the Dukes of Savoy straddled the Alps and had become also Kings of Sardinia.

The Napoleonic conquest had pulled the country together. Bonaparte was hardly the deliverer he proclaimed himself, but he reduced the country's political divisions from fifteen to five, crushed brigandage, made law and justice uniform and effective. In the eyes of Mazzini, despite war and political despotism, the Napoleonic domination had "elevated our souls." With it had arisen, as a picture in the distance, "the oneness of Italy, the object of all our efforts." After Napoleon's fall the diplomats restored former conditions as far as possible, but the atmosphere had changed.

It is to the Mazzini period and the Mazzini spirit that Browning's "Italian in England" belongs, the vivid picture of the man hidden in the aqueduct: "That second time they hunted me/From hill to plain, from shore to sea/The Austrian bloodhounds"; the girl accepting his message; the priest in the confessional to whom she courageously passes it. And then the exile in which the patriot, grown old, dreams of seeing Italy once again, and discovering perhaps on some small farm among his children the girl who with him had dangerously served "that dear, lost land,/Over the sea, the thousand miles."

Not improbably this exile would still be primarily a Florentine, bitterly hating the Austrians, a Neapolitan resenting the Bourbon tyranny—or even a Sicilian hating the Neapolitans through whom that tyranny extended to Sicily—for after Napoleon's fall former conditions had been restored. But the desire for a United Italy was growing, felt by men who later became bitterly opposed to one another's way of seeking it.

Pius IX had imbibed the ideas of an exiled patriot, Gioberti, who wanted a federated Italy of which the Pope would be the natural leader. Mazzini, another exile, was a republican, desiring an Italy totally unified, with no Pope and no kings. His religion was God and the People. His country he said had been murdered, and he wore black always as a sign of his grief. Still he accepted for a while the idea of papal leadership, and Garibaldi, the soldier of fortune who later conquered Sicily and Naples with an army of one thousand in a period of weeks, now offered the Pope his sword.

At this time Pius wanted no swords; this white-robed, humorous and emotional churchman fancied he could adapt the principles of liberalism to a situation infinitely more complex than he realized. "A Liberal Pope," said Metternich aghast, "is an impossibility." Austria was not going to relax her hold; the Bourbons had learned nothing; the

King of a united Sardinia and Piedmont was dreaming the dream—to be made reality for his son by Cavour—of becoming himself the ruler of a united Italy. And in France, Napoleon III was prepared to help whatever side would mean advantages to his own country.

The Pope's initial reaction against Austria, when Metternich increased the Austrian garrison inside the States of the Church, encouraged the revolutionaries to believe he was wholly on their side. He became almost insanely popular. But they *would* not, he constantly repeated learn to distinguish between the Pope, father of Christendom, and the Italian devoted to his own country. He appealed to Austria to think of Italy as a sister land in the Christian world. "Both are our daughters and very dear to us."

The first round in the fight for which all were preparing went to Austria, challenged by the united kingdom of Piedmont and Sardinia.

The Pope believed himself obliged to maintain the States of the Church; they made him independent of earthly rulers and were at that time secured by a vast multitude of Catholics in all the countries of Europe. They were in the Pope's eyes "the seamless robe of Christ," which he must keep untorn even as had the Roman soldiers on Calvary. With these views he allowed his own tiny army to march with the forces of Piedmont, stipulating that they should fight in defense of the Papal States only if these were invaded. But their commander gave a very different impression, casting the Pope in the rôle of Peter the Hermit in a crusade for the freedom of Italy.

Piedmont had been far too confident. They were up against greater forces far more ably led, and the Austrians twice inflicted heavy defeats on them, after which King Charles Albert resigned his throne into the hands of his son Victor Emmanuel.

Pope and King were identified—and discredited—in this defeat; the revolutionaries now took matters into their own hands. Pius had given the Romans a constitution; their Prime Minister, De Rossi, was not only a layman but an unbeliever, an able man working hard both for peace and the unification of Italy. But he was assassinated, a bishop shot at an open window, the Pope's guard disarmed. The Pope fled to

Gaeta and Garibaldi's army marched in. A triumvirate, of which Mazzini was one, took over the government of the city.

The rulers of the world had small sympathy with this situation. It was in "the year of revolutions" (1848) that it began, when none of them felt very secure. Even Queen Victoria, vigorous Protestant though she was, sent the Pope a message of sympathy; and *The Times* thought him a "splendid fellow" because he had modeled his newly given constitution on that of Britain. Napoleon discovered that the Pope's cause was popular with French Catholics of the left as well as of the right, and he finally decided that his best policy was to support him. So French bayonets brought Pius back, and drove Garibaldi into exile.

He was prepared to defy France, Austria, and Spain, but his small army was overwhelmed and he had to fly. His sick wife was with him and died in his arms. After years of wandering Garibaldi bought the north end of the island of Caprera whence he could look and dream and prepare, if Italy should again call him. "I am terrified," he said, "of the likely prospect of never again wielding sword or musket for Italy." But, visiting England, it was he who had the wisdom to advise Mazzini henceforward to work with Victor Emmanuel. Italy was not yet ripe for a united republic, and Piedmont-Sardinia was the only state strong enough to be their leader when the struggle was resumed.

Casa Guidi Windows (Part I written in 1848, part II in 1851) is written from the viewpoint of one side in the crusade, first with an immense optimism, later with a profound disappointment. Elizabeth Barrett Browning's prejudices against any sort of ecclesiastical ruler ran deep; those against the head of the Catholic Church were almost insurmountable, but she briefly hoped in Pius: ". . . this country saving is a glorious thing," well done if by a common man, excellent by a rich one, by a king sublime, improbable by a priest:

> A pope? Ah there we stop, and cannot bring
> Our faith up to the leap, with history's bell
> So heavy round the neck of it—albeit
> We fain would grant the possibility
> For *thy* sake Pio Nono!

One feels it must have been almost a relief to her when the bright hopes of the revolutionaries were disappointed and the Pope lost his place in the cast of this tremendous drama. But the real disappointment came over Florence and its people. She had taken the singing of a child beneath her window, *"O bella Liberta, O bella,"* as a symbol, but now she demanded of the nation itself:

> Didst thou, too, only sing of liberty
>> As little children take up a high strain
> With unintentioned voices, and break off
>> To sleep upon their mothers' knees again?
> Couldst thou not watch one hour. . . .

Outside Piedmont recruitment had been poor for the armies of liberation: ". . . to leave our piazzas, shops and farms/For the simple sake of fighting was not good/. . . . Desire was absent that provides great deeds."

Her much-loved Florentines did not understand "The serious sacred meaning and full use/Of freedom for a nation."

Elizabeth was not as deeply implicated in the cause of Italy at this date as she became later. She felt, looking back in 1858 upon the rebellions of 1848, that they had been only a preparation—a "dress rehearsal." Yet even at this time it is interesting to note the sustained intensity of her poem. It has been said that we owe to her the most dramatic lines in Browning's "Italian in England": "I would grasp Metternich until/I felt his red wet throat distil/In blood thro' these two hands." Not that Browning could not himself be intensely dramatic, but he is far more skilled at painting a picture that includes an intensity made greater by the fact that beauty, details of daily life, and the whole surrounding atmosphere are in it. Elizabeth's letters, but Browning's poems, transport us to the Italy of their affections:

> What I love best in all the world
> Is a castle, precipice-encurled,
> In a gash of the wind-grieved Apennine . . .
> . . . a sea-side house to the further South

Where the baked cicala dies of drouth, . . .
                              For, what expands
Before the house, but the great opaque
Blue breadth of sea without a break? . . .
A girl bare-footed brings, and tumbles
Down on the pavement green-flesh melons,
And says there's news today—the king
Was shot at, touched in the liver wing,
Goes with his Bourbon arm in a sling:
—She hopes they have not caught the felons.
Italy, my Italy!

Even at this earlier stage Elizabeth found it hard to abandon the tragic note, but she still saw the sorrows of Italy—much more than she did later—as implicated in the sorrows of a suffering world. She scorned the more fortunate part of humanity which was in 1850 "a Fair-going world." The splendors of distant lands were pouring into "the gorgeous Crystal Palace," while she was looking at "the poor who sit in darkness," at the England of brothels and of child labor, at the America of slavery, and at the slavery of nations:

Annihilated Poland, stifled Rome,
Dazed Naples, Hungary fainting 'neath the thong,
    And Austria wearing a smooth olive leaf
On her brute forehead.

12 Life, Death, and Danger

Robert neither eats nor sleeps when he is anxious.

ELIZABETH BARRETT BROWNING

Elizabeth's age and her health were both against her, but despite all fears their first and only child was born in March, 1849. "Our blessed Ba," wrote Browning to her sisters, "gave birth to a fine strong boy." The doctor assured him "without flattery, the little creature is the very model of a beautiful boy. . . . Was it not dear of Ba to refuse to look at the babe till I could show it her? . . . the little hands and fingers are wonderfully strong"—and all the usual rest of it.

The baby was christened Robert Wiedemann Barrett "without godfathers and godmothers," wrote Elizabeth to Mrs. Jameson, "in the simplicities of the French Lutheran Church." But when he began to speak he (naturally?) resisted all attempts to call him Wiedemann; he turned it into the rather charming "Penini." This was presently shortened to Pen, and to all his friends he remained Pen Browning for life, calling himself more formally Robert Barrett Browning. The financial strain on his parents Mr. Kenyon insisted on meeting by the gift of £100 a year.

Browning had told Elizabeth that "he didn't believe he had the least touch in him of paternal instinct"; but when Pen was only nine days' old he was writing ecstatically to the Barrett sisters of his size, his strength, his astonishing quantity of hair. "I have just got three little tufts cut off,—for you and Miss Tripsack [Trepsack], and my own Mother . . . he follows lights and noises with his little great eyes and even hands—and when I make a chirrup to him with my lips, fairly takes hold of my nose!—All indubitable signs of his being what Mr. Disraeli calls the 'Coming Man.' "[1]

But the waiting and watching had been an immense strain, and hardly had Browning begun to recover from it in the joy of parenthood when the news came from England of his mother's death. The shock was too great—death treading thus on the heels of life. The bond between mother and son had been a close one. Browning had told Elizabeth of his own great physical resemblance to his mother (though this is hardly borne out by Alfred Domett's description of her head—so square that it always made him think of a tea caddy). Domett noted Browning's affectionate and courteous manner, revealing his deep affection; he felt how intensely united a family they were. "There was something peculiarly thrilling," Elizabeth wrote, "to a nature like his in the discord between the joy and the grief, in the thought that we were rejoicing here while his mother was dying." For a while he could hardly bear to look at his own child; his joy seemed almost literally turned into grief. He put aside comfort at first "passionately," she told Mrs. Jameson. "Now it begins to rise into sight again."[2]

Elizabeth, who loved her hard and unloving father so persistently, could understand and deeply sympathize. She wrote to her sister of the love so full in her husband's nature, of the sadness of his exile. For long his sleep was broken, his sadness almost constant. And he wept to an extent mysterious to our generation. He always did cry easily: when listening to great music or watching tragedy, when hearing his wife's poetry read, when reading his own (and the audience cried with him), even when visiting the room where Petrarch died. A far more prolonged grief was witnessed by those who passed him blindly weeping in the London streets months after his wife's death. The intense vitality which had resurrected Elizabeth was now pouring for the first time in his life into the realization of death. And after all we are judging as from another world in a century so different. The athletes of Homer wept, and at Trafalgar Nelson and Hardy kissed each other good-by not without tears.

Fortunately, as the hot weather approached, Florence became no place for Elizabeth or the baby. Husband and wife went in advance of the nursery party to find a good place for the summer. Lerici, Elizabeth tells us, "seemed good for Robert," but she was relieved to find it too expensive; the scene of Shelley's drowning recalled too keenly her own personal tragedy.

Shelley being for Mrs. Miller the King Charles's head which cannot be kept out, she will have none of this. Ignoring Elizabeth's view that Lerici suited Browning, she says that the associations there were "intolerable" to him. He had left "no written record" on a first visit to Italy of "what *must have been* [italics mine] psychologically its capital experience"; nor had he told anyone that what he "followed . . . looked for" in the streets of Pisa were "the footsteps" of this poet of "old conflicts, old betrayals": yet these things too she says. It is not merely the lack of evidence I find strange; it is the counterevidence of Elizabeth's words, *and* of Browning's Essay on Shelley [see Chapter XV]. Its writing would have been intrinsically impossible for a man in the mental state Mrs. Miller depicts.

One fact, highly dramatized, betrays the dreamlike texture of the whole. A "small, weightless object carefully packed and labeled" appears in Sotheby's Catalogue of a sale of Browning's effects; and Mrs. Miller's book ends with the words, "It was a flower plucked from Shelley's grave."

So it was. But it might as easily have been the laurel leaf from Byron's garden or the ivy from his grave, picked half a century apart. It might have been the plaster mask of Keats; Edmund Kean's green purse given to Browning by Forster, or the lock of Milton's hair the gift of Leigh Hunt—or supremely Elizabeth's (of which he had felt unworthy) "so much of you—all precious that you are—as may be given in a lock of your hair—I will live and die with it." Browning, though his thought reached into the age of Existentialism, remained sentimentally a Victorian. A reviewer wrote lately that, rummaging in the *Times* office, he found a thickly black-edged envelope. In it were two locks of Disraeli's hair. [Presented by Queen Victoria?] The tribal customs of a past age can only puzzle a later generation.

Robert and Elizabeth were surprised to discover in the reputedly worldly and anglicized Bagni di Lucca a glorious and almost inaccessible retreat. Three villages together constituted Lucca, and in a house above the highest of the three the Brownings made their temporary home. They spent two later summers there.

The black and white of a chessboard. Browning would use this simile in "Bishop Blougram's Apology" for the faith and unfaith in a man's soul; Elizabeth would use it of her husband's moods. Both of them tended to extremes—Elizabeth having, as she said, "a sad heart and a merry mind," Browning living habitually on the white squares of life's board, yet when on the black intensely aware of their blackness.

This was probably the first time Elizabeth had had to be the support to Robert instead of Robert to her. Fortunately her sympathy with his feelings was unfailing. For even after their arrival at Lucca he was writing to Sarianna as though, since his mother's death, he cared little for life. Years later, after their father died, Browning noted that his sister's mourning had in it no bitterness, for she had been a perfect daughter. Most of us suffer as he did with the longing to remake an unchangeable past.

Elizabeth wrote twice to her father-in-law and Sarianna, begging them to come and make their home with her and Robert; the refusal must have been something of a relief.

Two happy letters to Mrs. Jameson on August 11 and 13 show both parents thrilled over Penini's first tooth, and record Robert's remark: "Well, I never thought I could care so much for a child." And to Mrs. Martin she writes that Robert is as bad as she is "watching every movement of the baby."[3]

The letters had become more cheerful, beauty and time were doing their work of healing. And Browning was meditating on the poem—the two poems—which grew out of his joy and his suffering: *Christmas-Eve and Easter-Day.*

"The beauty of the scenery and walks," writes Elizabeth, "is something past description; and Robert and I enjoy it to the uttermost only wishing we could draw to us all those whom we love. . . . Think of his twice snatching me up and carrying me up a long steep—long enough and steep enough to incur the risk of breaking a vessel in the chest or heart. I was so frightened that fatigue would have been nothing at all to it, and quite seriously angry."

On a longer expedition Elizabeth rode a donkey "along the dry beds of exhausted torrents, the loose rocks crumbling around us. At the top you look round on a great world of innumerable mountains, the faint sea beyond them. . . . Wasn't it daring of us to take Baby?" Perhaps more daring of Robert to take Ba on a ten-hour expedition.

Browning wrote to Leigh Hunt from Bagni di Lucca in October, 1857: "I never suspected the existence of those 'Sonnets from the Portuguese' till three years after they were written; they were shown to me at this very place eight years ago." He it was who "thought of the subterfuge of a name."[4]

Many years later (in 1864) he looked back again, seeing the same vivid picture, and in a letter to Julia Wedgwood he wrote:

> Yes, that was a strange, heavy crown, that wreath of Sonnets, put on me one morning unawares, three years after it had been twined—all this delay because I happened early to say something against putting one's loves into verse; then again I said something else on the other side, one evening at Lucca—and the next morning she said hesitatingly: "Do you know I once wrote some poems about *you*"—and then—"There they are, if you care to see them"—and there was the little Book I have here—with the last Sonnet dated two days before our marriage. How I see the gesture, and hear the tones—and, for the matter of that, see the window at which I was standing, with the tall mimosa in front, and little church-court to the right.
>
> . . . The publishing was through me—in the interests of the poet, I chose they should be added to the other works, not minding the undue glory to me, if the fact should become transparent. . . . The Portuguese—purposely an ambiguous title—was that Caterina who left Camoens the riband from her hair.

"A strange heavy crown" it must certainly have been, to face the publication of poems expressing that intensity, not of love so much—

for that they both expressed in their lives always and he was not backward at expressing it in poetry—but of an admiration, a setting of herself
so far beneath him, against which he had always fiercely striven. He
never forgot for a moment that the world was very very far from sharing
her estimate, and it must have taken a great deal of love for his wife, a
great deal of concern for her fame, to make him willing to publish such
lines as

> Thou, bethink thee art
> A guest for queens to social pageantries,
> With gages from a hundred brighter eyes
> Than tears even can make mine, to play thy part
> Of chief musician. What hast *thou* to do
> With looking from the lattice-lights at me,
> A poor, tired, wandering singer, singing through
> The dark, and leaning up a cypress tree?
> The chrism is on thine head,—on mine the dew,—
> And Death must dig the level where these agree.

I fancy had they not both been profoundly convinced that his
future fame was certain, these sonnets would have gone unpublished.
Certainly neither guessed how very very far in the future it would be,
that she would not even live to see it. And Browning, who steadily
maintained that his wife *was* the greater poet, is said to have declared
he dared not keep for himself alone the finest sonnets since Shakespeare.
Such a judgment, if he did indeed pronounce it, does more credit to
Browning's heart than to his head. But this need hardly surprise us.
From Bagni he was writing to Mrs. Jameson of his wife's "entirely
angel nature, as divine a heart as God ever made; I know more of her
every day; I who thought I knew something of her five years ago."
Elizabeth wrote to the same friend of his improvement in health and
spirits and how "Robert and I go out and lose ourselves in the woods
and mountains, and sit by the waterfalls on the starry and moonlit
nights. . . . We are both enjoying this great sea of mountains and our
way of life here."

Soon there were hopes of another baby and on December 21, Elizabeth writes of having avoided a miscarriage. "We ought to groan

elegiacally, or at least 'make the best of it' philosophically, when we talk of a possible second baby thirteen months after the first, instead of which we are just *pleased* like stupid people. Our English friends will hold up their hands in compassion I am sure."

The "disappointment and vexation" of a miscarriage were taken "philosophically," "Wiedemann does for us very well. . . . Robert and I contend who shall not cross him in any of his wishes—we are each of us dreadfully afraid of being the unpopular person . . . his royalty fails to corrupt him: he is full of love . . . huggings and kisses till Flush says 'something too much of this', and walks away from an excess of demonstration which he considers in bad taste."

Thus to Mrs. Martin. And to Mrs. Jameson she speaks of looking in amazement at this tiny living, thinking being "much as a savage does at a ticking watch—can it be alive. . . . Robert has much my feeling and we are never tired of examining him."[5] Apparently the first disappointment after Pen had no serious effect on Elizabeth's health. But, after yet another miscarriage in July (of 1850), Browning wrote to Mr. Kenyon that the doctor said "she had lost above a hundred ounces of blood within the twenty-four hours," and that "not one in five thousand women would suffer to the same extent. . . ." He had received Kenyon's letter "after sitting all night by the little patient white face, that could smile so much more easily than speak." She certainly had all the courage in the world, for before the end of September came another, her last, and worst, miscarriage. Whether she could survive was in doubt. She was "on ice for three days, . . . Robert and Wilson both up all night," for six weeks she could not walk across the floor. "Nobody (in the body) ever looked more ghastly than I did." But they went into the hills near Siena, and she made so swift a recovery that we soon find her visiting churches and boasting of having "walked to the top of San Miniato."

In these months of life and death and danger Browning had written and published two of his greatest poems, inspired certainly in part by intensity of emotion after the birth of his son, the death of his mother, the mortal danger of his wife.

G

13 Christmas-Eve and Easter-Day

Christ's place indeed is with the poets.

OSCAR WILDE

CHRISTMAS-EVE

A WORLD of thought and emotion is in the background of these poems, both spoken in the first person, both "poetry of experience."[1] In "Christmas-Eve" the narrator shelters from the rain in the porch of a chapel as the sermon is beginning. The poem opens vividly with a description of repulsion by and revulsion from a chapel at once like and unlike the Clayton-Ready-Irons experiences of Browning's boyhood.

> They eyed me much as some wild beast
> That congregation still arriving . . .
> In came the flock: the fat weary woman,
> Panting and bewildered, down-clapping
> Her umbrella with a mighty report,
> Grounded it by me, wry and flapping,
> A wreck of whalebones . . .

Followed her the

> Little old-faced peaking sister-turned-mother
> Of the sickly babe she tried to smother

> Somehow up, with its spotted face,
> From the cold, on her breast, the one warm place . . .

Wincing at the door with "the gruff/Hinge's invariable scold/ Making my very blood run cold," he looked and listened: "humbly knew himself improper,/But could not shrink up small enough," as

> . . . the dingy satins
> Of a female something, past me flitted,
> With lips as much too white, as a streak
> Lay far too red on each hollow cheek;
> And it seemed the very door-hinge pitied
> All that was left of a woman once,
> Holding at least its tongue for the nonce.
> . . . from each that entered,
> I got the same interrogation—
> "What, you the alien, you have ventured
> "To take with us, the elect, your station?
> "A carer for none of it, a Gallio!"—
> Thus, plain as print, I read the glance
> At a common prey, in each countenance.

Thus must the boy Browning have felt, for all his bravado, when publicly rebuked by the Reverend Clayton. Today he retorts:

> But still, despite the pretty perfection
> To which you carry your trick of exclusiveness,
> And, taking God's word under wise protection,
> Correct its tendency to diffusiveness,
> And bid one reach it over hot ploughshares,—
> Still, as I say, though you've found salvation,
> If I should choose to cry, as now, "Shares!"
> See if the best of you bars me my ration!
> I prefer if you please, for my expounder
> Of the laws of the feast, the feast's own Founder . . ."

His old exasperation is back at the narrowness, the bigotry, which no love for his mother could exorcise. He had set the scene very differently from his boyhood's chapels: the creaking doors, the poverty-

stricken flock, the outcasts of society, but here were the same spiritual
experiences, the same mental processes to be observed—and observing
them he was, with a good deal of contempt:

> These people have really felt, no doubt,
> A something, the motion they style the Call of them;
> And this is their method of bringing about,
> By a mechanism of words and tones
> (So many texts in so many groans)
> A sort of reviving and reproducing...

The sermon for Browning is mere unmeaning sound, and he asks:

> After how many modes, this Christmas-Eve,
> Does the self-same weary thing take place?
> The same endeavour to make you believe,
> And with much the same effect, no more:
> Each method abundantly convincing,
> As I say, to those convinced before,
> But scarce to be swallowed without wincing
> By the not-as-yet-convinced . . .

More and more impatient: "I very soon had enough of it./The hot
smell and the human noises" . . . "That placid flock, that pastor vocifer-
ant."

So he "flung out of the little chapel"—but not, as we shall learn,
in physical fact: he is still there and still aware even of the preaching,
with an awareness overlaid yet not erased, by a series of visions.

On these visions whole books could be written—on their relation to Moses and the burning bush, for instance, to the visions
in Isaiah VI and VII, and to Peter's "Depart from me, O Lord, for
I am a sinful man." Any two readers will read differently, both
perhaps truly. I can but follow the line of the poem as I see it. In
the course of it will come two further experiences of a religious
assembly—High Mass at St. Peter's, depicted with an intensity no
Catholic poet has even approached, and a Liberal Protestant lecture
at Göttingen, conveying with equal vividness the opposite extreme of a

rather pallid religion. These three are for Browning clearly the key modes of Christianity. At the end he will feel that the chapel, by far the least attractive in his description, is what God wants for him.

Free—for now—of the Chapel he turns to nature, through which: "my faith sprang first! . . ./—In youth I looked to these very skies,/And probing their immensities,/I found God there . . ."

Passing beyond the first lesson of God's power he finds love too, discovers:

> That he who endlessly was teaching,
> Above my spirit's utmost reaching,
> What love can do in the leaf or stone,
> (So that to master this alone,
> This done in the stone or leaf for me,
> I must go on learning endlessly) . . .

—learning the why of man's brief day on the "stupid" earth, which

> Suffers no change, but passive adds
> Its myriad years to myriads,
> Though I, he gave it to, decay,
> Seeing death come and choose about me,
> And my dearest ones depart without me . . .

The realization of eternity, of the vision of God face to face (and in Him of all we have loved), is met by the first immense experience of this poem. A moon rainbow was forming, typical surely of the white light which Browning felt he so often broke up into its prismatic hues:

> It rose, distinctly at the base
> With its seven proper colours chorded,
> Which still, in the rising, were compressed,
> Until at last they coalesced,
> And supreme the spectral creature lorded
> In a triumph of whitest white,—
> Above which intervened the night.

The white light is Anima's vision, prepared for often by anguish, leaving after it exhaustion and bewilderment. That he is imaging a tre-

mendous spiritual experience no student of the poem can doubt. He said
later that the one thing he had *seen* was the lunar rainbow. But in the
poem, beneath the white moon: "Another rainbow rose, a mightier, . . .
Rapture dying along its verge./Oh, whose foot shall I see emerge?" It is
a vision of Christ. But at first rejoicing and longing, like St. Peter, to
build "service-tabernacles three" where "I may worship," he realizes that
the figure is turned away from him, that he had perhaps lost Christ
through despising (as he so heartily had) the uncouth worshipers in
the chapel. Catching at His garment's hem he cries:

> "But not so Lord! It cannot be
> That thou, indeed, art leaving me—
> Me, that have despised thy friends! . . .
> I thought it best that thou, the spirit,
>   Be worshipped in spirit and in truth,
> And in beauty, as even we require it—
>   Not in the forms burlesque, uncouth,
> I left but now . . ."

His prayer is answered—

> The whole face turned upon me full
>   And I spread myself beneath it . . .
> So lay I, saturate with brightness,
>   And when the flood appeared to ebb,
> Lo I was walking, light and swift,
>   With my senses settling fast and steadying.

He is swept across the world to St. Peter's in Rome and views:

> As the swarming hollow of a hive,
> The whole Basilica alive!
> Men in the chancel, body and nave,
> Men on the pillars' architrave,
> Men on the statues, men on the tombs,
> With popes and kings in their porphyry wombs,
> All famishing in expectation
> Of the main-altar's consummation. . . .
> Earth breaks up, time drops away,

> In flows heaven, with its new day
> Of endless life, when He who trod,
> Very man and very God,
> This earth in weakness, shame and pain,
> Dying the death whose signs remain
> Up yonder on the accursed tree,—
> Shall come again, no more to be
> Of captivity the thrall,
> But the one God, All in all,
> King of kings, Lord of lords,
> As His servant John received the words,
> "I died, and live for evermore!"
>
> Yet I was left outside the door.

This line opens a fresh stanza. Browning feels that the Church he has seen at a worship he so magnificently describes has

> Departed from the founder's base:
> He will not bid me enter too,
> But rather sit, as now I do,
> Awaiting his return outside. . . .
> I see the errors; but above
> The scope of error, see the love—

The vision passes and Animus takes over, sometimes, I cannot help feeling "leaving its bright accomplice all aghast." It was almost impossible that Browning's conscious mind could have approved the Mass through which had come to him vision and inspiration. But it was a pity that reaction should carry him into talking of "raree shows" and "posturings and petticoatings." He could not accept intellectually a system to which he had not in fact applied his intellect.

But he had realized that love of men is called for by Christ's love, and: "Cautious this time how I suffer to slip/The chance of joining in fellowship/With any that call themselves his friends," he finds himself in the lecture hall at Göttingen University where a "hawk-nosed, high-cheek-boned Professor . . . three parts sublime to one grotesque," is lecturing, coughing (and spitting). "With a wan pure look, well-nigh celestial," this "sallow virgin-minded studious/Martyr to mild enthusiasm" is discussing "the Myth of Christ," of what value and "whence . . . derivable . . . (since plainly no such life was liveable)." He asks:

> Whether 'twere best opine Christ was,
> Or never was at all, or whether
> He was and was not, both together—
> It matters little for the name,
> So the idea be left the same.

Unlike the motley gathering in the chapel, his audience is "not a bad assembly neither,/Ranged decent and symmetrical/On benches . . ." We can almost see them with mildly admiring looks as he patronizes apostle and evangelist:

> . . . understanding
> How the ineptitude of the time,
> And the penman's prejudice, expanding
> Fact into fable fit for the clime,
> Had, by slow and secure degrees, translated it
> Into this myth, this individuum,
> Which, when reason had strained and abated it
> Of foreign matter, left, for residuum,
> A Man! . . .

"The vesture still within my hand"—that vesture which the Gospel tells us brought healing—Browning felt

> I could interpret its command.
> This time he would not bid me enter
> The exhausted air-bell of the Critic.
> Truth's atmosphere may grow mephitic
> When Papist struggles with Dissenter, . . .
> Each, that thus sets the pure air seething,
> May poison it for healthy breathing—
> But the Critic leaves no air to poison;
> Pumps out with ruthless ingenuity

> Atom by atom, and leaves you—vacuity . . .
>   (If mere morality, bereft
>   Of the God in Christ, be all that's left.)

Had Christ demanded of his followers:

>   "Believe in good,
>   In justice, truth, now understood
>   For the first time?"—or, "Believe in me,
>   Who lived and died, yet essentially
>   Am Lord of Life?"

Yet the question remains—*how* accept, how acknowledge, how worship? He does not feel inclined to go on with ". . . further tracking and trying and testing./" 'This tolerance is a genial mood,' " until the time and place " 'Where I may see saint, savage, sage/Fuse their respective creeds in one/Before the general Father's throne.' "

God "by God's own ways occult,/May—doth, I will believe—bring back/All wanderers to a single track."

But that track is not yet laid. Meanwhile, although:

>   I cannot bid
>   The world admit he stooped to heal
>   My soul, as if in a thunder-peal
>   Where one heard noise, and one saw flame,
>   I only knew he named my name.

Can the poet rest in a "genial mood" of tolerance for all religions? No he must, as modern usage has it, be committed, and this commitment he believes best met in a worship "Where earthly aids being cast behind,/His All in All appears serene/With the thinnest human veil between."

He finds himself back in the chapel "bolt upright/On my bench as if I had never left it." There he realizes that treasure can as well be carried in an earthen as in a golden vessel:

>   But the main thing is, does it hold good measure?
>   Heaven soon sets right all other matters!—
>   Ask, else, these ruins of humanity,

> This flesh worn out to rags and tatters,
> This soul at struggle with insanity,
> Who thence take comfort . . .

Only once in these experiences had Browning been swept off his feet, and that was by the Mass in St. Peter's. Intensely critical of both chapel and lecture hall he was sheerly exalted by the silver trumpets, the worshiping crowd, the sense of a Presence. Now he reacts, hoping that the Pope may forgo "today's buffoonery," while for the professor he prays: "May Christ do for him what no mere man shall,/And stand confessed as the God of salvation!"

And the poem ends with the poet prepared to sing "The last five verses of the third section/Of the seventeenth hymn of Whitfield's Collection,/To conclude with the doxology."

EASTER-DAY

"Christmas-Eve" concerned different ways of approaching God through Christ. This poem is tackling a different problem—the difficulty of believing at all:

> . . . could you joint
> This flexile finite life once tight
> Into the fixed and infinite,
> You, safe inside, would spurn what's out . . .

But life is not thus: it *is* finite, as yet unfixed, scrappy, profoundly imperfect, and to the man who longs for a world "perfect and entire," a world "quite above faith," the poet answers:

> No. The creation travails, groans—
> Contrive your music from its moans . . .

Perhaps one reason why Browning's fundamental ideas are so furiously debated is that so far as he can be spoken of as belonging to a category, it is one highly suspect by extremists at both ends. He was fully and richly a Christian humanist, and while some Christians suspect humanism, even more humanists deny the possibility of the union. This he understood—in both doubts he all but shared with an immense energy of imagination. It is not surprising that this poem begins: "How very hard it is to be/A Christian!"

This is the profounder and more difficult theme of "Easter-Day." Elizabeth felt she must reassure others—and perhaps herself—that Browning had *not* become an ascetic: It was (he said) one side of the question. This remark should be borne in mind by the critics who affirm that, in "Easter-Day" anyhow, Browning cannot be speaking as himself. Never is Browning more himself than when arguing with himself—and this argument is on two levels.

Intellectually it is hard to be a Christian because of the very nature of faith. "Blessed are they," Christ says, "who have *not* seen but have believed." "Faith," says the Epistle to the Hebrews, "is the substance of things hoped for, the evidence of things not seen." As Browning had reminded Elizabeth, to believe is not as easy as to breathe, "but there is no reward prepared for the feat of breathing and a great one for that of believing." Writing now of "how very hard it is to be/A Christian!— hard for you and me"—he goes on to treat the problem at a second level. The world around us not only challenges the Christian intellectually; the immense attractions of this world challenge him morally—and the one challenge reinforces at every step the power of the other. Browning already realized that he was in a post-Christian world, and he is haunted in this poem by the thought of the ease with which the martyrs died when Christ was still alive for them.

The carrying out of life's aims is never easy, but the Christian's aim is higher and is constantly obscured by fits of cold doubt: "You must mix some uncertainty/With faith, if you would have faith be." And, on behalf of the soul most shaken by doubt, he exclaims against the fallible judgments of men.

> . . . shall we award
> Less honour to the hull which, dogged
> By storms, a mere wreck, waterlogged,

> Masts by the board, her bulwarks gone
> And stanchions going, yet bears on,—
> Than to mere life-boats, built to save,
> And triumph o'er the breaking wave?

There seems from all evidence to exist a kind of pattern in human psychology after a bereavement. At first the lost wife, mother, friend, is vividly present: in prayers, in dreams, in daily life. Then comes the ache of emptiness when this realization of immortality—or as some think simply this psychological effect of grief and memory—becomes dimmed. Gradually the joy of life clamors to be felt; the sense of loss remains, but less poignantly; the vision of meeting again in a future life grows dimmer. And this can easily bring with it almost a wish to forget, to be able once more to enjoy daily delights intensely, fully.

And there is struggle in the mind alike and the senses: Shall we at the end: ". . . start up, at last awake/From life, that insane dream we take/For waking. . . ." Or will life indeed be followed by judgment— and if so, how defend what we made of it?

> . . . I resolved to say,
> "So was I framed by thee, such way
> I put to use thy senses here!
> It was so beautiful, so near,
> Thy world,—what could I then but choose
> My part there? . . .
> Is it for this mood
> That Thou, whose earth delights so well,
> Hast made its complement a hell?"

In this mood, a mood known to every Christian who has found joy in life and in the world, he hears the words: " 'Life is done,/Time ends, Eternity's begun,/And thou art judged for evermore.' "

But what is the judgment? Precisely to stay forever in the world he has chosen—

> "This world,
> This finite life, thou hast preferred,
> In disbelief of God's plain word,

To heaven and to infinity. . . .
                                    Thou art shut
Out of the heaven of spirit; glut
Thy sense upon the world: 'tis thine
For ever—take it!"
                              "How? Is mine
The world?" (I cried, while my soul broke
Out in a transport.) "Hast thou spoke
Plainly in that? Earth's exquisite
Treasures of wonder and delight,
For me?" . . .

"All partial beauty was a pledge
Of beauty in its plenitude:
But since the pledge sufficed thy mood,
Retain it!"

But "the eye is not filled with seeing, nor the ear with hearing." Painters
try to abstract the one face

With its one look, from throngs they saw.
And that perfection in their soul,
These only hinted at? The whole
They were but parts of? . . .
What visions will his right hand's sway
Still turn to forms, as still they burst
Upon him? How will he quench thirst,
Titanically infantine,
Laid at the breast of the Divine?

Music, in Browning's eyes the highest of the arts, he tries—and
poetry. But none of the gleams "made visible in verse," the hints and
intuitions which " 'pull the more into the less/Making the finite
comprehend/Infinity,' " none of this is enough for the spirit of man:
" 'else were permanent/Heaven on the earth its gleams were meant/To
sting with hunger for full light.' "

Again he asks—in this poem as in the last—dream or vision? What,
as he looks back, might have been only a "strange Northern Light," had
seemed, like the moon rainbow, the setting for a great personal revela-

tion: Across the sky: "Sudden there went,/Like horror and astonish-ment,/A fierce vindictive scribble of red/Quick flame..."

"Christmas-Day" had shown Christ as Saviour. But when this gift of the world was chosen "He stood there. Like the smoke/Pillared o'er Sodom, when day broke,—/I saw Him."

The gift did not bring its anticipated fullness of delight, and whether one believes or not in the supernatural, Browning is here driving home a fact of common human experience. An almost boundlessly rich woman, with power of choice to go, do, have, anything and everything she wanted, once made me see her mere effort of choice as the agony it had become. At that very time letters from blitzed England spoke of joy in waking alive to the song of birds or the sight of flowers. Class barriers were broken down, petty feuds healed, and human love was constantly manifested in sacrifice.

It is not only the "spirit's hunger . . . unsated not unsatable" for beauty, truth, the fullest use of senses and intellect, that has failed: eyes suddenly opened he cries: " 'I pray,—/Leave to love only!' " It was the problem of the boy Browning—and now of the man suffering from the loss of a mother, loved indeed but selfishly, by one overabsorbed in the discovery of the world. Now has come the unsought discovery of love—not human only but divine.

> "Love is the best? 'Tis somewhat late!
> And all thou dost enumerate
> Of power and beauty in the world,
> The mightiness of love was curled
> Inextricably round about,
> Love lay within it and without,
> To clasp thee—but in vain! Thy soul
> Still shrunk from Him who made the whole,
> Still set deliberate aside
> His love! . . ."

These two poems are Browning's first clear intimation of belief, not merely in a general idea of incarnation but specifically in that of the Son of God. Could man " 'who was so fit instead/To hate, . . . invent that scheme/Of perfect love?' " In the cloud-wrapped judge he had dis-

cerned "pity mixed/With the fulfillment of decree." That mysterious
fulfillment—the gift made eternal of the world deliberately chosen.
Now he is crying out for the old frustrations of a life reaching beyond
itself: " '. . . leave me not tied/To this despair, this corpse-like bride! . . .
Be all the earth a wilderness!/Only let me go on, go on,/Still hoping
ever and anon/To reach one eve the Better Land.' "
And mercy prevails over judgment:

> I knew Him through the dread disguise
> As the whole God within His eyes
> Embraced me.
> > When I lived again,
> The day was breaking—the grey plain
> I rose from, silvered thick with dew.
> Was this a vision? False or true?

For the rest of his life the dread will remain—dread of too much
ease, too smooth a path:

> "happy that I can
> Be crossed and thwarted as a man,
> Not left in God's contempt apart, . . .

> And think, "How dreadful to be grudged
> No ease henceforth as one that's judged.
> Condemned to earth for ever, shut
> From heaven!"
> > But Easter-Day breaks! But
> Christ rises! Mercy every way
> Is infinite,—and who can say?

Almost more than with any other does one feel the intolerableness
of the heckling that Browning alive or dead has been forced to endure
over this poem. His critics are demanding a John Stuart Mill to give
them logic instead of poetry, and it is hardly surprising that he should
have refused to acknowledge his identity with a man (or men) absorbed in vision (or dream) where Anima was working at a level deep
even for that ever-deep and mysterious source of inspiration.[2]

As reported by Sharp, *Christmas-Eve and Easter-Day* was, according to one eminent cleric, "the most Christian poem of the century"; to another "the heterodox self-sophistication of a free-thinker."

Elizabeth said that her husband's grief for his mother's loss was assuaged by the realization that her God was his God, her Saviour his Saviour—and to some degree one understands, after reading these poems, the mockery such a claim has called forth.

Psychology is a modern science. Had it been developed earlier many of the worst evils of the more-or-less Christian centuries would have been avoided. Browning was ahead of his age when he recognized what his contemporary, the scientist Pasteur, also saw when he claimed to have the faith of a Breton peasant—and hoped one day to have that of a Breton peasant's wife. This does not mean (any more than does Newman's saying that all men have a reason, though not all men can give a reason) that he despised the mind's processes. Still less does it mean what Browning in his later years sometimes appeared to say—that love can be a substitute for mind.

What it does mean is—and this is surely what Browning held when he wrote *Christmas-Eve and Easter-Day*—that the approach to God, the apprehension of Him as Creator and Redeemer, is not the act of *one* faculty, heart or mind, but of a total human person. His mother was more than unlikely to understand what he himself could only imperfectly express; there could never have been between them the meeting of minds so richly present with Elizabeth; but as *persons* they loved and understood each other. And as persons God understood them both, even if in their worship they spoke different languages. If Catholic and Protestant had realized this fact of human nature, half the world's persecutions might have been avoided, though it would not, I suppose, have inhibited the persecutors who see God only as a mythical enemy to human progress.

14 Two Checkered Years

We called the chess-board white,
—we call it black.

"BISHOP BLOUGRAM'S APOLOGY"

*C*HRISTMAS-EVE AND EASTER-DAY was poorly enough received. The publishers had timed it for the Easter of 1850 and two hundred copies were sold immediately. After this the sales slackened and as late as 1864 his publisher's account shows copies of this first edition still on hand. Of the reviewers De Vane says, "Whether they praised or blamed they generally misunderstood." This was almost invariably Browning's fate: "he has recklessly impaired," wrote the *Athenaeum* in an otherwise favorable review, "the dignity of his purpose by the vehicle chosen for its development." He was too Christian for the unbeliever, too flippant for the commonly solemn believer, too new for contemporary fashion.

But Joseph Milsand in the *Revue des deux Mondes* wrote with enthusiasm and understanding of Browning's religious philosophy, and with this French Protestant a warm friendship began when the Brownings went to Paris in 1851.

The years between marriage and the publication of *Men and Women* were full and rich, but Duckworth in his *Browning: Background and Conflict* notes the curious irony that the man who in his old age was said to have "dinnered himself away" had written in 1846: "I am convinced that general society depresses my spirit more than any other cause." It was Browning not Elizabeth who in their first months in Italy shunned the English-speaking society that tended to seek them out. Gradually they learned to select, but after two years of marriage Elizabeth told Arabel she had not been able to persuade Robert to dine out once. She writes, however, to Henrietta: "Last week five evenings out of the seven, we had somebody here . . . people fall in for coffee and talk."

"Here" was Casa Guidi; and in Florence, in Bagni di Lucca, in Rome, in Siena were friends who "looked in," friends to whose villas or apartments husband, wife, and presently child went together, or else Browning walked over by himself. Elizabeth grew so much stronger that she was able to walk with her husband many hours at a time. Among their friends were the American sculptor, William Wetmore Story, with his wife and children, who joined them at Lucca one year and had a neighboring villa at Siena another. Then there was "young Lytton" (later Lord Lytton)—son of the famous Edward Bulwer—who himself wrote under the penname of Owen Meredith.[1] On the Brownings' second visit to Lucca he occupied their spare room. "He lost nothing from the test of house intimacy with either of us—gained in fact much. Full of all sorts of good and nobleness he really is," wrote Elizabeth; and Lytton on his side was deeply grateful to her for her liberality in offering "to receive me and *my pipe*," and wrote to Browning: "It has been a great Era in my life to have met and known you and I often ask myself with shame if I am really worthy to seek your friendship."

It was Browning's only fault, Story noted, that he did not smoke— but Tennyson was wedded to the habit and when he could not find a particular tobacco in Florence "he was so disquieted . . . that he turned back to England and never went to Rome." Alfred Tennyson the Brownings much liked; and Frederick his brother, a lesser poet, became a great friend. Frederick spoke of Browning as "a man of infinite learning, jest and bonhomie and moreover a man of sterling heart that reverbs no hollowness."

The summer of 1850 was spent at Siena. Henry James, writing the biography of Story, sought in "the cluster of Siennese villas" an answer to "unanswerable questions" about "Robert Browning and Walter Savage Landor, and other spirits of the general scene . . . on the high terraces, meant for soft evenings and in the cool bare echoing rooms where shutters were pulled open for me to violet views." He felt as he gazed and dreamed a pang "not so much of accepted loss as of resented exclusion." There they stand still those old cool houses "on their communicating slopes, behind their overclambered walls and their winding accommodating lanes; there they stand in the gladness of their gardens . . . and in that wondrous mountain ring . . ."

No one better than James can help one to recreate those Italian days as the friends wandered leisurely through the lanes, drank tea on the terraces, or picnicked in the woods.

In 1851 the Brownings decided they must go to England. The journey went well. "The only sort of excitement," Elizabeth told her sisters, "that can be said to agree with me is the excitement of travelling." She could "bear more than many strong women."

From Venice she wrote to Arabel of "the fantastic beauty of the buildings, the mysterious silence of the waters, St. Mark's piazza by gaslight, with its great populace swept up and down as if by the breath of music, the moon on the lagunes and the gondolas passing in and out of the shadows with their little twinkling lamps."[1] Penini was chiefly pleased with what he called "the holy pigeons" in the piazza—and here as in Florence the mingling of classes thrilled Elizabeth: "I do love Christ's equality, the beating of heart to heart, the response of hand to hand."

The climate did not suit Browning, but did he write there "A Toccata of Galuppi's?" Anyhow they stayed a month, went on by Milan, the Lakes and Paris, meeting, in Paris, Tennyson—just made Poet Laureate. He had left England, Elizabeth reported, "because you English have hunted him half to death. He says you are the greatest nation in the world and the most vulgar—and he hopes to have a little peace and liberty away from you." At Milan, Elizabeth climbed to the top of the Cathedral, an amazing sign of her new vitality, but to Arabel she wrote from Paris "the dreadful joy of seeing you again requires a little strength."

Both husband and wife had been at once longing for and dreading the return. Browning felt unable to face the home where his mother's absence would become too aching a void. Elizabeth longed yet hardly dared to hope for reconciliation with her father. The atmosphere is reflected in her abundant letters; Henrietta came to London to see her; George, at last reconciled, came around often to their lodgings and became "mine untle" to Pen; Arabel she saw constantly. And with the courage of despair, in almost daily secret visits to Wimpole Street, she even took the risk of meeting her father.

Finally, she tells Mrs. Martin, "I could not leave England without trying the possibility of his seeing me once, of his consenting to kiss my child once. So I wrote, and Robert wrote. . . . In reply he had a very violent and unsparing letter, with all the letters I had written to Papa through these five years *sent back unopened, the seals unbroken*. . . . He said he regretted to have been forced to keep them by him until now, through his ignorance of where he should send them. So there's the end. I cannot, of course, write again. God takes it all into His own hands, and I wait."

Meanwhile they had been received with real enthusiasm by many friends old and new; word pictures abound in contemporary memoirs, but mostly of Elizabeth. Browning is recorded as "talking loudly and with vivacity," her silence is variously interpreted: that she had not much chance of speaking, that she could speak only seriously or on serious matters. She had, said Sara Coleridge, "a weak plaintive voice," but there was "something very impressive in her dark eyes and brow."

Tennyson offered them his house and so did Browning's old friend Arnould. Fanny Kemble called and left tickets for her Shakespeare reading; Barry Cornwall (Mr. Procter) called daily "till business swept him out of town."

"Mr. Forster of the 'Examiner' gave us a magnificent dinner at Thames Ditton in sight of the swans; and we breakfast on Saturday with Mr. Rogers. . . . I can't tell you what else we have done or not done. It's a great dazzling heap of things new and strange. . . . Such kindness on all sides."

Thus Elizabeth chronicles to her old friend, Mrs. Martin. But "the sort of life is not perhaps the best for me and the sort of climate is really the worst."

They spent an evening with Carlyle, who, according to Henry James's father, showed his affection for Browning in the only way he ever showed it to his friends—by a condescending pity: "Poor John Mill," he would say, "Poor little Browning." But all the same he did frequently speak with warm admiration both of and to Browning.

To a friend visiting Italy he had written on February 16, 1851: "If at Florence you know the Poet Browning (one of the bravest and most gifted of English souls now living) I will send my affectionate remembrance to him." These words Browning annotated in 1885: "Written to a friend of his, who showed it to E.B.B., who characteristically would preserve what I ought to destroy." On their side, both Brownings venerated the old lion—"one of the great sights in England" said Elizabeth; and Browning wrote to him of "my five years' hunger for the sight of you and Mrs. Carlyle."

Above all—even above Carlyle—was for Elizabeth the reunion with "good joyous Kenyon" as her husband dubbed this dear friend and cousin.

Despite his initial shrinking Browning was far more completely happy than his wife. "I do believe," she wrote, "he would have been capable of never leaving England again, had such an arrangement been practical for us." He had as yet no torn feelings about the family that was left him: it was, said Elizabeth, "pure joy to him with his family and friends."

But an English winter was too perilous and before the end of September they left for the continent, accompanied by Carlyle.

In the volume entitled *Last Words of Thomas Carlyle* we find this: "Excursion (futile enough) to Paris" described at some length, curiously illustrating the then problems of foreign travel. Advice must be sought as to "passports, routes, conditions"—and such advice was so confusing that Carlyle welcomed the information that the Brownings too were going to Paris. He "walked to their place—had during that day and the next consultations with these fellow pilgrims," and postponed his own journey a day "for the sake of company who knew the way to travel. Such rumours, such surmises; the air was thick with suppositions, guesses, cautions. . . . The Brownings and their experience and friendly qualities were worth waiting for. Fare to Paris 22/-, wonderful. Thither and back 'by return ticket' £1.12—such had been the effect in prices of this 'Glass Palace' and the crowds attracted to it . . . and so away we went, Browning talking very loud and with vivacity, I silent rather, tending towards many thoughts."

Noting the "torpor of seasickness" as "a sorry phase of humanity," he goes on to describe how Browning, despite suffering from it, struggled with porters and customs men for their luggage, "brought it in all safe about half past ten and we could address ourselves to desired repose." Next morning, again, it was Browning who "did everything; I sat out of doors on some logs at my ease and smoked," and on arrival at Paris "the brave Browning fought for us, leaving me to sit beside the women. . . . I walked out to smoke . . . cigar ended I went in again. Browning still fighting (in the invisible distance). . . . Our luggage visible at last . . . Browning visible with report of a hackney coach; we think it is now over; rash souls, there is yet an endless uproar among the porters . . . even Browning has at last grown heated." And to Elizabeth he said, "Ah it's a triumph for these fellows to have a poet to do just their will and pleasure—that's the way in this world—The earthborn order about the heaven-born and think it's only as it should be."

Securing a cab for himself, French money and the key of his trunk from Browning, Carlyle at last got off to the hotel where he was to be the guest of the Ashburtons. He states, with an exclamatory note, that it was the most expensive in Paris, costing £45 for the week's stay of the Ashburtons, their two servants and himself. But he slept badly, disapproved strongly of the French and their theater ("their canine libertinage and soulless grinning over all that is beautiful and pious in human relations were profoundly saddening to me"). "I withdraw to the Brownings before seven. Great welcome there and tea in quiet. B. gives me (being cunningly led to it) copious account of the late 'revolutions' in Florence—such a fantastic piece of Drury Lane 'revolution' as I have seldom heard of." Next day: "Decide to vanish to Browning," whom he also misses sorely on the return journey but is comforted, after all the "passport showing; crowded botheration; steamer overflowing," by the "admirable silence, method and velocity" at London Bridge.

Carlyle wrote warmly from London: "Adieu dear Browning; commend me to the gentle excellent Lady and remember me now and then." They wanted him to come back, but he had had enough of Paris. Browning pleaded: ". . . won't you reconsider the matter . . . we here have had all the good fortune in your journey with us, and visits to us; the weather is admirable . . . the perfection of fresh warm clearness and we get all that to ourselves too." Beginning to write on Shelley, he has some of Carlyle's thoughts in mind: "I shall always hope—for a great incentive—to write my best *directly to you* some day."[2]

Meanwhile he set to work on this very important essay and Elizabeth told Arabel that he had "taken to his new room with green curtains, and sits there half in sun and half in shade 'doing' his Shelley to his heart's content . . . 'I feel in *such* good spirits' he says."

Did Browning know, when he wrote this essay, about Shelley's desertion of his wife, Harriet Westbrook? W. G. Kingsland states in *Robert Browning, Some Personal Reminiscences* that Browning told him he had only learned the facts later—and to Shelley's biographer, Dowden, Browning wrote of learning them about 1858. W. M. Rossetti's memory was of having been told—also by Browning—that he saw Harriet's letters when he was writing. But it was a good deal later, as De Vane notes, that he began to be seriously shaken about Shelley.

Looking at the internal evidence of the essay—if Hookham the bookseller did show Browning the letters at that time, it would be he who added the mitigating circumstances, related there, of Shelley's excitement approximating almost to madness, of the laudanum bottle, of his hallucinations visual and aural. All this Browning mentions, and he says also that Shelley would not wish his own name cleared at the cost of another's, which at least suggests that Browning had been told, too, how Harriet, poor woman, had first left Shelley. She had hoped confidently that he would follow her, but the fact by itself suggests at least a question mark. Surely the blackest blot on Shelley's character came later—his proposal that the three—Mary Godwin, he and Harriet—should live together, and the borrowing of money from his wife when he returned with his mistress to England. Hearing about these, rather than reading the letters, could be the point at which Browning finally gave up the idol of his adolescence, whose influence had faded by his twentieth year but whose poetry he still ranged with that of Keats. With a total realization Browning could hardly have been "in *such* good spirits" as he sat in sun and shade " 'doing' his Shelley."

The story of Harriet was not, of course, the whole of Shelley; there was his immense generosity to Godwin, the fantastic father of his second wife, who combined cadging with reproaches, and accepted money with a grandiloquent assumption of high-mindedness. There was his indignant rage at the oppression of Ireland; his response to any human need, even by self-sacrifice, where it did not impinge upon his sexual desires. There was in him a true compassion for the needy only too rare in the age of complacency and the class of sufficiency to which he belonged, and this appealed to the Browning who had written in *Sordello* of the "sad dishevelled shape" borne by mankind in his own vision. At moments one seems to hear in this essay some broken notes from what might have been a marvelous dramatic monologue.

Browning in his essay sees Shelley already emerging from the atheism of his youth on the way to a full Christian faith. This has been smiled at as akin to Cardinal Wiseman's belief that Browning might himself end up a Catholic. Neither idea is intrinsically absurd. To Herford it appeared that Christian thought in some respects has "ranged itself with Shelley," so that what he might have adopted "would have been sufficiently unlike that which he assailed." Yet, too, he sees that for Browning "the essence of Christianity lay at this time in something not very remote from what he revered as the essence of Shelleyism—a corollary as it were implicit in his thought."

Dowden in his smaller *Life of Shelley* goes further, seeing an immense change between the hostility and defiance of his boyhood at the sight of York Minster and the days when, Dante in hand, he would sit "a docile rebel . . . in the fragrant gloom" of Milan Cathedral. Dante and the other medieval poets had become Shelley's companions. He read Ariosto at Lucca, he translated scenes from the *Magico Prodigioso*

Elizabeth Barrett Browning, from the bust by W. W. Story. Sculpted after her death, it shows her in her girlhood

The Casa Guidi, Florence

The Drawing Room at the Casa Guidi, From a painting by George Mignaty

Robert Browning,
1855. From a painting
by D. G. Rossetti

Pen and his Pony

of Calderon, regretting that the "grey veil" of his own words should fall over those "perfect and glowing forms." Dowden notes, with the same interest as did Browning, if not an immediate approach to Christianity at least that "his imaginative delight" was "so little troubled by the ardours of the great Catholic poet," while Edmund Blunden has pointed out an almost personal devotion to Christ shown in *Prometheus*:

> Remit the anguish of that lighted stare;
> Close those wan lips; let that thorn-wounded brow
> Stream not with blood: it mingles with thy tears!

Christ's true followers are described as:

> The wise, the mild, the lofty and the just,
> Whom thy slaves hate for being like to thee,
> Some hunted by foul lies from their heart's home, . . .
> Some linked to corpses in unwholesome cells.

This is much like an attack on official Christians in defense of the Christian ideal. Perhaps Browning was not so absurd after all.

When the Brownings left London for Paris that autumn they were shortly followed by his father and sister. To Browning his father told a story of being persecuted by a neighboring widow, Mrs. Von Müller, and of his doubts concerning her moral character. Browning, with characteristic impetuosity and with the trustfulness he always felt toward those he loved, acted as foolishly as well might be; the one thing to do (he felt) was to bring the matter to an end forthwith. His father, he wrote to Mrs. Von Müller, had informed him of the manner in which she had annoyed him and of the persecution he had undergone for some time. But Mr. Browning senior had also written her a letter in which he spoke of "breaking off the match" on account of her "misconduct" from the time she was a girl: and (he asked) was the certainty of her first husband's death established when she married Von Müller? Browning knew nothing of this or other letters, but he must soon have learned that Mrs. Von Müller was bringing an action for breach of promise against his father.

Paris had brought relief to Elizabeth's cough, and both poets were busy enough. Browning is said to have written three poems in three days: *Love among the Ruins,* greeting the New Year on January 1, 1852; on January 2, *Women and Roses;* and on the third *Childe Roland.* In old age he told a friend that *Childe Roland* had taken two days to write. The amount of ink spilled in trying to find roots from which that poem grew is truly fantastic. Years later Mr. Nettleship of The Browning Society, after asking Browning three times about the poem's meaning and being told each time that it was just a kind of dream, managed to write eighteen pages expounding it. Browning laughed heartily and said no doubt it was all there, though he himself did not know it. "A quite obvious and naturally supernatural *dream,*" says Saintsbury, "one has dreamt things like it but inferior."

Legitimate as it is to examine the writings of a poet to discover meanings hidden from himself and even to search his subconscious, it has been decidedly overdone in Browning's case. I hardly dare to suggest that Browning's intense anxiety over his father's situation had some bearing on *Childe Roland.* Great writing, poetry especially, arises from intensity of feeling—and the feeling may be of all sorts. More than plain grief do prolonged anxiety and uncertainty, dogging the imagination, bring nightmares persisting into the day.

One can imagine husband and wife puzzling over what *had* really passed between old Browning and Mrs. Von Müller that could give ground for an action. Whatever the issue the publicity would be a hideous thing.

Both Brownings had an exaggerated fear of any invasion of their private lives—lives which through circumstances had become all too public. The appearance of Miss Mitford's Memoirs this winter shattered Elizabeth, for they told the story of that grief of which never to any human but her husband could she speak—the drowning of Bro. "I am morbid, I know," she wrote to Mrs. Jameson, "I can't bear some words even from Robert." And to George: "I felt inclined to go off to Egypt and burrow in the sand somewhere—She might as well have cut off my fingers as a proof of friendship."

In Paris they met and liked Dumas, but a great disappointment for Elizabeth was the failure to establish a friendship with George Sand.

Their introduction to her had come from Mazzini via Carlyle, who described her as the "Highpriestess of Anarchy." She was, he said, living now outside Paris "within sound of the 'Church Bell' she has lately *christened* at her Curé's request. After all I participate in your liking for the melody that runs thro' that strange 'beautiful incontinent' soul,—a *Modern* Magdalen, with the 'seven devils' mostly still in her." But in his journal he had earlier written (1840): "In the world there are few sadder, sicklier phenomena for me than George Sand and the response she meets with." And he described her circle as "a new Phallus worship, with Sue, Balzac and company for its prophets and Madame Sand for a virgin."

Browning had no liking for any of it and Elizabeth describes him as "a little proud" about making advances: "he wouldn't have our letters mixed up with the love letters of the actresses, or perhaps given to the 'premier comique' to read aloud in the green room." Also the weather was frightful. "But I represented to him that one might as well lose one's life as one's peace of mind for ever, and if I lost seeing her I should with difficulty get over it."

So Robert wrapped his wife up and got her into a closed carriage. It had been very good and kind of him "to let me go at all . . . She [George Sand] seems to live in the abomination of desolation— . . . crowds of ill-bred men who adore her *à genoux bas*, betwixt a puff of smoke and an ejection of saliva. . . . A noble woman under the mud be certain."

Browning was by no means certain—especially with a wife prepared to "adore" in this atmosphere of smoke and spitting—which she had abominated at Florence in the person of Father Prout. But he was generous and Elizabeth says, "We both tried hard to please her . . . only we always felt we couldn't penetrate—it was all vain." Robert had seen George Sand seven times, she writes later, but " 'can't get on with her,' he declares—'the ice breaks—and then there's a new frost.' "

Had he, one wonders, discussed the redoubtable lady with Milsand, who did not like her at all, and who spent the evening with the

Brownings at least once a week? "Robert and I really *love* him—there's no other word for it," Elizabeth wrote to Arabel. "I would let him marry *you*." Other friendships were made this year—with Lady Elgin, with whom Elizabeth was at one about "spiritualism, mesmerism, clairvoyance, visions and the like"; with Mr. Carré, a minister from Jersey "of the Newman St. Connexion," whose cures "in the name of Christ" she had no difficulty in believing but who thought evil spirits came through séances and hoped she would keep her heart pure from them.

Robert, she remarks in one letter, "was quite vexed that I wouldn't stay the Communion at the Church—he does dislike going out in that way." They did not, however, go to Carré's but to the French Independent Church; and she, at least, could not agree with Carré's sacramental views, thinking it "a clear scriptural doctrine that the 'priesthood' is absorbed into Christ's life and dignity." She could not "accept as small 'retail' popes such men as Mr. Owen and Mr. Carré."

Hoping that Arabel does not disapprove of the scamps they know and the table rapping ("nothing scarcely is too high or too low for me"), Elizabeth goes on to her dismay at having discovered "the profoundest infidelity" in the intellectual world. Mrs. Jameson had told her that in England nobody believes. "As to Germany you know how they tear the scriptures to pieces, with teeth and nails. The French socialists *use* Jesus Christ and deny him in the same sentence. To them he is crucified between Robespierre and Marat."

Perhaps the spiritualism which seems more and more to surround her, in Italy, England, France, above all among her American friends, but in which at this date she still called herself only a "potential believer," was for many a substitute for the Christianity they had lost.

Husband and wife were both hardly recovered from an attack of grippe when, in May, Browning's cousin James Silverthorne died, and he decided to go to England for the funeral. Elizabeth looked so pale and distraught that he gave up the idea. And she certainly tried to persuade herself that it was in Robert's own interests that she should keep him from the journey and the misery of a funeral at the scene of his mother's grave. One sees her building up her case as she writes, and a tirade follows against fixing "on such a subject" as funeral ceremonies: "in no paroxysm of anguish could I identify or appear to identify the dust there and the soul there."

Robert and Elizabeth were back in London when the case was brought against Mr. Browning. They were not present in court but read next morning the long report in *The Times*.[3]

Held before Lord Campbell and a special jury it is sad enough, even for an outsider, as a picture of the folly that could be reached by a man who had been for so many years a devoted husband. And at that date the fact that he must have begun this courtship so shortly after his wife's death would appear especially horrifying. What must it have meant 'for his son to read letters beginning: "My dearest, dearest, dearest, dearest, dearest, much-loved Minny"—and to realize that his father's own counsel could do no better than ask for a mitigation of sentence in consideration of the fact that his client was "a poor old dotard in love"? It was alleged, too, that the engagement with Mrs. Von Müller had been broken by the older Browning only "under the influence of his son."

This is the view taken by Cyrus Mason, who declares that his uncle really did want to marry the widow and that she, too, was attached to him. If so, why had he run away? Unfortunately, *The Times* report does not give the fifty long letters read in court, which in point of style and intelligence were favorably commented on by Lord Campbell. But it does give the evidence of Mrs. Von Müller's son-in-law, Samuel Sutor, which adds to the puzzle. Mr. Browning had evidently returned to London *after* his son had written to Mrs. Von Müller; for Mr. Sutor, who had seen the letter, says, "I asked as he was not then under the influence of his son, whether it was his intention to carry out his original views with Mrs. Von Müller. His reply was 'What do you mean?—Marry Mrs. Von Müller?—Certainly not.' I then said I had no other course to pursue than to send him a letter from a solicitor."

One unmentioned element in this story is the influence of Sarianna on both father and son. What had she said to her father? Few daughters desire a stepmother and Sarianna had been devoted to her mother. Her view of the case would have been presented both energetically and plausibly to Robert and Elizabeth. The impression given by the existing evidence is of a perplexed and vacillating man, of scales on which the weights changed constantly, of a man moreover whose intellect was far stronger when turned on books and ideas than on matters of practical life. Missing his wife, he would perhaps have liked more than a daughter! Yet he had clearly very real doubts concerning the woman who attracted him. The evidence that remains is too slight for any certain conclusion to be drawn from it. I am not writing a novel and real life is full of open questions.

It is almost impossible to exaggerate the agony suffered by Robert Browning and Elizabeth, as they imagined *The Times* report spread out in front of Mr. Barrett on the Wimpole Street breakfast table—or being read by Mrs. Jameson and Miss Mitford, by Carlyle and by their "dear Mr. Kenyon." Inside the Browning family Cyrus tells us that poor Reuben found on his desk at Rothschild's Bank next morning ladies' gloves and other tokens showing that there, too, the report had not gone unnoticed.

Browning had not, his wife said, "apprehended the real character of the letters . . . felt it to the heart of his heart and could scarcely raise his head after the blow of that dreadful newspaper." But to his father he went, "loved and pitied him." Damages had been set at £800 and the mystery is not lightened when we see Mr. Browning deciding to escape the alternatives of payment or debtors' prison by migrating to Paris. His son went over to install him there and then handled in England the business of disposing of the house his father had recently acquired. The old man, separated from home, friends, books, became ill and depressed, and his son grew more and more careworn. Even the kindness of friends, and the bitter-sweet of stolen visits to Arabel, could not make this a happy time for Elizabeth. As for Pen, since Wilson had gone home to her family both summers, he feared that his mother, too, would leave him and was convinced that a "mitaine" haunted Wimpole Street.

Miss Mitford and Elizabeth had corresponded over the *Memoirs*, Elizabeth apologizing for her own oversensitiveness and recognizing the "affectionateness and tender consideration" with which Miss Mitford had received her distressed remonstrances. Theirs was a very old friendship and an intimate correspondence went on for the rest of their lives.

But meeting this summer was a problem: while Wilson was away, Penini could not be left and, with all the people to be seen in London, Browning was deeply engaged. "He will like to see *you*," wrote Elizabeth, "and besides, he would as soon trust me to travel to Reading alone as I trust Penini to be alone here. I believe he thinks I should drop off my head and leave it under the seat of the rail-carriage if he didn't take care of it." So both were to go, but Wilson's overprolonged visit to her family prevented this half-dreaded, half-hoped-for meeting.

Browning did visit his old friend W. J. Fox—reconciled with his wife after Eliza Flower's death in 1846. Sarah's death had followed her sister's two years later. It could hardly have been a visit to lighten Browning's heavy thoughts in that painful year.

A more cheerful side is seen in the christening of Tennyson's son Hallam. Elizabeth could not go but, as Browning held the baby and tossed it in his arms, Tennyson remarked, "Ah, that is as good as a glass of champagne to him." And to Kenyon, Browning wrote later from Florence: "I felt all those spark-like hours in London struck out of the black element I was beset with, all the brighter for it." They met Charles Kingsley, too, that summer, "original and earnest," said Elizabeth, "and full of a genial and almost tender kindliness." They lunched with the Ruskins and were introduced by Mrs. Carlyle to Mazzini. "Oh such a fuss the Brownings made over Mazzini this day," wrote Mrs. Carlyle. "My private opinion of Browning, is, in spite of Mr. C's favour for him, that he is 'nothing' or very little more, 'but a fluff of feathers!' *She* is *true* and *good*, and a most *womanly* creature."

Mrs. Andrew Crosse gives at least a suggestion of why Mrs. Carlyle had taken so strong a dislike to Browning, when she describes him holding her kettle in his hands absorbed in conversation. "Can't you put it down?" said Mrs. Carlyle—and Browning did—on her new carpet where it left an indelible mark.

"See how fine he has grown," said his hostess bitterly. "He does not any longer know what to do with a kettle."

"Ye should have been more specific," said Carlyle.

Mrs. Crosse herself writes more warmly of the husband than of the wife. Elizabeth had a "distinctly hard-featured, non-sympathetical aspect," her lower jaw betrayed the "strength of obstinacy." Her talk was that of a reader: "the habit of conversing in a one-sided way with the best books which is vastly different from conversing with the best men." She felt, too, that while Browning's humanity was never at fault, "her womanly nature leads her to hate the sinner and to scold him overmuch."

Later, after a tea party at Forster's, Mrs. Carlyle seemed dubious even about Elizabeth. "I like Browning less and less; and even *she* does not grow on me." But to Elizabeth, Jane Welsh Carlyle appeared "full of thought and feeling and character," and at that date Mazzini was one of her heroes "with his pale spiritual face and intense eyes. He made me melancholy with his vain dreams and perilous assumptions and set me wondering on what turf of Italy he would lie at last with a bullet through that noble heart of his. Oh, it must come to this, be sure. He does not understand, he does not see while the simplest of us can see and understand." Later his failure to understand caused many deaths, and his early admirers would grow embittered as Mazzini from his English exile sent others to their fate in Italy.

When Mrs. Carlyle called upon Elizabeth, she brought with her an American friend, Mrs. Twisleton, to whom Elizabeth confided at a later meeting that her disposition was so anxious she was always building "dungeons in the air." This time on leaving London she felt, she told Arabel, as though her soul had been dragged through a hedge and had "left some torn shreds of itself on the thorns."

Paris, too, had its cares, but "Our old friends the Corkrans here," she wrote, "have out of love to us, quite adopted Mr. Browning as the grandfather of their children, and Mrs. Corkran professes to have quite fallen in love with his simplicity and other qualities." This would make it easier to depart as they ought before it grew too cold. And "Do you know, Arabel," wrote Elizabeth, "I was quite touched and sorry to leave poor Mr. Browning and Sarianna in Paris. His simplicity and affectionateness drew me a good deal . . . He can't understand any of it . . . struggles against facts and necessities . . . said dolefully that 'he knew it had been a trouble to me.' *'Of course it has,'* said Robert, *'What did you imagine?'* " Whereon Elizabeth felt obliged to assure him, "I wasn't troubled at all and rather liked it upon the whole."

Her pen flows on, not only when settled, at home, more or less, in this city or that, but on the journeys. The little desk with fitted inkstand would serve in the least hospitable of hotels or even in the diligence. Elizabeth always wrote on her knee.

"Oh Arabel," came a letter from Genoa on November 5 (for so astonishingly late had the fine weather tempted them to stay on in Paris), "I have repented, Robert has repented, everybody has repented taking the Mont Cenis route." The cold had been bitter, they were three nights without taking off their clothes. Pen alone, "a gypsy child," she felt, "had enjoyed everything."

And then in answer to her sister's curiosity—"Oh Arabel—'have we quarrelled?' 'How often have we quarrelled?' We are famous for quarrelling, are we not? That is because we love one another too much to be contented with temporising—It seems foolish to talk of such things—but for a man to love a woman after six years as he loves me, could only be possible to a man of very uncommon nature such as his—I cannot tell you what his devotion and tenderness are to me at every hour . . ."[4]

15 An
Anglo-American Circle

We were all bachelors together.

ELIZABETH BARRETT BROWNING

IT IS not surprising after two such years to find Elizabeth rejoicing at being "home again" at Casa Guidi. At first it seemed to Browning quiet almost to deadliness, but soon the circle of friends[1] were around them once more and both were absorbed in their work, the main interruptions being caused by Elizabeth's uncertain health.

After one bad attack she writes to Henrietta: "Poor darling Robert ... his nights have been diversified by keeping up the fire, boiling the coffee, and listening to the horrible cough which made sleep out of the question for either of us. Nothing could exceed his tender patience."

Browning's hopes, so often dashed, had begun to revive. To Milsand he wrote in February, 1853. "I have not left the house one evening since our return. I am writing—a first step to popularity for me—lyrics with more music and painting than before." To Forster, in June, he speaks of "a number of poems of all sorts and sizes and styles and subjects ... the fruits of the years since I last turned the winch of the wine press. ... I hope to be listened to, this time, and I am glad I have been made to wait this not very long while."[2]

Interesting that the time seemed now not very long. I think Browning always lived fully *in* the happiness or unhappiness of the hour. To William Allingham, he wrote in July: "We have been in Florence quietly in the old place after the old way, some eight months—gone like one!"

William Allingham was a minor poet, an Anglo-Irishman employed in Her Majesty's Customs, full of a passionate admiration for great literature, forming friendships with Leigh Hunt, Carlyle, both Brownings and above all Tennyson. There is an interesting ambivalence in his attitude to Browning, reflected in the *Letters* and *Diary*. Browning was, he told Leigh Hunt, "the Turner of poetry," but "more of an Italian than an Englishman which I think is a pity." And to Arthur Hughes he wrote: "The only quality Browning wants, to be perfect, is a little stupidity." But he had found *Sordello* "a piece of rich confusion, confusing one most confoundedly,"—and in later entries in the *Diary* grave doubts are expressed of "a want of solid basis . . . yet I always end by striking my breast in penitential mood and crying out 'O rich mind! wonderful Poet! strange great man.' "

Browning's letter to Allingham of July 3, 1853, tells something of the months that have gone so fast:

> The weather was milder than ever in winter, wetter than common in spring, and is now hotter than uncommon this great summertime; and what with rain and heat the greenness is such greenness, the color such color!—but you can't see them—tho' you have a right, if ever man had. I wish you the sight of a million fire-flies—lizards, as your love may desire, and a scorpion or two for the truth's sake—(they get under the windowsill of the room here). Then, plate-fulls of the fruit of that Japanese Pear which is a flower-tree in England and here a producer of great yellow knobs half plum, half apple, and the brilliantest Japan besides. But the best will be when we go (I take your arm in spirit you observe) to a villa up in the hill country next week . . . 'Tis in Giotto's country, the Mugello.

"The heat has come in like a tiger with a spring," wrote Elizabeth to Arabel about this time. It was a happy letter, for Robert had been remarking that "we two being married just seven years I looked exactly seven years younger than when we married." Penini had been telling her that if she didn't eat more she would be a little baby when he was a great man and he would have to carry her. Pen, she admitted, got his own way with her, but Robert was strictly obeyed; there must be in him "a potentiality of wrath" for "he spoils the child as much as I do."

They had a new servant, Ferdinando Romagnoli (who, she hoped, would "make Wilson comfortable"), having just got rid of one who both smelled and looked terrible. "We have practised a hair's breadth of Christianity in keeping this man so long," said Elizabeth. They gave him a present as well as the month's wages and he was very grateful.

To Lucca they went—and there were the Storys and Lytton, with whom an amazing expedition was undertaken. Elizabeth wrote to George:

> The distance is six miles off, but the ground being absolutely per-
> pendicular, the guides forced to walk at every animal's head to pre-
> vent a general precipitation, you can scarcely calculate the amount
> of necessary fatigue. Said I to Mr. Lytton as we approached home—
> "I am dying, how are you?" "A quarter of an hour ago," he an-
> swered, "I thought I should have to give it up, altogether, but now
> I am rather better." Think what the fatigue must have been to
> bring such an answer from a young man one & twenty who had
> ridden the whole way. Certainly he is very delicate. For a week
> afterwards I could not stir from the house but I never suffer per-
> manently when the weather is so exquisite.

In Henry James's biography of Story we are told of less strenuous pleasures, of his taking tea with the Brownings and staying till almost midnight; of going "backward and forward," writes Elizabeth, "to tea-drinking and gossiping at one another's houses," while "our husbands hold the reins." And Story describes the picnic which inspired Browning's "By the Fireside":

> The day was glorious, and after climbing an hour we arrived at
> a little old church. . . . The grand limestone mountains spring
> sharply up, with deep patches of purple shade and little grey towns
> perched here and there on the lower spines. Under the trees here

we spent nearly an hour, and then took our donkeys and horses again, and, after an hour and a half, passing over wild and grand scenery, with mountain-streams dripping and tumbling, and now and then over beds of red-veined jasper, we rounded a height bold and rugged as the Alps and saw before us the soft green velvety dome of Prato Fiorito, adorable name, covered with its short golden grass. Here we lay for half an hour and talked and gazed. . . .

A few days later

The whole day in the same woods with the Brownings. We went at ten o'clock carrying our provisions. Browning and I walked to the spot, and there, spreading shawls under the great chestnuts, we read and talked the live-long day, the Lima at our feet, babbling on, clear and brown, over the stones, and the distant rock-ribbed peaks taking the changes of the hours. In the afternoon we took a long walk through the grove and found wondrous *fungi,* some red as coral.

Story was a poet after his fashion, though some accused him of trying to set his feet in the too-big prints of his friend. Here he has set the scene in prose for Browning's poetry, for every detail of those rides, the rose-flesh mushrooms, the gray church, the heart of the woodland, Browning wove into the love story still so fresh and new that he could dream of a wondrous ending:

> My own confirm me! If I tread
> This path back, is it not in pride
> To think how little I dreamed it led
> To an age so blest that, by its side,
> Youth seems the waste instead? . . .
>
> But who could have expected this
> When we two grew together first
> Just for the obvious human bliss,
> To satisfy life's daily thirst
> With a thing men seldom miss?

Americans increasingly became the Brownings' friends, or, arriving in Europe as admirers, visited and described them. George Stillman Hillard in *Six Months in Italy* writes of Browning as "simple, natural, playful," Mrs. Browning all genius and sensibility. "Her tremulous voice," he wrote, "often flutters over her words like the flame of a dying candle over the wick. I have never seen a human frame which seemed so nearly a transparent veil for a celestial and immortal spirit."

Nathaniel Hawthorne in his *Italian Notebook* describes her as "a pale small person scarcely embodied at all," as elfin rather than earthly but "sweetly disposed towards the human race." To almost all these more casual acquaintance she appeared of far more importance than the husband, whom Lockhart approved of as "not at all like a damned literary man." Trollope, while he had never seen Browning "rough or uncourteous to the most exasperating fool," noted a "lurking smile" that made the utterers of platitudes and illogicalities a trifle uncomfortable.

Robert Lytton, at this time British attaché in Florence, cherished a romantic attachment to both husband and wife, whom he called in moments of special intensity "My king and my queen": "If all who know you feel as I do, they must ever seem drawn to lean on you and draw life and warmth from your great-hearted presence." At a reception given by him on the terrace at his Bellosguardo Villa were English, and American friends, and one Italian, the historian, Pasquale Villari: "We were all bachelors together," writes Elizabeth. She and Lytton were united in looking for "a new revelation and evangel . . . here are all the symptoms that preceded the Christian era and then as now the world seemed used up." Lytton's father would thirty years later be a founding member of the Society for Psychical Research and already was writing to his son of manifestations—one supposedly by Byron. It was "what some great Poet, gone mad, might write from Bedlam, preserving in his mental chaos all the mechanism of the art."

The absence of Italians from their circle is a little surprising. Margaret (Fuller) Ossoli, Jessie (White) Mario, and Mary (Thornton) Tassinari were Italian by marriage only; their husbands are barely mentioned. The Brownings had met Mazzini in London, admired but later repudiated him; Massimo d'Azeglio visited them in Rome, Gordigiano painted Elizabeth, and the poet Dall Ongaro translated her poetry. But only Pasquale Villari really belonged to the Florentine Circle—and his wife, Linda White, was English.

This Anglo-American group, whether believing or unbelieving, were constantly playing with spiritualism, and at this time Browning himself possibly thought of it almost as a game. He could count on his own power (as Elizabeth complained) of ruining a too successful séance by his laughter. Later he asked George to destroy all Elizabeth had written on the subject; but husband and wife never read each other's letters and I doubt if he yet guessed how overexcited hers were becoming—especially when she first met William Burnet Kinney, United States representative at Turin. Mr. Kinney was going through a process of conversion and told Elizabeth of "accounts from America of the most extraordinary character." Robert himself, while rebuking Elizabeth for credulity, confessed (she told Arabel) that "half his nature was taking my part and that therefore he had to strive against himself and me—which vexed him all the more."

Young Lytton meanwhile, probing for the "new evangel," was fascinated by another Florentine resident, Seymour Kirkup, from whom I found a letter at Balliol reminding Browning of his own unusual psychic powers. While Browning at this time denied any personal experiences, he many years later told a curious story of an Italian nobleman, brought one day to the Casa Guidi, who boasted of clairvoyant powers. Asking for some personal belonging of Robert's, he was given a pair of sleeve links, and exclaimed: "Something about these cries out 'murder!' " The links were taken from the dead body of a great uncle of the poet's who had been murdered long ago on his estate in Saint Kitts. Kirkup would certainly have refused to accept Browning's explanation that, while no one in Florence knew about the sleeve links, the shrewd Italian was guided by "the involuntary help of my own eyes and face."

Kirkup lived on in Florence till 1880 but already in 1853 he was an elder in their community. He had by his experiences been converted from materialism to belief in a spiritual world, but Elizabeth wrote to Henrietta: "to my mind, the man was somewhat hasty, after having heard in vain the mystical knockings at all the doors and windows of the universe his whole life long to come round suddenly through a rap on the door by means of a clairvoyante." And to Lytton she spoke of the futility of the supposed revelations—but also of the importance of continued experiment. She could not leave the subject alone, and Lytton was excitedly drawing her on.

"There is a real *poem*," she wrote a little later, "being lived between Mr. Kirkup and the 'spirits' so called. . . . And such a tragic face the old man has, with his bleak white beard. Even Robert is touched." According to Hawthorne, report called Kirkup a necromancer, talking with dead kings and emperors, talking even with Dante. His former medium's daughter (reputedly also his) he adopted, and through her would talk to her dead mother and other spirits. But however touched by the old man, whatever Browning's own potential, he would have no truck with spirits, and he used to recount with gusto how he caught Kirkup's medium cheating him.

Elizabeth's keen conviction of a surrounding world, from which signals reach us through those specially endowed to receive them, had been sharpened by the experience of her last meeting with Margaret Fuller, who had dined with them in the spring of 1850 the night before sailing for the States. She gave Pen a book inscribed "in memory" of her own small son who was going, too; she seemed full of fears and forebodings. And the ship sank. Just as Elizabeth had lost her brother did she lose a friend, not yet intimate but one to whom she was attracted by a strong sympathy.

But Lytton had been critical. Margaret Fuller was "only a petticoated pedant after all, with now and then blind notions of a restless heart tumbling and beating uneasily beneath a heap of books and dry dust of erudition." How right she had been to marry "that good-natured, adoring uncultivated count. . . . I was more interested in Madame Ossoli than in Margaret Fuller."[3]

Women at that date expected criticism when struggling for a life of freedom and full intellectual development, but no one sympathized more keenly than Elizabeth with intellectual—or sexual—rebellion. The lack of intellectual training for women, the domination by husbands, the lack of sympathy for the "fallen woman," stirred her to rage. She was irritated by the excitement over Florence Nightingale, for such work as nursing had always been admittedly feminine.[4] She does not appear to have recognized the vastness of that great woman's organizing powers, of the creation of a new world in hospitals, barracks, even homes. Elizabeth could not imagine why the quiet and conventional Jane Austen was so immensely admired, while Browning disliked the extravagant humor in Martin Chuzzlewit. He did not, it is true, mention Sairy Gamp or Betsey Prig, it is the American scenes he detests— but Pecksniff too: there was perhaps a lack of complete humor in his make-up despite the plausible claim made by Herford that he was the Dickens and the Balzac of poetry in the creation of so wide a variety of men and women.

Compared with Jane Austen's the experience of both husband and wife was wide, compared with Dickens', it was narrow. These were only passing criticisms, but there seems a tendency to look out for the extraordinary; I can imagine Browning today studying with zest men who turn into women, women who turn into men, homosexuality and perversions. There was a fund of sanity in him, but there was something that had responded to the darker side of Wanley's *Wonders of the Little World*. As to Elizabeth, she knew, she told Arabel, too much of books in proportion to life. The life in a Jane Austen novel appeared so narrow: *Aurora Leigh* shows her in greater sympathy with Charlotte Brontë.

Elizabeth's health, the dawnings of what later became her fanatical excitement over spiritualism—and Pen. While he was still almost a baby, Browning had objected to his being so dressed that visitors mistook him for a girl, to his being taken to parties beyond his proper bedtime, to the spoiling, the lack of discipline with which this overexcitable and invalid mother treated her overexcitable only child. One friend had begged her seriously not to make "an idol" of him. She embroidered fantastic jackets for him, let his golden curls grow long, decorated his hat with an immense feather. She tells her sisters something of this, and that she means to have her way. Pen, she says, is as yet a "sort of neutral creature." If put into boy's clothes, he would look like "a small angel

H*

travestied." But while Pen was so young, did it much matter? And Browning certainly spoiled them both. There was so much leeway of tenderness to be made up for her, her health and happiness were always his first consideration.

These were clouds, but very light and small on a horizon glowing with hope, while she was writing *Aurora Leigh* and he *Men and Women* amid "the old magnificent mountains and chestnut woods and great moonlights," as they lingered on at Lucca while the Storys preceded them to Rome. Browning wrote on October 7, 1853: "This poor place has given up the ghost now, and we really want to get away." He had heard "more about the fever at Rome than I care to infect this paper with." In emulation of Story's pencil—"so happy at bridge-sides and bits of rock and water"—he, too, is making sketches "that may bring back this last happy time when the darker days arrive, as they will, I suppose."

This letter was sadly prophetic, for the Roman fever struck their friends. The Storys' small boy sickened first—and died. The Brownings took the little girl into their apartment. But she, too, had got the fever. On December 21, Elizabeth wrote to Mrs. Jameson:

Ah dearest friend! You have heard how our first step into Rome was a fall, not into a catacomb but a fresh grave, . . . I doubt whether I shall get over it, and whether I ever shall feel that this is Rome. The first day at the bed's head of that convulsed and dying child; and the next two, three, four weeks in great anxiety about his little sister, who was all but given up. . . . It was not only sympathy. I was selfishly and intensely frightened for my own treasures . . .

Rome was certainly unhealthy, with constant recurrences of fever. Months later Lytton wrote in great agitation: "I pray God you are both well; if so, make haste and come out of that doomed city."

Edith Story has described how Thackeray visited her sickroom and read her *The Rose and the Ring* (not yet published). Her door was guarded by "the steadfast tramp of Pen Browning who was acting as sentinel outside my door to prevent 'other horrid maladies' from coming in." Pen also reproved Anne Thackeray for making too much noise.

Edith had several setbacks in Rome, so when she was a little better, the Storys decided to move to Naples. But at Velletri, their first stop, she had a bad relapse, was "in a state of all but insensibility." Story sent an urgent message, begging Browning to come and be with them at the end. Elizabeth dreaded his going and Pen gave vent to "the most piteous screams and sobs." Elizabeth hardly slept that night and did not know, she said, when she had had "such a concussion of nerves."

The next afternoon Browning returned all smiles with news that the child was much better. Elizabeth in a letter to Arabel showed a surprising lack of sympathy. She blamed Story for not facing up to the situation "in all manliness and fortitude," especially as he had with him at Velletri a wife, two servants, three physicians and "full pecuniary resources."

Certainly Browning had his problems, but they both seem to have enjoyed much of that winter in Rome. In an undated letter to Mrs. Story, Elizabeth writes of listening to the Miserere in the Sistine Chapel "very overcoming in its ejaculatory pathos. Then we have made various Campagna excursions with Mrs. Sartoris and Mrs. Kemble, dined in bosky villas and pinewood forests, and done the proper honour to your glorious opal mountains in the distance." In another letter to Arabel she speaks of Browning having been at fourteen, and she at "some five or six," of these excursions, one of which gave us "Two in the Campagna" (C. Day Lewis told me that of all Browning's lyrics he would choose this as the most perfect.)

Elizabeth wrote to Miss Mitford: "The talk was almost too brilliant for the sentiment of the scenery, but it harmonized entirely with the mayonnaise and champagne!" The party wandered off in various directions, but says Browning: "We sat down on the grass, to stray / In spirit better through the land, / This morn of Rome and May . . ."

Rome was socially a more worldly city than Florence, and more abounding in important English visitors. "If anyone wants small talk," wrote Elizabeth, "by handfuls of glittering dust swept out of salons, there's Mr. Thackeray besides."

"I think Mrs. Browning," wrote Anne Thackeray enthusiastically, "is the greatest woman I ever knew in my life." Browning she described

as "a dark short man, slightly but nervously built with a frank open
face, long hair streaked with grey and a large mouth which he opens
widely when he speaks, white teeth, a dark beard and a loud voice with
a slight lisp, and the best and kindest heart in the world."

But to Thackeray, Elizabeth was not attracted. "As to the society,"
she wrote to Arabel, "it rains lords and ladies for the especial benefit of
Mr. Thackeray perhaps." And to Henrietta (December 30, 1853):
"Mr. Thackeray . . . 'can't write in the morning without his good dinner
and two parties overnight.' From such a soil spring the Vanity Fairs!
He is an amusing man-mountain enough and very courteous to us—but
I never should get on with him much, I think—he is not sympathetical
to me." Nor to Lytton, who, transferred in 1854 to Paris, wrote often
to his "dearest ones." He had met Dickens and was "impressed by a
something powerful and electrical about him of vigorous intelligence
and goodness," but Thackeray, though "very kind and civil to me," he
could not like "very cordially."

In Rome the visitor in the mid-fifties seemed less aware of the
Risorgimento than anywhere in north Italy. Perhaps this was in part
because Rome cried aloud her own past at every step—the Forum and
the Colosseum, the ruins and the monuments, the very stones unheeded
or built into shrines and churches, themselves speaking of a second
civilization with years counted in many hundreds. And the Campagna

> . . . with its endless fleece
> Of feathery grasses everywhere!
> Silence and passion, joy and peace,
> An everlasting wash of air—
> Rome's ghost since her decease. . . .
>
> Such life here, through such length of hours,
> Such miracles performed in play,
> Such primal, naked forms of flowers,
> Such letting nature have her way
> While Heaven looks from its towers!

Again, leafing through *Men and Women,* one becomes aware of
the variety of thought stirring in Browning's mind; of the power of the
prismatic rays into which the white light he sought was more commonly broken. "Holy Cross Day," introduced by an extract from a
Bishop's secretary of 1600 concerning a compulsory yearly sermon to
the Jews of Rome, has a laconic note: "The present Pope abolished this
bad business," which serves to remind us how long an evil period in the
Church's history prolonged itself, to remind us of *how* evil it was.

> "God spoke, and gave us the word to keep,
> Bade never fold the hands nor sleep
> 'Mid a faithless world,—at watch and ward,
> Till Christ at the end relieve our guard.
> By His servant Moses the watch was set:
> Though near upon cock-crow we keep it yet. . . .
>
> "Thou! if thou wast He, who at mid-watch came,
> By the starlight, naming a dubious name!
> And if too heavy with sleep—too rash,
> With fear—O Thou, if that martyr-gash
> Fell on thee coming to take thine own,
> And we gave the Cross, when we owed the Throne—
>
> "Thou art the Judge. We are bruised thus.
> But the Judgment over, join sides with us!
> Thine too is the cause! and not more thine
> Than ours, is the work of these dogs and swine,
> Whose life laughs through and spits at their creed!
> Who maintain Thee in word and defy Thee in deed! . . .
>
> "We withstood Christ then? Be mindful how
> At least we withstand Barabbas now!
> Was our outrage sore? But the worst we spared,
> To have called these—Christians, had we dared!
> Let defiance to them pay mistrust, of Thee,
> And Rome make amends for Calvary!"

They had meant to go to England the summer of 1854, and in May left Rome for Florence. "Such nights we have between starlight and firefly-light, and the nightingales singing," wrote Elizabeth to Miss Mitford in June, herself longing to stay in Casa Guidi, but "constrained by duty and love" to go northward to their two families. But in July she writes: "Our reason for not going to England has not been from caprice, but a cross in money matters. A ship was to have brought us in something, and brought us in nothing instead, with a discount; . . . unable even to 'fly to the mountains' as a refuge from the summer heat. . . . That we should be able to sit quietly still at Florence and eat our bread and maccaroni is the utmost of our possibilities this summer."

"A comfort," she wrote to Sarianna, "is that Robert is considered here to be looking better than he ever was known to look." In a fit of depression, however, he had shaved off "his whole beard, whiskers and all," so horrifying Elizabeth that she demanded, under pain of all being at an end between them, that he grow it again "directly." But the beard "grew *white*, which was the just punishment of the gods."

Meanwhile he was trying to raise the necessary funds for their journey by letting Casa Guidi for a year, "which if the thing happens, will give us a lift." It has been said that another reason for the delay was that *Aurora Leigh* was not completed, and certainly the whole matter of manuscripts is something so changed by the invention of the typewriter that we have again to stir imagination to realize a different world. Everything not only written but *copied* by hand. Elizabeth at one point describes her husband as dictating his own completed manuscript for four hours daily "to an amanuensis." Only when a copy existed could the manuscript be trusted to an uncertain post. Sarianna copied for them both; Elizabeth and their friend Isa Blagden copied for Browning —and there was no such thing as taking a carbon. When they did go to London the following year, *Aurora Leigh* was still not finished, but Browning was able to hand *Men and Women* to his publisher.

London and Paris, Pisa and Florence, Siena, Le Havre, Lucca and Rome, weeks spent in leisurely travel from one to another Italian town, how incredibly changed a life for the woman who had spent years in a single room. But for Browning the change was even greater, for he had assumed a huge responsibility while Elizabeth remained the cherished, cared-for woman she had always been. Browning must now not only run his own life but hers, too. Both had in different ways been spoiled; both had been surrounded by a family, now almost totally lost. And if ever a life reminded two humans that we have not here a lasting city, it was this one of constant change—a "tent life" as Elizabeth once called it.

But with all the moves, the Brownings recognized a home at Casa Guidi. Florence was too hot in midsummer, too cold at midwinter for full comfort, but the Casa was the place they had furnished; it held their books and pictures; it was the best place for writing; it was the place where Penini had been born and which he loved. To picture their lives it is well to visit Rome and Siena, it is essential to muse awhile in the Casa Guidi, formerly known as Palazzo Guidi, the Brownings having chosen to change a mere palace into a home.

The street on which the living rooms look out is surprisingly narrow. The Church of San Felice seems oppressively close. There was just room, Elizabeth said, for two people to walk along the "terrace" abreast, and this is proof positive that Browning had kept his early slimness and that she did not wear a crinoline! I should call it a balcony rather than a terrace. The outlook on the court is pleasant, especially if shrubs and flowers are growing there, but the court is not large. The windows being at the end of exceptionally long rooms make the rear curiously dark even under a Florentine sky.

Miss Borchardt, secretary of the Linguistic Society of Florence, has put loving care into as full a restoration as may be of the rooms on this side which are rented by the Society, and imagination can easily replace the long table and upright chairs needed for their meetings with the rather splendid, rather heavy desks, sofas, armchairs, and book cases of the Browning era; can clothe the walls with the tapestries (bought for a few hundred lire), seen many years later by Anne Thackeray in Browning's London home. "Mythologies and metaphors and gardens and browsing flocks; the gods in Olympus and looking down upon a golden age . . . a messenger comes flying from the clouds.

We see far away blue hills and the towers of an ancient city; and is not that a distant gibbet depicted with a figure hanging to it just outside the city wall?" Browning's large desk is at Baylor University, and most of the furniture was photographed from the sketch made after Elizabeth's death. The long dining and drawing room, Elizabeth's equally long bedroom and tiny study, the kitchen with an odd little room above it, accessible only by a rope ladder in the days when it was the bedroom of Ferdinando, their second and permanent Italian manservant—all are on the San Felice side of the house. Looking on the Via Maggio and the Pitti Palace is Browning's room.

One wonders whether he at least did not crave at times for wider spaces, for he had not come from imprisonment in a London bedroom but from an open-air life, a large garden, a lot of walking and riding. He still walked constantly, sometimes with Elizabeth, sometimes alone, observing the streets and markets and churches, watching and overhearing the men and women.

A vivid picture is painted of the years 1854 to '57 in the *Letters and Memories* of a young American sculptor, Harriet (or Hatty) Hosmer, whom the Brownings had come to know on their first visit to Rome. At that date the Englishman, Gibson, regarded as a sculptor of genius, had taken this brilliant girl as a pupil; presently she would have her own studio with workmen under her; her works would sell for as much as £1,000; she would be "taken up" on a big scale by the English aristocracy. Kate Field, who would end up owning her own newspaper in Washington, wrote enviously of her a few years later: "Lady Ashburton got down on her knees to Hatty Hosmer the other day, and gave her a magnificent ring, a ruby heart surrounded with diamonds. Why she went on her knees is a mystery. Is not Hatty lucky? She is fortunate in everything." But Elizabeth relating the same story in a letter to Isa (probably of May 1860) attributes the gift (and posture) to Lady Marian Alford.

In 1854, at the outset of her career, very popular in the American and English circle in Rome, Hatty horrified the Italians by walking and even riding about quite alone. Gibson's letters to her begin "Dearest" or "My Little Hat" and are signed "your slave." Fanny Kemble writes: "My very dear little Capellina," both Brownings "Dearest Hatty." Elizabeth writes of Hatty as "the young American sculptress, who is a great pet of mine and Robert's and who emancipates the eccentric life of a perfectly emancipated woman by the perfect purity of hers. . . . She lives here all alone (at twenty-two); dines and breakfasts at the cafés precisely as a young man would; works at 6 o'clock in the morning till night, as a great artist must."

Harriet lived in Rome, but in a letter from Florence, Elizabeth writes of her in "a house of emancipated women." Miss Hayes was there, the translator of George Sand, who " 'dresses like a man down to the waist' (so the accusation runs). Certainly there's the waistcoat which I like—and the collar, neckcloth, and jacket made with a sort of wagtail behind, which I don't like. . . . They are both coming to us tonight, with Miss Blagden who occupies the apartment under theirs."

Isa Blagden was English and a novelist, never very famous and today forgotten except as the close friend of both Brownings. "A dozen or more good and dear women," Lytton wrote, "must have gone to the making of that one little body." With Miss Blagden stayed later the Irish feminist and reformer, Frances Power Cobbe, who observed how Isa and Browning "wrangled playfully." Miss Cobbe found him "always full of spirits, full of interest in everything from politics to hedge-flowers, cordial and utterly unaffected . . . a ripple of laughter round the sofa where he used to seat himself, generally beside some lady." Mid enthusiastic talk he "would push nearer and nearer till she frequently rose to avoid falling off."

The Brownings' acquaintance with Frances Cobbe began later than their friendship with the Storys, Lytton, and Frederick Tennyson; and one sees again both in an allusion to Elizabeth's pain-worn face and in the remarks about Robert's "wrangling" with Isa, the appearance of the light clouds looking in the earlier fifties no bigger than a man's hand. For in those bright days Elizabeth had reached the peak of her improved health, and spiritualism, the main subject of the wrangling, had only just begun to absorb her attention. They were a gay group of friends especially when Hatty joined them. Much of the summer of 1854 she passed with Isa, walking down to the Brownings' for break-

fast, playing with Pen, studying under Browning's guidance, breath-
lessly admiring Elizabeth. After her departure came letters from both
husband and wife. Says Browning:

> Writing to you, dearest Hatty, is almost like breaking a spell
> and driving you away, or at least putting in evidence for the first
> time that you are really gone, out of sight, out of hearing, out of
> reach. You won't, then, come in any more of a morning, or after-
> noon, in the old way? I can tell you, and you will believe it, I think,
> that often and often Ba and I have seen you, on the queer chair at
> the little end of the table, on the sofa, and in all old places of yours.
> You are dear and good to speak to us, as you do, and to feel, as you
> say, for us. Come back to us, at any distance of time, and you'll see
> whether we love you less, *more* it won't do to promise. Meantime
> both of us wish you well, with our whole heart.

Elizabeth sends messages from Pen and misses sorely "the third
coffee cup" at their breakfast table, while Browning asks, "What of the
Greek now, pupil of mine. . . . We see next to nobody, but make up a
rare fire and get on with our work. . . . Yet we had rather be idle and
have you."

In the Roman winter Harriet writes: "How often did I climb the
cold, cheerless, stone stairway which led to their modest apartment on
the third floor of 42 Bocca di Leone. Nothing cold or cheerless, however, when their door was gained."

On a later visit to Florence, again staying with Isa, Hatty would
sometimes have Browning's company in her pre-breakfast walk to the
Casa Guidi. Expressing a wish one morning to ride in the caretta of
Girolomo, their purveyor of vegetables, she received a ready assent from
him. "*Andra andra,*" he said of his donkey, and it proved only too true.
First the footboard slipped from beneath their feet, next the seat slid
perilously backward, while the vegetables shot out on either side of
the cart. Determinedly the donkey galloped—not to the Casa Guidi but
to the home of Girolomo, halting so abruptly at the gate that they were
almost thrown to the ground, while Mrs. Girolomo voiced sympathy.
And worst of all the donkey would budge no more: "I did not say," re-

marked Girolomo, "that he would *come,* only that he would *go.*" Disheveled and famished they made their way home on foot, where Browning demanded breakfast before he would tell the tale.

This he did dramatically, reproducing, with the help of the Casa Guidi furniture, a rope and a few boards, the caretta and its donkey. Stocking it with vegetables from the kitchen he mounted on his improvised seat and re-enacted the morning's catastrophe. Hatty writes:

> Browning, who was a capital actor and possessed the keenest sense of the ridiculous, was inimitable in his role, pouring forth in Greek, Latin and the vernacular a torrent of threats, entreaties, and exhortations, addressed indiscriminately to the donkey, to Girolomo, and to San Antonio, while the clattering feet of the donkey, produced by an ingenious device indicating gradually accelerated speed, heightened the general effect and formed a running accompaniment to the recitative. A fine touch of realism was introduced by the vegetables, which, at stated intervals, but with utter disregard of Mrs. Browning's safety, were hurled about the room. No detail was lacking which could render illusion perfect, the catastrophe being reached in the sudden centrifugal impetus caused by the abrupt halt at the vineyard gate.

> "Nothing does Ba so much good as a good laugh," said Mr. Browning, gazing with satisfaction at her helpless condition and at her face glistening with tears, "and I will set this down as the laugh of her life."

Turning from Hatty to the memories of Mrs. Hugh Fraser, an English diplomatist's wife, is startling indeed. She comes on the scene a little later, when Elizabeth was obsessed by the question of Italian liberty. Pen (called "Penry" by Mrs. Fraser) "was constantly with us" in "a little company of children." She describes him as "beautifully dressed," but rather spoiled and inclined to be bossy with the other children. On Browning she is lyrical: ". . . his face was a noble one, clear and pale . . . his voice I remember well. It was deep and joyous as the wind when it sang through our cypresses."

But meeting Elizabeth was "an awesome experience," coming from

the blazing sun "into a great dark room. . . . Everything was intense—
the heat, the enthusiasm, the darkness, and I tried hard to get keyed
up. . . . The poetess was everything I did not like . . . great cavernous
eyes . . . big bushes of black ringlets . . . her face was hollow and ghastly
pale . . . why should that nice happy Mr. Browning have such a dis-
mally mournful lady for his wife . . . lacking in humour and terribly
sentimental?"

Mrs. Kinney, wife of William Burnet Kinney, visiting Casa Guidi
in 1854, thought it strange that Browning "never will allow that she
is ill, but now he must see it and feel it. . . ." An article in the *New
York Home Journal* had described Elizabeth as "a crooked, dried-up
old woman, with a horrible mouth." Mrs. Kinney rushed to her defense, writing of her "beauty of spirit," but not denying that "her frame
is shattered by disease." Browning was furious. " 'I see well enough yet'
as Benedick says—'without spectacles, and yet see nothing of the
matter.' " She should, he claimed, have described his wife as "beautiful
in person"—and he never forgave her well-meant intervention.

Mrs. Kinney's horror at hearing both Brownings proclaim George
Sand "a great woman" reflects perfectly the Victorian outlook which
they so frequently outraged, for they admitted that she had a series of
lovers. Lust, Elizabeth said, was no worse than intemperance or glut-
tony. George Sand's mind was "godlike," and she was kind and charitable. But, said Mrs. Kinney, "lascivious," with her unlawful loves.

"Love," exclaimed husband and wife together; "she never loved
anyone but herself."

Mrs. Kinney admired Mrs. Browning, but was critical of him.
Browning "labors in all he writes—not to *polish,* but to roughen it." He
was too "impulsive, often abusive in speaking of others and unsparing
in his ridicule and contempt of many whom the world calls poets," but
"she is good, never speaks ill of anyone and is kind and gentle, conciliat-
ing with all."

Mrs. Kinney was not alone in her view. The only opinion on record
that Elizabeth was critical, Robert kind, came from Mrs. Crosse. There
was as noted the lurking smile with which Browning could make the
fool feel himself just that. At Pisa an English couple had been spread-

ing unkind gossip about Elizabeth: she gave herself airs, had been too proud to return their call. Browning visited them and talked blandly of gossip he had heard, repeating their own words to them as of unnamed malicious folk while he watched them writhe. His language could be as violent in abuse as in enthusiasm, though most of the extreme instances recorded belong to his later life. But there certainly was in him "a potentiality of wrath." To the end of his life a friend noted how his face would blanch at a mention of Home, the medium or, sadly enough, of Harriet Hosmer, for this was one of the tiny handful among Browning's friendships which did not last.

Hatty Hosmer loved both Brownings, thinking Elizabeth "the most perfect human being I have ever known." A beautiful small sculpture of hers is their clasped hands, which perhaps suggested to the poet the lines in "James Lee's Wife":

> "As like as a Hand to another Hand!"
> Whoever said that foolish thing,
> Could not have studied to understand
> The counsels of God in fashioning
> Out of the infinite love of his heart,
> This Hand . . .

Hatty thought Elizabeth's face "plain of feature," but redeemed by "wonderful dark eyes, large and loving and luminous as stars." But in the "large full lipped mouth" she thought there might be found "the key to some of Mrs. Browning's less delicate verse"—an allusion to the startling Victorian view which discovered coarseness in Elizabeth's attempts to bring social evils into the sight of those who should be working to cure them.

If the "later years," in which Harriet Hosmer's biographer tells us she was writing, mean that period in which she and Browning had quarreled, her description of him is not ungenerous:

> Years have passed, and photography now reveals to us a face of great intellectual power, but also the face of the comfortable man of the world, tinged, perhaps, with a certain sense of success, but in the days of which I write, he dwelt apart from the every-day world;

he stood, I think, on a higher plane, fulfilling in every sense the ideal we have formed of a poet. The broad forehead, the black and slightly waving hair, the keen and clear gray eyes, the fresh complexion of faintest olive hue, and very slight, as yet, the delicate frame. There were the genial, cheery voice, the unfailing joyous spirits of youth, the unique conversational gifts, witty, grave and gay by turns, with, over all, a manner as charming as any verse he ever penned. Accustomed as we now are to the halo which surrounds their names, it is difficult to associate their present popularity and fame with the *poco curante* mood in which they were then regarded. They lived a life of seclusion, unappreciated, unobserved. It is not too much to say, that outside a purely literary coterie, and their modest circle of personal friends few had heard their names. But what cared those great spirits for the outer world? They lived in a world of their own, happiest when alone therein.

16 Men and Women

Even now, as I am speaking . . . there glides through the room the pageant of his persons . . . men and women that live.

OSCAR WILDE

"ROBERT'S poems are magnificent," wrote Elizabeth to Henrietta in April, 1855, "and will raise him higher than he stands. We are up early working, working. Penini's lessons I never neglect—then I write.—Then dinner—then I criticise Robert's MSS. Altogether I have scarcely breath for reading. . . . Everybody admires at me for looking so well. How can I ever hope to be pitied, I who am always dying and it makes no difference?"

Browning had written to his publishers in 1853: "I shall give you something saleable one of these days—see if I don't," and his hopes for *Men and Women* ran high. For it contained his richest expression of the twofold ideal unfolded in prose in his essay on Shelley. Never have the objective and subjective poet, as he described them in this essay, been more fully fused than in himself. Milsand had already noted this, and there are flashes of likeness between what he wrote of Browning and what Browning wrote of Shelley; as we read the essay, our tendency is to forget Shelley and concentrate, as did Carlyle, on its author. Carlyle thought little of Shelley, "an extremely weak creature, and lamentable, much more than admirable. Weak in genius, weak in character . . . a poor thin, spasmodic, hectic, shrill and pallid being . . . something void, and Hades-like in the whole inner world of him. . . . In a word, it is not with Shelley but with Shelley's Commentator that I take up my quarters at all: and to this latter I will say with emphasis, Give us some more of *your* writing, my friend." He found in Browning "the authentic sound of a *human* voice" amid the "cackle" of the universe. "I honour and respect the weighty estimate you have formed of the Poetic Art; and I admire very much the grave expressiveness of style (a *little* too elaborate here and there), and the dignified tone."

Hastily withdrawn because the letters it was to introduce proved to be spurious, this essay should indeed be reprinted as an introduction to Browning's collected poems.

The "inexhaustible variety of existence," the "soul's delight in its own extended sphere of vision," "an irresistible sympathy with men" compelling him to offer them his "own provision of knowledge and beauty"—all this, in what Browning called the "objective" poet, sets him "on labour as other men are set on rest."

The "subjective" poet, gifted also "with the fuller perception of nature and man, is impelled to embody the theme he perceives, not so much with reference to the many below as to the one above him, the supreme Intelligence which apprehends all things in their absolute truth. Not what man sees, but what God sees—the Ideas of Plato, seeds of creation lying burningly in the Divine Hand—it is toward these that he struggles."

He is "rather a seer" therefore than a "fashioner"; yet "it is with this world, as starting point and basis alike, that we shall always have to concern ourselves: the world is not to be learned and thrown aside, but reverted to and relearned. The spiritual comprehension may be infinitely subtilised, but the raw material it operates upon must remain."

The two faculties of the objective poet and the subjective might issue from the same man "in successive perfect works," but "mere running in of the one faculty upon the other, is of course, the ordinary circumstance." In *Pauline*, in *Paracelsus*, in *Sordello* and *Pippa*, in the *Dramatic Romances and Lyrics*, in *Christmas Eve and Easter Day*, Browning had shown powers both subjective and objective, but the world around remained unresponsive, deaf, and blind. No wonder that he felt it was "the bestowment of life upon a labour, hard, slow and not sure." But "the misapprehensiveness of his age is exactly what a poet is sent to remedy; and the interval between his operation and the generally perceptible effect of it, is no greater, less indeed, than in many other departments of the great human effort. The 'E pur si muove' of the astronomer was as bitter a word as any uttered before or since by a poet over his rejected living work, in that depth of conviction which is so like despair."

Carlyle, more perceptive perhaps despite his growls than many a smoother critic, had realized the danger of a profound discouragement: "I liked the Essay extremely well indeed"; he wrote "a solid, well-wrought, massive, manful bit of discourse; and interesting to me over and above, as the first bit of *prose* I had ever seen from you;—I hope only the first of very many." Thus his letter began, for here was Browning writing in prose as he had advised. But verse or prose—"Seriously, dear Browning, you must at last gird up your loins again; and give us a right stroke of work . . . in whatever form your own *Daimon* bids. Only see that *he* does bid it; and then go on with your best speed."

Browning had obeyed his mentor by writing the best work of the best ten years of his life. I should like to adjure anyone reading this book to lay it down at this point, take up Browning's *Poetical Works* and reread *Men and Women*—every one of that marvelous and all-inclusive collection. In the Murray or Macmillan editions it is a little troublesome to find them all because of the various places where Browning (inadvisedly) has distributed them, but most are in *Dramatic Lyrics* and there is a date guide at the book's end. Even knowing them well already (some by heart) I found this rereading of the utmost value to a deeper understanding of Browning—and of the Shelley Essay which probably preceded most of these poems.

First for one's imagination come the incredible riches scattered by the objective poet: Lippo Lippi seeing

> The value and significance of flesh, . . .
> The beauty and the wonder and the power,
> The shapes of things, their colours, lights and shades,
> Changes, surprises— . . .
> This world's no blot for us,

Nor blank; it means intensely, and means good;
To find its meaning is my meat and drink.

Lippo is surely Browning on canvas, striking out new ways of
seeing and saying, doubted by his Prior as Browning was by his world.
Anything odder than comparing him to Andrea del Sarto, the "faultless
painter," I can hardly conceive. Browning's art was crammed with
faults, roughnesses, elisions, obscurities. Andrea says, "All is silver grey
/ Placid and perfect with my art." And he sighs longingly for his wife
to do what Elizabeth was doing ceaselessly for Browning. Had she, says
Andrea, "but brought a mind! / Some women do so. Had the mouth
there urged / God and the glory! Never care for gain."[1]

Turn from the smooth-running lines of these two poems to "Master
Hugues of Saxe-Gotha," an imaginary composer, to observe Browning
in riotous high spirits expressed triumphantly by the meter and by what
Chesterton has called a "frantic" astronomical image:

> Hallo, you sacristan, show us a light there!
>   Down it dips, gone like a rocket.
> What, you want, do you, to come unawares,
> Sweeping the Church up for first morning-prayers,
> And find a poor devil has ended his cares
>   At the foot of your rotten-runged rat-riddled stairs?
>   Do I carry the moon in my pocket?

Next go to the change in meter, meaning, imaginative power of
that astonishing poem: "A Toccata of Galuppi's." One longs to quote it
all—the glimpse of Venice through the masks and balls and lovemaking
("Then more kisses!"—"Did *I* stop them, / When a million seemed so
few?") Back to the plaintive music "sigh on sigh" which

Told them something? Those suspensions, those solutions—"Must we die?"
Those commiserating sevenths—"Life might last! we can but try!"

And then in the final verse the poet with all his vital energy turns
upon the musician, who yet has imposed his own mood of gloom:

"Dust and ashes!" So you creak it, and I want the heart to scold.
Dear dead women, with such hair, too—what's become of all the gold
Used to hang and brush their bosoms? I feel chilly and grown old.

Even Carlyle did not fully understand, as none of Browning's critics of this period did at all, the fierce strain of poetic creation, the long period of gestation preceding it. We know of Browning's brain-and-liver fever, reducing him to a "shadow of a shade" around the time of the publication of *Pippa Passes;* of several other attacks of illness, during one of which he wrote "Artemis Prologuizes" (note the nightmare quality of that poem), and a great deal more not subsequently recorded; of another when he felt impelled to recite all the poems of Donne, of yet another which preceded the writing of *Paracelsus*. As we look at the years in Italy when he often appeared idle, something may indeed be attributed to a despondency following apparent failure, but far more to the fact that production of the highest quality must be spaced widely and irregularly, must grow in the mind as plant or baby from seed, before it can in its maturity be set down on paper:

> He stood and watched the cobbler at his trade,
> The man who slices lemons into drink,
> The coffee-roaster's brazier . . .
> He took such cognizance of men and things,
> If any beat a horse, you felt he saw;
> If any cursed a woman, he took note;
> Yet stared at nobody . . .

In most of these poems we see the "running-in" of subjective and objective; one can certainly imagine Browning "digging in his own soul" and himself speaking to God in much of what he wrote, but in his greatest poetry the two elements are most fully fused. "He would not," says Herford, "trumpet forth truth in his own person . . . he let it struggle up through the baffling density, or glimmer through the conflicting persuasions of alien minds, and break out in cries of angry wonder or involuntary recognition."

Two results are especially noteworthy: Browning's people are never lay figures, and to make them live he recreates not alone the thoughts which they utter, but the scenery, the circumstances, their fellowmen. Turn from his painters and musicians to the Arab physician Karshish, to the Greek poet Cleon, and with each you find a different world as well as a different man; human longings and divine responses are there always, but the settings are vividly various. Yet, too, for anyone who thinks that Browning's faith was just something imposed on him by, or caught from, his mother and wife, it must be baffling to find the different minds going by such different roads and all seeing God on their road and at its end. I began to reread *Men and Women* with just the human pictures in view, and I ended by wondering whether any poet has lived who named God more frequently—from a defense of painting "Adam's wife" naked as He created her, right up the scale to David singing of Incarnation and Redemption, or the "corregidor," who in his ceaseless pacing of the streets, his "cognizance of men and things" had been

> Thro' a whole campaign of the world's life and death,
> Doing the King's work all the dim day long,
> In his old coat and up to knees in mud,
> Smoked like a herring, dining on a crust,—
> And now the day was won relieved at once! . . .
>   Bless us all the while
> How sprucely we are dressed out, you and I!
> A second, and the angels alter that.

Elizabeth and he writing together did not always show each other what they wrote, and it is fascinating to find in *Aurora Leigh* the lines: "Earth's crammed with heaven / And every common bush afire with God." For thenabouts Browning was writing in "Transcendentalism"

> He with a "look you!" vents a brace of rhymes,
> And in there breaks the sudden rose herself,
> Over us, under, round us every side,
> Nay, in and out the tables and the chairs
> And musty volumes, . . .
> Buries us with a glory, young once more,
> Pouring heaven into this shut house of life.

Browning saw mud as well as stars; indeed, the stars shone in the mud at times and pseudo-stars fell as if from the sky. Beauty surrounded him in those years. One must return to Italy to become fully aware of the two poets as they lived, especially of the Browning of *Men and Women*. In the noise of the modern city it is hard to see him half dreaming at a street corner, aware still of stalls and barrows, vendors and buyers:

> River and bridge and street and square,
>> Lay mine, as much at my beck and call,
> Through the live translucent bath of air,
>> As the sights in a magic crystal ball.

The very markets are beset today by the motorist, the pedestrian's life not worth an hour's purchase. Even inside the churches the crowds seethe hour by hour, sight-seeing, with their guides telling them what to see. In a great church where Michael Angelo's last Pieta has found its home or where the walls are covered with frescoes, the apse with mosaics, the windows glowing with glass, you trip over their feet and are deafened by their voices. But learn which are the quiet hours—and in Rome in San Prassede, his "Church of peace"; or Santa Maria Maggiore with its marvelous vista of pillars; in the black and white Cathedral of Siena; in the Florentine churches, most of all familiar to him, you can still picture Browning drinking in beauty, observing absurdity, studying men and women of today, of the Renaissance, of the Middle Ages, of time and of eternity.

> On the arch where olives overhead
>> Print the blue sky with twig and leaf,
> (That sharp-curled leaf which they never shed)
>> Twixt the aloes, I used to lean in chief,
> And mark through the winter afternoons,
>> By a gift God grants me now and then,
> In the mild decline of those suns like moons,
>> Who walked in Florence, besides her men.

And out in the countryside, forsaking the be-motored high roads, wandering through hilly wooded bypaths you can still, as in "By the Fireside," find the quiet he lived in:

> But at afternoon or almost eve
>> 'Tis better; then the silence grows

> To that degree, you half believe
> It must get rid of what it knows,
> Its bosom does so heave.

Returning to the men and women, it is obvious enough that they are mostly, with considerable emphasis, men *and* women—sex apparent as a source of profound joy and grief, of conflict ending in peace or never ending, of the most agonizing problems in the human predicament. What is Browning telling us about sex in these poems and from what throne—or what prison—is he speaking? This last question would have appeared an absurd one till quite lately, yet Dowden wrote many years ago of a pitfall which the biographer should beware: a failure to realize that the fulness of his own happiness sharpened the poet's insight into the causes which may wreck the relations between men and women. One of these, already spoken of, is the "world's coarse thumb / and finger." In "Respectability" and "The Statue and the Bust," as again later in "Youth and Art," hesitation, delay, arise from worldly fears—whether of lack of money or loss of name. And here it is obvious enough that Browning speaks of a battle which ended in victory for Elizabeth and himself.

But there is another victory to be won as the years pass: victory over the problem of a real, a profound difference between the sexes, rendering them, as has been said, almost in essence incompatible. I fancy that in all men and women of genius this becomes less prominent, most such women having more of the male in them than their sisters, most such men having more in them of the woman than their fellows. Anyhow Browning could see exquisitely from the woman's viewpoint: read again "A Woman's Last Word," the ending in peace of a difficult giving:

> —Must a little weep, Love,
> (Foolish me!)
> And so fall asleep, Love,
> Loved by thee.

The tendency to give—a profound generosity flowing from love—he sees as stronger in woman than in man. But the first longing is

stronger in man, the initial resistance in woman. In "A Serenade at the
Villa" Browning depicts the lover serenading his mistress:

> Oh, how dark your villa was,
> Windows fast and obdurate!
> How the garden grudged me grass
> Where I stood—the iron gate
> Ground its teeth to let me pass!

And again in "Love in a Life" and "Life in a Love" "While the one
eludes, must the other pursue," "So the chase takes up one's life, that's
all."

But when he has won his prize it is man that tires soonest, and this
is depicted above all in the exquisite lyric "In a Year" where the woman
ponders how the very things, the looks, the gestures, which once awakened love now bear a part in killing it:

> Dear, the pang is brief,
> Do thy part,
> Have thy pleasure! How perplexed
> Grows belief!
> Well, this cold clay clod
> Was man's heart:
> Crumble it, and what comes next?
> Is it God?

A few of the lyrics concern sex but not marriage. "A Light Woman,"
snatched by a man to save his friend, a woman he does not want for
himself and in the taking has lost the friend: ". . . a pear late basking
over a wall; / Just a touch to try and off it came," but now

> With no mind to eat it, that's the worst!
> Were it thrown in the road, would the case assist?
> 'Twas quenching a dozen blue-flies thirst
> When I gave its stalk a twist.

"A Pretty Woman" was Mrs. Jameson's niece Gerardine, and the
poem shows that Browning who had rather violently repudiated the
idea that any man could wish to marry so mindless a girl had ended
with an appreciation of "just a flower":

Then how grace a rose? I know a way!
Leave it, rather.
Must you gather?
Smell, kiss, wear it—at last, throw away!

Andrea del Sarto had married a woman as light as the one, as mindless as the other of these two, and Browning shows by contrast the woman he had won, to whom the best lyrics in the book are dedicated "Love Among the Ruins," "My Star," "One Word More" and most notably "By the Fireside." Yet he writes, too, of the problems and dangers surrounding the happiest of marriages. One of these is rather specially fascinating for a reason also connected with biography, and casts light on an important element in Browning's character. He shows in "Mesmerism" his very real fear of one element in spiritualism in which he firmly believed—the power of the soul to reach, to affect, to dominate other souls, in ways invisible, incomprehensible. Elizabeth had urged many years back the wonderful cure of her friend, Miss Martineau, as an argument in favor of mesmerism, but to Browning it was clear that the soul was owned by God alone, that no man must attempt to pass outside the human framework set by his Creator.

This awareness of human limitation becomes vivid in both "The Guardian Angel" and "Two in the Campagna." It is not before man or woman that Browning is bowing down in the Church at Fano: While asking the angel as God's minister to help that aching head of his "which too much thought expands" (and his wife "my angel" had, as he later wrote to Julia Wedgwood, "with her two little hands" once charmed away such distress and sent him into a peaceful sleep), the poem is a cry from the limited to the limitless, from the created to the Creator.

In like manner "Two in the Campagna" is very far from being a confession that the love, so triumphant in poems written around the same time "By the Fireside" and "One Word More," was in fact beginning to fail.[2] *The* problem of life Browning held was to pull the infinite into the finite—to fill time with eternity. His doctrine of the infinite moment is precisely the recognition that only for moments can this be done; here on earth at least "the good moment goes." But it goes to return again. It was there in the Campagna, it was there overwhelmingly by the ruined chapel in the mountains of "By the Fireside"; it was there in "One Word More" as the moon rose over Florence and he, leaving the world of men behind him could

> Cross a step or two of dubious twilight,
> Come out on the other side, the novel
> Silent silver lights and darks undreamed of,
> Where I hush and bless myself with silence.

But in the Campagna he has realized human limitations:

> Infinite passion, and the pain
> Of finite hearts that yearn.

An intending student of Browning should surely begin with this and the two earlier similar collections *Dramatic Lyrics* of 1842 and *Dramatic Romances and Lyrics* of 1845. With these also we are vexed by his tiresome habit of rearranging, but the order in which they were written, though interesting, does not greatly matter for their understanding. Of his *Dramatic Romances and Lyrics* he spoke in 1845 as "this dancing ring of men and women hand in hand"—and all three contain some of his famous dramatic monologues.

This form does not, of course, belong to Browning alone, but no one else has I think used it so powerfully. "In England," says Ezra Pound, "Browning refreshed the form of monologue or dramatic monologue or 'Persona,' the ancestry of which goes back at least to Ovid's *Heroides* which are imaginary letters in verse, and to Theocritus, and is thence lost in antiquity."[3] A glance at Theocritus (in translation) does not suggest that he gave much to Browning, and while Sappho's letter is good fun, Browning is infinitely more entertaining and profound than is Ovid. But when trying to write plays, he confessed that his problem was caring far more for character than for action; his plots would lag while his characters talked.

To Oscar Wilde it seemed that Browning was "the most supreme

I

writer of fiction . . . from the point of view of a creator of character he
ranks next to him who made Hamlet." Giving us a living procession of
Browning's characters, Wilde comments, "His sense of dramatic situa-
tions is unrivaled." Wilde does not, as T. S. Eliot does, contrast the
characters in the plays, who are impossible to remember, with the
speakers of the monologues, who are impossible to forget. But it is
Wilde who makes in advance the best comment on Eliot's judgment
when he says: "Browning might have given us a Hamlet, who would
have realised his mission by thought. . . . He made the soul the pro-
tagonist of life's tragedy and looked on action as the one undramatic
element of a play."⁴ And this is partly because the monologue is *not*
the same thing as a soliloquy; it is self-revelation made in a sort of
dialogue.

Robert Langbaum who has drawn out this distinction brilliantly in
his *Poetry of Experience* suggests a comparison with Pope's *Eloisa to
Abelard,* or we might recall Hamlet's "To be or not to be," for in a
soliloquy the speaker is arguing with himself, is resolving, maybe
changing his outlook, his intended action. In a monologue there is no
change of viewpoint; the speaker is justifying himself, explaining himself, showing off to a gallery of one or more. And this is where the
element of dialogue comes in; surely we can see and hear not only
Blougram but Gigadibs, not only the Bishop but the "nephews" he is
talking to, we can see the men to whom Karshish and Cleon were
writing, the passer-by who flashed his light into Lippi's face, Andrea's
wife listening not to her husband but for the cousin's whistle. Robert
Langbaum rightly says that the "Soliloquy of the Spanish Cloister"
should in fact be called a monologue; in his self-justification the speaker
has given us the first taste of something more deeply penetrated in
Guido in *The Ring and the Book*—an evil man hating a good and simple
one just because of his goodness, and all unconsciously revealing that
goodness and simplicity.

The dramatic monologue Langbaum sees as a form, little understood
at Browning's date, especially suited to ours: ". . . it imitates not life,
but a particular perspective towards life, somebody's experience of it."
And it is the more true in that it

imitates the structure of our own experience in which illumina-
tions burn at the centre with certainty and then shade off into
ambiguity and doubt. Abt Vogler's instant of doubt makes the
ecstatic instant believable by providing it with a recognizable setting. . . . Far from weakening our confidence in the vision, the
incompatibility throws us back upon the more intense instant as
the primary certainty; while the judgment that proceeds from the
less intense instant appears as a problematical speculation.[5]

Edwin Muir gives us two other useful hints about a poet, "second,"
he claims, "only to Shakespeare and Chaucer" in his rich variety.
Browning's contemporary world was shocked by his "love for the curious" and "for the violently ordinary," which "brought unexpected
material into his poetry, and along with it, to deal with it, a vast new
vocabulary." For Browning cared immensely for activity. "He could
not," says Muir, "have seen with composure Tennyson's man come
and till the field and lie beneath. He would have concentrated on the
tilling of the field with an agricultural passion." He had a technical
interest in all human activity. "When he wrote of painters, or priests,
or lovers, or imposters, he wrote with a professional appreciation of the
importance of their modes." Love being for him "the highest activity . . .
he devoted his most intense imaginative consideration to it."

Another element, often disputed, seems to Muir undeniable by a
reader of his lyrics—the sheer music, "tentative and casual music in
which the thought seems to be experimentally finding its proper expression: almost a hand-to-mouth music." Everything in Browning's
work is, Muir feels, "an enquiry beginning with a Perhaps and con-
verging circuitously upon one of the cardinal truths in which he
believed." Hence "this free, faintly interrogative, street music," of
which "he was a master. . . . He used it with consummate ease and
variety."[6]

Look then for people, look for music in *Men and Women*; you will
find both.

17 Conviction
So Like Despair

Because the seeming solitary man
Speaking to God may have an audience too . . .

THE RING AND THE BOOK

BY MAY of 1855 Elizabeth had written more than seven thousand lines of the endless *Aurora Leigh,* Browning was still adding to *Men and Women,* and that summer found them in London seeing the same old friends and many new ones. "Tomorrow," she wrote to Henrietta, "we breakfast with Mr. Kenyon to meet half America and a quarter of London." She told George: "In America he [Browning] is a power." Had the United States agreed to international copyright—or had Browning had there an admirer to do for him what Emerson did for Carlyle—the Brownings would have been wealthy. Alone among the great English writers at that time, Carlyle received for years more money from his American than from his English publishers. Before *The French Revolution* had brought him anything in England he had received £400 from the States. In the cause of England's prophet America's prophet proved himself a good man of business, too. As it was, an occasional publisher would pay the Brownings a little for sheets in advance (this happened with *Aurora Leigh*), but wide pirating went on to the end of their lives. Elizabeth wrote to Mrs. Jameson in an undated letter of July or August:

The best news I can send you is that Robert has printed the first half volume ... the work looks better than ever in print. ... He has read these proofs to Mr. Fox (of Oldham), who gives an opinion that the poems are at the top of art in their kind. ... Let me see what London news I have to tell you. We spent an evening with Mr. Ruskin, who was gracious and generous. ... Robert took our young friend Leighton to see him afterwards, and was as kindly received. We met Carlyle at Mr. Forster's, and found him in great force, particularly in the damnatory clauses.

Elizabeth then had read *Men and Women* in manuscript. She says so often that they did not show each other what they were writing that this has been accepted too literally. She sometimes copied for him, he sometimes read unpublished poems aloud to her, and even to some of the Florentine circle; she had read a good deal of *Dramatis Personae,* published only after her death. When and how did she show her work to Robert? He had read the first six books of *Aurora Leigh* by March, 1856, months before publication; when he talks to their publisher of "looking after commas" for her this may refer either to manuscript or proof.

They were too busy, between proofs and the completing of *Aurora,* and too poor besides, to accept multitudinous invitations to country houses—from Sir Edward Lytton, the Custs, the Martins, the Alfred Tennysons and many others. The Barrett family had been shot away instantly by Papa—this time to Eastbourne, and there the Brownings hoped to follow them, since it would be hardly out of their way to Paris where the winter must be spent.

With all his generosity Mr. Kenyon sometimes forgot to send his yearly gift on the appointed date. Elizabeth writes "we are at the end of our purse and can't travel any more, not even to Taunton, where poor Henrietta, who is hindered from coming to me by a like pecuniary straitness, begs so hard that we should go." It was difficult even to "return visits to the hour, and hold engagements to the minute, when one has neither carriage nor legs, nor time at one's disposal. . . ." Yet "people may live very cheaply and very happily if they are happy

otherwise." Another member of the Barrett family had been added to
the disinherited. "Alfred is just married at the Paris Embassy to Lizzie
Barrett . . . the third exile from Wimpole Street, the course of true love
running remarkably rough in our house."

There were the Procters to be seen (Barry Cornwall his pen name
was); his sharp-tongued wife, a little like Jane Carlyle, faithfully
visited by Browning all through his later life; and the daughter Adelaide
Anne, minor poet reputed to outsell Tennyson, with a face, said Elizabeth, "worth a drove of beauties." She is best known today by "The
Lost Chord."

Of Tennyson's latest volume report declared: "The sale is great,
nearly five thousand copies already." The italics are Elizabeth's. And no
doubt both husband and wife had high hopes of something similar for
Men and Women—infinitely superior surely to *Maud* and appealing to
far more various tastes. On one historic occasion a group had the opportunity to compare both poems and poets, while Dante Gabriel Rossetti
made surreptitious sketches of them and William Michael Rossetti sat
listening and taking notes. It was the second day the Laureate had
spent with the Brownings. Elizabeth wrote to Mrs. Martin, he "dined
with us, smoked with us, opened his heart to us (and the second bottle
of port), and ended by reading *Maud* through from end to end and
going away at half past two in the morning."

"Oh Hatty," wrote Browning to Harriet Hosmer, "why were you
not here in London first, and you should have heard Alfred Tennyson
read 'Maud' to us, and Mrs. Sartoris sing, and Ruskin and Carlyle talk,
our three best remembrances."[1] Elizabeth thought Tennyson's reading
"like articulated music." *Maud* was his favorite; my own parents often
listened to it. Did he say to Elizabeth as he sometimes did to my mother,
"Give me your hand that some electricity may pass from you to me?"
And then he would perhaps forget the hand he held and wave it
ardently in time with the music of his reading! As he finished he would
say, "No one knows what *Maud* is till they hear me read it." Elizabeth
talks of his "unexampled *naïveté!* Think of his stopping in *Maud* every
now and then—'There's a wonderful touch! That's very tender. How
beautiful that is!' Yes, and it *was* wonderful, tender, beautiful, and he

read exquisitely in a voice like an organ, rather music than speech."

Browning gave them "Fra Lippo Lippi," and it is interesting to compare Elizabeth's rapture over Tennyson with the judgment of Henry James who, not present that night, had later opportunities to listen to both poets. Tennyson was often called "the Bard," and bardic Henry James found him. It should have been, he felt, a "prodigious occasion . . . I pinched myself for the determination of my identity and hung on the reader's deep-voiced chant for the credibility of his: I asked myself in fine why, . . . I failed to swoon away under the heaviest pressure I had doubtless ever known the romantic situation bring to bear." The great man remained the Bard, but "The character was just a rigid idiosyncracy."

James felt Browning to be not at all a bard but totally a poet. He read

> with all the exhibition of point and authority, the expressive particularisation, so to speak, that I had missed on the part of the Laureate; an observation through which the author of *Men and Women* appeared, in spite of the beauty and force of his demonstration, as little as possible, a Bard. He particularised if ever a man did, was heterogeneous and profane, composed of pieces and patches that betrayed some creak of joints, and addicted to the excursions from which these were brought home; so that he had to *prove* himself a poet, almost against all presumptions, and with all the assurance and all the character he could use. Was not this last in especial, the character, so close to the surface, with which Browning fairly bristled, what was most to come out in his personal delivery of the fruit of his genius? It came out almost to harshness; but the result was that what he read showed extraordinary life. During that audition at Aldworth the question seemed on the contrary not of life at all. . . ."[2]

Would James have felt the same at this date? Tennyson was the Laureate, the great success; Browning so much the failure that in discussions prior to Tennyson's appointment several names had been mentioned, including his wife's, but his own never. At the peak of his fame, the absurd Home, the spiritualist, could never have thought up such an explanation as he gave of Browning's uneasiness when "spirit hands" at a séance hovered around his wife's head and finally placed a wreath of flowers on it. Browning, said he, had been observed to place himself in the way in the obvious hope that the crown would rest on his own head. Home gave in *Incidents In My Life* a highly colored account of the incident. Browning briefly remarked that he had later seen Home and "relieved" himself. He had done so yet more fully in "Mr. Sludge, the Medium."

Betty Miller gives in "The Séance at Ealing" (*Cornhill* magazine, January, 1957) a vivid description of the evening,[3] quoting at some length the letter Browning wrote immediately after it. Unwilling to embarrass his hosts he did not, as Home later claimed, rise from his seat; but he did look under the table and around it and was, he admitted, unable to account for some of the phenomena. That there had somehow been cheating Browning was convinced, but Home refused his request for another séance and in later years Browning convinced himself that he had spotted the tricks in this one. (Pen said that his father often told him so.) As Chesterton did not fail to see, the idea of Browning running round the room in the hope of spirit hands placing a wreath on his own head adds to the scene a pleasing touch of low comedy.

But for Browning, as he watched his wife's face, there could be no comedy—it was for him the first scene in a near-tragedy. For some years the group of friends had experimented, some in fun, some seriously, at table-turning and calling up spirits, real or imaginary. But now he was witnessing something deadly serious as Elizabeth submitted to the forces of a preternatural world at the hands of the first skilled practitioner she had encountered. Had he been as certain as he tried at times to believe he was, that it was *all* mere cheating, he would have feared it far less. Now he was seriously alarmed.

A friendship with Ruskin had sprung up on the Browning's last stay in London when they visited Denmark Hill and saw the Turner collection which Elizabeth found "divine." Ruskin wrote: "You are the only husband and wife whom I write single letters to this way, but I never think of you two separately—never of one without the other: I like getting those nice double letters too—a bit of white and brown like a black-cock's breast."

The muscular Christian, Charles Kingsley, bracketed the two men together as objects of his dislike:

> Leave to Robert Browning
> Beggars, fleas and vines;
> Leave to squeamish Ruskin
> Popish Appenines . . .

Although Ruskin had praised with such enthusiasm the Bishop ordering his tomb, it was Elizabeth's poetry he loved best. "I am going to bind your poems in a golden binding and give them to my class of working men—as the purest and most exalting poetry in our language," he wrote in March, 1855. And a month later, trying to revive the medieval art of illumination, he had rejected a canto of Dante's in favor of Elizabeth's "Catarina to Camoens" with which his best workman was to create "one of the most glorious little burning books that ever had leaf turned by white finger . . . with deep blue and purple and golden embroidery."

"My husband is very much pleased," Elizabeth replied, "and particularly that you selected 'Catarina' which is his favorite among my poems for some personal fanciful reasons besides the rest."

Ruskin wanted her, however, to outlaw the "long compounded Greek words"—especially "nympholeptic," "When you have succeeded in all your designs upon the English language, I might perhaps most graphically describe it as

> Tesseric, pentic, hectic, hiptic,
> Maeno-daemonic, and dyspeptic,
> Hippid-ic, Pippid-ic, East-wind-nipped-ic,
> Stiffened like Styptic, doubled in dyptych,
> Possi-kephaly-cheresecliptic

The last line by the way (he concluded) really is a triumph of expression."

At the height of his fame as an art critic, self-chosen spokesman for

the Pre-Raphaelite Brotherhood, Ruskin would have seemed the very
person to welcome a novelty in the world of poetry as great as was
Turner in that of art, and not dissimilar in what he claimed for the
painter—that he tried to depict reality "irrespective of any conventional
rules," as did artists before Raphael and not since. Like Browning,
Ruskin was a devotee of Carlyle; and all three shared the experience of
talking to the deaf world of their age. "Every day," Ruskin had written
in *Modern Painters,* "convinces me more and more that no warnings
can preserve from misunderstanding those who have no desire to understand."

Yet some of the pre-Raphaelites felt an element of this lack of desire
in Ruskin's attitude to their poet. Rossetti read Browning's poetry
aloud to him "in a rich voice." But he wrote to William Allingham:

Ruskin on reading *Men and Women* (and with it some of the other
works he didn't know before) declared them rebelliously to be a
mass of conundrums, and compelled me to sit down before him
and lay siege for one whole night; the result of which was that he
sent me next morning a bulky letter to be forwarded to B. in which
I trust he told him he was the greatest man since Shakespeare.

An immensely intelligent wife proofreading, friends like the Rossetti
brothers, Fox, and Milsand, who thought Browning's poems "super-
human," created a warming atmosphere. In Paris the glow continued,
with Milsand's information that about half the book was being translated for the *Revue des deux Mondes* and a letter from his publishers
telling him of initial sales good enough to clear expenses. High spirits
and the joy of being in Paris carried both husband and wife through
the trial of finding themselves in rooms of which the only asset was
yellow satin furniture, the apartment having been chosen by a zealous
friend who described the satin as "worthy" of two poets. Penini had to
sleep on the floor in his parents' room, and trunks remained unpacked
till they could move two weeks later.

The rooms had been taken, Browning wrote to Hatty Hosmer,
"against our will and protestation." It was "—an apartment with no

bottom (for carriages were under it), no top (for the roof tiles were over it), no back (for there was an end to the house with the end of our room)" yet it was gaily he added that after two months' misery "we carried our dead and wounded to this pleasant house," 3 Rue de Grenelle. Here Anne Thackeray soon found them out. "A little warm, shabby apartment," she writes, "with a good fire always burning, and a big sofa, where she sat. . . . Mr. Browning would come in and talk. Pen was a little boy with long curls, and some of the grand gentlemen from Mrs. Sartoris' used to come in and sit by the fire."

Despite the exhausting effort of mounting *"au cinquième,"* Elizabeth as well as Robert visited the Corkrans. Their small daughter Henriette, told to expect two poets, pictured them excitedly as dressed in togas and crowned with laurel leaves. Her disillusionment was boundless. Elizabeth, small, pale, and panting after the climb, gave no signs of genius; her husband dressed in brown with his loud voice and commonplace speech suggested a successful businessman; he devoured plum cake most unpoetically. But he gave great solace to little Henriette by dismissing as rubbish the ghostly visitants in whom her mother believed as firmly as did Elizabeth. Robert Browning, she felt, was far less like a poet than his gentle absent-minded father, but he would make short work of a ghost. Henceforward night frights were to be banished; she would repeat to herself, "Mr. Browning, who is a great man, says it is all nonsense."

The first cheerful information about sales was followed by a long silence. But then his publisher, Edward Chapman, seems never to have written a letter he could possibly avoid writing, so Browning was not unduly disquieted. More worrying were a few reviews that he had seen. On December 17, he wrote to Chapman:

> I was anxious to know . . . if the book continues to do well, and how well; the notices will come, I suppose next month. Meanwhile don't take to heart the zoological utterances I have stopped my ears against at Galignani's of late. 'Whoo-oo-oo-oo' mouths the big monkey—'Whee-ee-ee-ee' squeaks the little monkey and such a dig with the end of my umbrella as I should give the brutes if I couldn't

keep my temper and consider how they miss their nuts and gingerbread![4]

Could the *Quarterly* have been the "big monkey" which had asked
of an earlier poem, "Why must it be *Pippa Passes* and not *Polly Passes*";
which felt that Browning ought like Tennyson to "make his own
country the background of his poems. . . . The mode of thought, without
being anti-English, constantly bears an indescribable savour of the
continent."

And was the "little monkey" *The Christian Remembrancer*, which
felt that a poet should preach sound morals and that "The Statue and
the Bust" showed it as better to commit adultery than to hesitate, delay,
give up; that "Fra Lippo Lippi" invited readers to sympathize with
"that licentious monk-artist . . . apologising with unctuous minuteness
for his shameless course of life." Browning's pictures of love "are coarse
passion; his idea of beauty sensual."

The animal noises continuing, Browning wrote to William Allingham of "leaning over the rail of the literary pond" where "Goosey
Fraser and Gander *Blackwood*" were cackling.[5] However, more than
counterbalancing these reviews, came warm praise from Carlyle, who
wrote of his delight over a first glimpse of the book and his eagerness to
read it through—"That old 'Corregidor' is a diamond"—and of how
on a Christmas visit the best entertainment offered him had been readings aloud of *Men and Women*, given by Lady Ashburton, whose
"melodious clear voice" was listened to with "rapt attention."

A letter from Leigh Hunt showed him of the same mind as Carlyle
and the Rossettis. Browning answered: "you put a flower in my breast
which I hardly dare look at, much less finger."

But what of the wider public? Browning wrote again to Chapman
on January 17, 1856, reproaching the man,

who has left me these two months without a word about the well or
ill doing of my poems. Now do, do pray, dear Chapman, let us have
the Christmas account to put a little life and heart into the end of
this bleak month. I have read heaps of critiques at Galignani's,
mostly stupid and spiteful, self-contradicting and contradictory of

each other. What effect such "rot" would have on me, in the case of the book being somebody else's, I know exactly, but how it works with the reading public, you must tell me if I am ever to know.

It may well have been this time a dislike of sending bad news that slowed Edward Chapman in writing, for *Men and Women* had stopped selling after the first spurt— a spurt representing probably the whole group of ardent Browningites who had hurried to buy on publication.

The Brownings left Paris for London at the end of June carrying with them *Aurora Leigh,* and a few days later Browning noted: "Read this book, this divine book, Wednesday night, July 9th '56." But both husband and wife felt a profound anxiety about its reception by the English critics and the English public. For not only did the poem tell the story of a raped girl left with an unwanted baby, but it laid open, too, a running sore in English life which society had decided to ignore. It was impossible that Elizabeth's sister Arabel who "overworks herself in London with schools and refuges and societies" could remain ignorant of London's underworld of pimps and prostitutes. And the Elizabeth Barrett who had written "The Cry of the Children" felt it a plain duty to speak out on this subject too. "If a woman ignores these wrongs," she wrote to her friend Mrs. Martin, "then may women as a sex continue to suffer them; there is no help for any of us—let us be dumb and die. I have spoken therefore, and in speaking have used plain words—words which look like blots . . . words which, if blurred or softened, would imperil perhaps the force and righteousness of the moral influence."

It is comic today to read these words and note what would have been thought a blot.

Elizabeth's husband had assured her that she "couldn't be coarse if she tried," but after all *he* had been called so in unmeasured terms— and she was a woman, that "gentler" and "weaker" sex who should go through life unaware of any but pleasant things, whose lives like her own poems, should be bound "in a golden binding with deep blue, purple and golden embroidery."

There was nothing they could do now but wait, and with all the swiftness of printers' work at that date they would be back in Florence long before publication.

Mr. Kenyon was in the Isle of Wight and he lent the Brownings his house in Devonshire Place, but this year there was not to be so much of London life, and the visit was overshadowed by a deep personal anxiety about Mr. Kenyon, as well as by the nervous fears for *Aurora's* fate. It was to be, little as they guessed it, Elizabeth's last visit to England.

They spent in the Isle of Wight "a happy sorrowful two weeks" with Arabel—who had again been hastily dismissed from London by her father as soon as he heard of the Brownings' arrival. The brothers, too, were at Ventnor and made a great fuss over Pen who "doubling his small fist" had threatened a boy of twelve: "I will show you that *I'm a boy*"—"great applause from the uncles," comments Elizabeth. Thence to Cowes to Mr. Kenyon and back via Taunton to see Henrietta—also, incredible as it would have seemed, for the last time.

Mr. Kenyon was plainly "very ill . . . Now and then he desires aloud to pass away and be at rest."

Elizabeth had dedicated *Aurora Leigh* to him and his death on December 3, 1856, cast a shadow over the poem's immense success, a success the degree of which astonished Elizabeth: "that golden-hearted Robert is in ecstacies," she wrote to Sarianna," far more than if it all related to a book of his own."

Kenyon left them £11,000, the larger part to Robert, and this (after a year of waiting for probate) relieved forever the habitual financial pressure. But Elizabeth, telling Mrs. Jameson of his death, wrote of the "sad, sad Christmas. . . . He has been in much what my father might have been, and now the place is empty twice over."

For Browning especially the legacy meant a great lightening of life's burdens. Elizabeth was amused by his detailed account book and the little heap of instantly paid bills. "You can't imagine," she wrote to Arabel, "how he lets his imagination buffett and torment him in the small uncertainties of life. . . . He says that he is anxious for *me* and not for *him*—but of what consequence is it whom one is anxious for, when the anxiety is perfectly unnecessary?"

With his present anxieties Elizabeth's sympathy was warmer, for

Robert's poetry was a great matter not a small one. Nor was she indifferent to the reviews of her own book, especially where they touched
the question of her character. Now in Florence was repeated the previous year's experience in Paris—Browning haunting the Reading
Room to bring back news of reviews, the post office to collect letters.
Some few periodicals stigmatized *Aurora Leigh* as coarse. Its heroine,
The Tablet wrote, was "a brazen-faced woman," and the reviewer
compared the story to a romance by a French pornographic writer. "The
world," wrote Arthur Clough, "rather cries Fye on *Aurora Leigh*—
which however has ardent admirers." One friend told Elizabeth that
" 'The mamas of England' in a body refuse to let their daughters read it.
Still the daughters emancipate themselves and *do*."

This was one explanation of the sales, for that first edition was gone
in a fortnight and the second a few months later. But there were other
reasons, too. Nearly all the important papers and reviewers hailed it,
even Mr. Aytoun in *Blackwood* "from the camp of the enemy (ar-
tistically and socially)." And, too, "Think of quite decent women
taking the part of the book in a sort of *effervescence* which I hear of with
astonishment. In fact, there has been an enormous amount of extravagance talked and written on the subject, and I *know it*, oh, I know it."

Typical of this extravagance was a letter from Robert Lytton full of
enthusiasm both for *Men and Women* and *Aurora Leigh*. Writing to
Browning he speaks first of being "overwhelmed" by a "power and
beauty . . . which surpasses even my most ardent hopes . . . limits are
not to be anticipated to the progression of which your genius is capable.
The last will be best with you. . . . I am haunted by all I have read: new
sensations of beauty, new thoughts of power from immeasurable
depths. . . ." But, alas for his critical judgment, he goes on to pronounce
Aurora Leigh "the solitary epic of the age," perhaps not inferior to
Milton and Dante, possibly even superior "by just so much as this age
is superior to theirs . . . this age of complicated sorrows and scattered
knowledge." He marvels how Elizabeth from her "little fireside sofa"
has "so silently acquired" such insight.

If Elizabeth was the woman I think her, she must have ground her teeth to find her "epic" put so high as to devaluate the otherwise true appreciation of her husband's undervalued masterpieces.

But Browning himself when writing of "this divine book," was not surely as wide of reality as in his exaggerated language about the *Sonnets from the Portuguese. Aurora Leigh* has in it some really great poetry and a great deal of acute observation. The absurd way in which the slum girl is made to talk as though she came from Cambridge, the plot, half copied (unconsciously) from *Jane Eyre,* the whole miserable Ninth Book cannot quite quench the excitement of passages where one feels the truth of Elizabeth's letter to Sarianna, acknowledging her debt to the greater mind companioning hers, yet urging too that she has kept her own profoundly personal outlook. *Aurora Leigh* though not the giant epic that so many proclaimed it, is well worth one or two readings.

Among the circle of friends in Florence, Frances Cobbe is representative in confessing that she did not dream Browning was as great a poet as Elizabeth.

> The utter unselfishness and generosity wherewith he gloried in his wife's fame—bringing us up constantly good reviews of her poems and eagerly recounting how many editions had been called for—perhaps helped to blind us stupid that we were! to his own claims. Never certainly did the proverb about the *irritabile genus* of Poets ever prove less true.

She wrote this many years later in her autobiography and added that in his days of fame Browning remained equally unassuming. Of Elizabeth she saw little. "But I am glad I looked into the splendid eyes which *lived* like coals in her pain-worn face."

But this year of 1856, as all hope of success for *Men and Women* vanished and he threw himself ardently into his wife's triumph, a note of bitterness is heard, chiefly about the idiot reviews "blackguardism from the 'Press,' all like those night-men who are always emptying their cart at my door . . . leave me to rub their noses in their own filth some fine day." In this same letter to Chapman (of December 3, 1856) he says that there is "such a thing to fear in these parts as a letter miscarrying."

But "If not, it's a shame of you, black and burning" not to have been at the trouble to send a line on how *Aurora Leigh* is going. He should not wait "for further notice from us (*Us*—I am the church-organ-bellows-blower that talked about *our* playing, but you know what I do in the looking after commas and dots to i's)."

POSTSCRIPT

> Hobbs hints blue—straight he turtle eats:
> Nobbs prints blue—claret crowns his cup:
> Nokes outdares Stokes in azure feats,
> Both gorge. Who fished the murex up?
> What porridge had John Keats?
>
> "Popularity"

Through this checkered story of hope, doubt, despair runs the thread of two correspondences, one with Ruskin, the other with Carlyle, which deepen the puzzle of the failure of *Men and Women*. For both men appeared to realize the greatness which had so struck Ruskin in the early dramatic monologue of a Renaissance bishop. He had too analyzed in *Modern Painters* a problem that was his and Browning's alike.

The worst of it is this kind of concentrated writing needs so much *solution* before the reader can fully see the good of it, that people's patience fails them and they give up the thing as insoluble, though truly it ought to be to the current of common thought like Saladin's talisman, dipped in clear water, not soluble altogether, but making the element medicinal.

But now with warm admiration he mingled a great deal of half-humorous attack on the obscurity of Browning's new volume, picking out especially "Popularity." This poem was later selected by Chesterton as a prime example of Browning's obscurity, resulting from a mixture of insane haste and the assumption that all the world shared his own multitudinous bits of recondite knowledge. He was, for instance, pained at Ruskin questioning his use of "orris" for "iris." "Why don't you ask the next perfumer for a packet of *orris*-root? Don't (sic) everybody know 'tis a corruption of *iris*-root?" In the same way he felt that everybody must know about the murex (translated in modern editions in a footnote to the poem as a mollusk from which the Tyrian purple dye was obtained). Ruskin, said Browning, was asking of poetry the explicitness and detail needed in a business contract. "Why you look at my little song as if it were Hobbs' or Nobbs' lease of his house or testament of his devisings, wherein, I grant you, not a 'then and there', 'to him and to his heirs', 'to have and to hold' would be superfluous.' "

Browning had found Ruskin's long letter (perhaps the one written after Rossetti's night siege) "over-liberal of praise here and there, kindly and sympathetic everywhere . . . the whole letter precious indeed." He had delayed in replying—his letter is dated from Paris, December 10 '55—because "the strife of lodging hunting" had been "too sore . . . south-aspects, warm bedrooms and the like." But now, set free to think, he pours out his own philosophy of poetry and combats Ruskin's desire for what has been well called "reading for runners."

For the deepnesses you think you discern,—may they be more than mere blacknesses! For the hopes you entertain of what may come of subsequent readings,—all success to them! For your bewilderment more especially noted—how shall I help *that*? We don't read poetry the same way, by the same law; it is too clear. I cannot begin writing poetry till my imaginary reader has conceded licences to me which you demur at altogether. I *know* that I don't make out my conception by my language; all poetry being a putting the infinite within the finite. You would have me paint it all plain out, which can't be; but by various artifices I try to make shift with touches and bits of outlines which *succeed* if they bear the conception from me to you. You ought, I think, to keep pace with the thought tripping from ledge to ledge of my 'glaciers,' as you call them; not stand poking your alpenstock into the holes, and demonstrating that no foot could have stood there;—suppose it sprang over there? In *prose* you may criticise so—because that is the absolute representation of portions of truth, what chronicling is to history—but in asking for more *ultimates* you must accept less *mediates,* nor expect that a Druid stone-circle will be traced for you with as few breaks to the eye as the North Crescent and South Crescent that go together so cleverly in many a suburb.[6]

Elizabeth had earlier stressed to Ruskin her disbelief in his view that poems could and should be written with the thought of general, instant comprehension. Now Browning asks, "Do you think poetry was ever generally understood—or can be?"

Later in the letter he answers his own question.

No they, [poems] act upon a very few, who react upon the rest: as Goldsmith says, "some lords, my acquaintance, that settle the nation are pleased to be kind."

Don't let me lose *my* lord by seeming self-sufficiency or petulance: I look on my own shortcomings too sorrowfully, try to remedy them too earnestly: but I shall never change my point of sight.

Ruskin had spoken of writing about Browning's poetry and he would be proud "to be recognized by you as you propose." But he begs Ruskin to

try and know me before you make up your mind—I aim widely and want more than a glance to take in all I endeavour at, hit or miss. With your letter came one from Carlyle—I hide his gold words as if I had stolen them, as I partly have,—but he looks to what suits his own sight, in what I show. So God makes him, you and me.

Ruskin's reply to this letter has disappeared, but another long one from Browning on February 1, 1856, discusses both his answer and *Modern Painters,* Vol. III, sent with it. This letter, too, Browning had received with delight "with its kindness and care about me." He finds in Ruskin's writing

an arrangement of rockets of various sorts and sizes which I see you stoop over and put the fusee to—some explode, some *catch* at the

rim and one is certain of them,—and if some few hang fire, seem-
ingly—they may no less go off of themselves when one least expects
it.... I witness to a great and noble lighting-up on the whole.[7]

Surely no bad description this of much of Browning himself! But
the most important element in the letter is the double confession, that in
the course of *Sordello* he had in certain passages spoken "in my own
person—not dramatically," and "knowing what my faith was and im-
measurably deeplier is" he would copy these out for Ruskin. All these
passages refer to that awareness of "Divine being or operation," which
Ruskin in his book had declared to be lacking in modern English poetry.

It is astonishing, leafing through *Sordello* in search of these passages,
to note how wide of the mark would have been one's guess. Not eternity
and time, not "the soul's absoluteness," not "This Human clear, as that
Divine concealed," not man, but nature

> The hermit bee
> Twirled so, and filed all day—The mansion's fit
> God counselled for—As easy guess the word
> That passed betwixt them, and became the third
> To (*God and*) the small, soft, unfrightened bee, as tax
> Him with one fault.

(*Alberic Romano was*)

> tied to a wild horse and trailed
> To death through rance and bramble-bush
> I take God's part and testify."

The insets are Browning's, and his testimony is to the nature whose
beauty and peace go on:

> Rustles the lizard and the cushats chirre
> Above the ravage.

But the final passage he chose was human—the

> child barefoot and rosy . . .
> Up and up goes he, singing all the while

>   Some unintelligible words to beat
>   The lark, God's poet, swooning at his feet.

By August of that year (1856) Ruskin was apologizing to Browning: "I was so ashamed of the way I had mangled that poem of yours that I dared not look you even by letter in the face." But by now he is sick of everything "except breakfast" and in no state "to attempt writing a letter to a poet. I don't see any use in poetry. I recollect you have written something nice about figs somewhere . . . after all there may be some sense in the kind of people who make railroads. . . . They say you are writing more poetry. I daresay I shall be very glad of this—someday—but I don't care just now." He has only enough animation left to wish the Brownings well "and to be sure that I am always affectionately Yours."[8]

Carlyle's real and profound belief in Browning, Browning's trust and belief in Carlyle brought forth yet another letter which one would give a great deal to be able to read. An irritating element in these correspondences is that we have Browning to Ruskin, Carlyle to Browning, but mostly suggestive indications only of the letters in between. Clearly this missing one from Browning was a real outpouring of soul to the man who was perhaps his chief ideal. How early Browning's letter was written we do not know, but in April, 1856 Carlyle is apologizing for his own delay in acknowledging a gift of *Men and Women* which came with it. He had read it "all, many of the Pieces again and again . . . able I was and am to give you *Euge!* Far beyond what I reckon you desire. . . . But you asked with so much loyalty, 'What shall I do to be saved, and gain the top of this sore upward course?'" He has long hesitated, having at length "renounced altogether the high thought of 'advising,' " having learned how "advice never fits the case; the case is not known to any Adviser, but only to the Advisee."

However, he will try—and what he had to say must have been heart-warming indeed of the

> excellent opulence of intellect in these two rhymed volumes: intellect in the big ingot shape and down to the smallest coin;—I shall

look far I believe to find such a pair of *eyes* as I see busy there in-
specting human life this long while. The keenest just insight into
men and things—and all that goes along with really good *insight*:
a fresh, valiant manful character, equipped with rugged humour,
with just love, just contempt, well carried and bestowed; in fine a
most extraordinary power of expression; such I must call it, whether
it be "expressive" *enough* or not. Rhythm there is too, endless
poetic fancy, symbolic *help* to express; and if not melody always or
often (for that would mean finish and perfection) there is what the
Germans call *Takt,* fine *dancing,* if to the music only of drums.[9]

Carlyle "in a private way" admits to himself "that here apparently is
the finest poetic genius, finest possibility of such, we have got vouch-
safed to us in this generation;" one which had "*grown,* in all ways since
I saw it last." It must *not* be lost in "the process of elaboration."

Such immense praise yet contained in it the seeds of the one criticism with which he felt he ought to be "equally honest. My friend it is
what they call 'unintelligibility!' That is a fact: you are dreadfully
difficult to understand." He is saying this in all sympathy; the cure is
not "easy, or the sin a mere perversity." He has himself had the same
struggle of "a man with very much to say," trying to say it in a world of
"the sordid, the prosaic, inane and unworthy. I see you pitching big
crags into the dirty, bottomless morass, trying to *found* your marble
work,—Oh it is a tragic condition withal!—But yet you *must* mend it
and alter." He will no longer forbid verse if Browning finds it "handier";
a man can be unintelligible in prose, too. One day Browning shall hear
his ideas of what poetry really is—meanwhile "Well, the sum of my
ideas is: if you took up some one *great* subject, and tasked all your
powers upon it for a long while, vowing to Heaven that you *would* be
plain to mean capacities, then—!—But I have done, *done.* Good be
with you always dear Browning; and high victory to sore fight!"

Author and publisher would contrive today to make known with
what excitement the foremost men of letters were admiring even when
they disagreed with Browning. Ruskin's opinion of a genius that had
caught the very heart of the Renaissance would have been printed on

the jacket of *Men and Women*. Leigh Hunt with a smile and Carlyle
with a growl would agree to let their words be used in advertisements.
But at that date books had no jackets. The art of advertisement was
hardly born, and Browning would have felt it in the worst possible
taste to send on private letters to his publishers. He did write to Chapman: "The half dozen people who know and could impose their opinions on the whole sty of grumblers say nothing to *them* (I don't wonder)
and speak so low in my own ear that it's lost to all intents and purposes . . ."

Why did not these friends, Carlyle especially, shout from the house-
tops instead of speaking "privately" to Browning and to themselves? He
lost much, I fancy, in those years through his absence abroad, but most
of all through his wife's fantastic popularity and a lazy, indifferent
publisher quite content that he should simply "look after commas and
dots to i's" in that best seller *Aurora Leigh*.

18 Friends, Family, and Frustration

Only one said, "I think the gesture strives
Against some obstacle we cannot see."

PRINCE HOHENSTIEL-SCHWANGAU

MR. BARRETT had characteristically refused to supply Kenyon's executors with Henrietta's address. She was to get a small legacy. But none of his strange acts, large or small, totally destroyed his hold on Elizabeth's affection. Relatives and friends had tried to bring about a reconciliation, but while saying he forgave his daughters, he declared that they had disgraced the family and to the last he refused to see them. Both had, of course, been cut out of his will.

In April, 1857, he died and Elizabeth wrote to Mrs. Jameson in July of "great bitterness which is natural. And some recoil against myself, more perhaps than is quite rational." She was beginning to recover and to "keep from vexing my poor husband who has been a good deal tried in all these things."

Imagination readily offers a picture of how much tried: to see his sick wife rending herself over the parent from whom she had with such difficulty been rescued; to hear her confess to a "sudden desolation" when all hope of a reconcilation—a hope she had deemed dead these many years—was again and finally extinguished.

Browning wrote to Hatty Hosmer a month after his father-in-law's death that Elizabeth had seen no one except Isa[1] and had not left the house: "She shall, if I have to carry her, before the week is out," he promised—and he did, indeed, bring his wife back to life, even if to a life less full than he had poured into her in Wimpole Street. We can hear an echo of the Love Letters: ". . . may you be better, less depressed. . . . Now *walk*, move . . . *anima mia dolce*."

Her heavy thoughts were not lightened by any of the family support commonly induced by a shared bereavement. Elizabeth's brothers had for years traveled freely—to Jamaica, to various countries in Europe, but never to Italy. She had always had to seek out these men who, perhaps out of fear of their father, had never come to her. Even now they did not stir; but Arabel, at last set free, she confidently expected, and wrote begging for a long visit. She was deeply disappointed to hear that Arabel had sold the Wimpole Street house only to buy a smaller one in Delamere Terrace. Her social work absorbed her, and her sister's pressure only hurt her feelings.

The countersuggestion was made that Elizabeth should go to England, now that the barrier to their free and full intercourse had disappeared. But her repugnance for England was certainly increasing as her strength diminished and the sisters were growing apart in many ways. It must have been a severe shock for Elizabeth to hear that Henrietta thought Browning's "Karshish" blasphemous. And Arabel was perhaps closer to the narrow Christianity of the chapels where Browning had suffered in boyhood, was more remote from the spiritual and intellectual world in which husband and wife were now living.

Elizabeth had to reassure both sisters that Pen would not become a Romanist; she allowed him to go into the churches, but Romanism was not catching like measles. Henrietta's husband urged Elizabeth to be definite as to what denomination she belonged to; Arabel was really afraid she was drifting toward Rome. "I who do not care," Elizabeth commented, "for Councils of the Church or any human authority, only for the scriptures and for experience, do not feel myself in danger."

There were in her eyes dangers far more serious than vagueness about the form of Christianity to be selected. She was, indeed, prejudiced against "Romanism," but in a letter to Mrs. Jameson she expressed herself with strange force against a deeper danger: "Tell me, is not the

Inquisitionist's burning of bodies to save souls really tender mercy by the side of the intolerance of those materialists, who for the mere aggrandisement of their barren doctrines will torture souls. . . . A fanatical religion is pitiable—but a fanatical infidel is hateful and horrible."[2]

To all definitely ranged in the ranks of this or that belief or unbelief the Brownings appear to have presented a puzzle. Their views were strong, yet their liberalism insisted that opposite views should be frankly expressed and listened to. Elizabeth could write more freely to Henrietta than to her dear Arabel about the problems which staying at Delamere Terrace would present for herself, for Robert, and for their hostess:

> There would be *gêne* on both sides. The irregularities of our house are scandalous—not immoral, observe, but scandalous. From morning till night people are running out and in—all sorts of people; and when we are in London we can't help it. There are men who come and talk—talk, some of them did last summer, till one in the morning—and the freest sort of philosophy is talked. Robert would be in agonies of annoyance, even if Arabel could bear it. Fancy Mr. Stratton elbowed on the staircase by Mr. So-and-So whose "aim in life" is to "subvert Christianity"!![3]

So to Lucca they went again that year, and here Browning's already frequent vigils were increased by the sudden illness of young Lytton, staying at the hotel nearby, with Isa Blagden, who insisted on nursing him herself. Browning wrote to Sarianna: "Through sentimentality and economy combined, Isa would have no nurse (an imbecile arrangement), and all has been done by her with me to help. I have sat up four nights out of the last five, and sometimes been there nearly all day besides. Imagine what a pleasant holiday we all have!"

Browning was devoted to Isa and put up with it all for her sake. She was fifteen years older than Lytton, but was probably in love with him, while he appeared deeply devoted to her. Lytton, however, was devoted to many women. Elizabeth wrote when early in 1859 they heard of his engagement: "Is it good for him indeed, Isa?—and is it not bad for HER indeed?—Pray be humane you who are magnanimous."

The Brownings never felt quite the same to him again. A little later

Elizabeth wrote: "Was ever a sinner who coquetted so with his sins? Poor Lytton. Strong enough for neither vice or virtue."

But that was in the future. Meanwhile, Lytton made a rapid recovery. The holiday began to look rosier and Browning told his sister of bathing "in the river, a rapid little mountain stream every morning at 6½ . . . The strength of all sorts therefrom accruing is wonderful . . . by the bye in this new book of Ruskin's, the drawing book, he says *Aurora Leigh* is the finest poem written in any language this century."

Wilson, married now to Ferdinando, seemed about to produce a baby and was returned to Florence for the better handling of the event. Whereupon Pen became ill—the same gastric fever as Lytton's, short but sharp. He sat up in bed looking like a wraith, but told his mother that their new maid "tells *novelle* quite finely! Stories of the devil and how he rides on a golden saddle and with a silver bridle. Per Bacco!"

Decidedly it was not one of the Browning's best summers, but about one incident he wrote with much pleasure to Leigh Hunt. He had discovered in the house of a Mrs. Sisted, known as Queen of the Baths, the original of "that divine little poem" of Shelley's "The Indian Serenade." Much interlined, "the characters are all but illegible. . . ." Browning had with a good magnifying glass "rescued three or four variations" which he encloses: "Are not all these better readings. . . . Then I give them you as you gave us Milton's hair."[4]

In March, 1858, Elizabeth writes cheerfully from the Casa Guidi. Robert had taken up homeopathy. He had been having "such violent attacks of headache that he talked of congestion on the brain," she told Arabel. But now "Not only is the liver quite relieved, but the irritability of his nervous system is calmed down to a degree which I should never have expected from any physical remedy." His appetite was better, his face showed the improvement, he had given up wine and was "the stronger and more cheerful for all his sacrifices."

That spring Home was expected in Florence and husband and wife had struck a bargain—he promising not to kill the medium in the street if she would promise not to go to a séance. At the last minute, however "Robert throws his arms round me, calls me 'Darling' and says that I shall do 'anything I like': but I won't be tempted out of our conventions, seeing that in spite of *nux vomica* Robert is still Robert."

They spent this summer at Le Havre, a place of few attractions. Sea bathing was advised for Elizabeth, Etretat proved impossible, and they needed a house where they could accommodate Arabel and a brother or two besides Sarianna and Mr. Browning. Milsand came for ten days and these were by far the best ten days for Browning. But both husband and wife felt the ugliness of the place, and both missed the sort of life led at Lucca or Siena in the villas and lanes and on the hills; above all they missed the Italian skies.

Browning wrote to Isa of Pen "minnowizing away among the Tritons," of his sister's enjoyment, and of the "fresh looks and rude health" of his father. "Best of all, Ba's improvement in health is incontestable and rapid." Yet he envied Isa up above Florence "where you so pleasantly perch. I shall never see anything so dear to me elsewhere."

A second letter laments the dull days, so filled in "doing the hospitable" that he has written no poetry. "I began pretty zealously—but it's of no use now: nor will the world very greatly care . . ."

Elizabeth, too, was missing the Casa Guidi. "Poor ghost of a Ba," she wrote to Fanny Haworth, "dislodged ghost. I long for my dear lower life in Florence and feel coldly the upper world here," despite "warm comfort and joy in holding my dearest Arabel's hand."

Two friends, shared by husband and wife, were very much alike in their circumstances, very different in character: Fanny Haworth and Isa Blagden. Both rather solitary, both with a small income, Isa was independent, managed to earn such luxuries as she wanted by her pen, and gave in her friendships at least as much as she received. Fanny was, Elizabeth felt, greatly to be pitied. Browning had hinted, years earlier, that she could do far better than she did as a writer. Elizabeth felt that her social ambitions had destroyed higher ones, and also that a fatal indecision blocked her from happiness. "Poor Fanny, she will stay in England and long for Florence."

Isa had many friends sharing the Bellosguardo villa's amenities and expenses. Fanny, after much vacillation, formed an alliance with one rich friend, bringing her ease and luxury. Elizabeth was much amused by this and other "female marriages," as she calls them with no faintest implication of what might today be suggested by such a term. She and Fanny corresponded regularly; and Browning reckoned Fanny as so much among his wife's "dear ones" that she had the right to a special letter about Elizabeth's death.

Of unknown and reputedly Eurasian descent, Isa had won a unique position for herself by force of character and by her unfailing kindness. "An eager little lady," said Henry James; "universally beloved," said T. A. Trollope; a "bright delicate, electric woman," Browning called her; and to Kate Field she was "Our Lady of Bellosguardo." The Brownings lent her the Casa Guidi when they were in Rome, and entreated her to think of their books and belongings as her own. Browning wrote to her constantly, telling her of every improvement in Elizabeth's health, to "set your own dear quick-beating heart at ease." To her he later expressed his rage over the unfairness in England to *Poems before Congress,* repeating the publisher's jest that he hopes "the apartments in the Castle of St. Angelo [Rome's Tower of London!] are comfortable." As with Ruskin both husband and wife write, and Browning, parodying "emphatic opera singers," ends one letter "T'abbracio, ti striiiiiiiiiiingo." He tells her he has been "a fool" to let Elizabeth catch cold, depicts Landor's behavior, sends every bit of gossip he can gather.

One long letter is devoted to a careful and encouraging criticism of Isa's writing; in another he admits his own many weak points, but also insists on his love of justice which should come before charity. Later he would refuse with characteristic crudity to subscribe to a fund for Mrs. Jameson's sisters; they had "sucked her dry" all her life, and now she is gone. "I don't feel inclined to offer the least squeeze from my nipples." With Isa Blagden, Browning is always in his shirt sleeves.

How one wonders did Barretts and Brownings mix at such close quarters? It was certainly in Paris that Elizabeth enjoyed Arabel most before the return to Italy.

William Allingham, who delighted in getting the friends he admired to talk of one another, records in his diary Tennyson's assenting to his description of Browning as "a vivid man," adding, "How he did flourish about when he was here." Now in Paris, calling on Thackeray at the Hotel Bristol, Allingham mentioned he had just been seeing Browning.

> "Browning was here this morning," Thackeray said. "What spirits he has—almost too much for me in my weak state. He almost blew me out of bed!"
> "A wonderful fellow, indeed!"
> "Yes, and he doesn't drink wine."
> "He's already screwed up to concert pitch."
> "Far above it. But I can't manage his poetry. What do you say?" (I spoke highly of it).
> "Well, you see, I want poetry to be musical, to run sweetly."
> "So do I"—
> "Then that *does for* your friend B.!"
> I spoke of Browning's other qualities as so splendid as to make him, as it were, a law in himself. But Thackeray only smiled and declined further discussion.
> "He has a good belief, in himself, at all events. I suppose he doesn't care whether people praise him or not."
> "I think he does, very much."
> "O does he? Then I'll say something about him in a number."[5]

Le Havre to Paris, Paris to Florence, Florence to Rome, Rome to Florence, Florence to Siena—the strain must have been considerable on the "unpractical" poet responsible for all practical arrangements, and for the care of a delicate woman, a child, and a household. For they always took maid and usually man, engaging furnished rooms, sometimes the same as in a previous year, sometimes looked for from a nearby hotel. The yellow-satin-furniture suite had conveyed its lesson: of their friends only the Storys could be trusted to discover anything suitable.

Many of the journeys were not without adventure. This year coming to France they had slept on the deck with nothing between them and the boards, to avoid a cabin packed with seasick passengers. Returning after a rather painful crossing of the Alps (Elizabeth, Browning wrote to Allingham, had had no food but a crust of bread for fourteen hours), they took ship from Genoa to Leghorn and in a *burrasca* "reeled about the sea in our little old Neapolitan boat." The journey took so long that they were given up for lost. Entering the Casa Guidi, Elizabeth met a friend who "stared at me aghast, as at a ghost of an old inhabitant of the house haunting the ancient place . . . Robert and I are delighted to feel here in a divine abstraction from civilized life."

But this "abstraction" would as usual be short lived. Only a month later, some American friends, Mr. and Mrs. Eckley, offered the Brownings their carriage for the journey to Rome. Insisting on paying for the hire of horses, they gratefully accepted the carriage. But of leaving Florence so quickly Pen remarked, "I must say it's the only *stupid* thing I ever did know you and Papa to do." On the journey two oxdrivers, hired to drag them up a mountain, had a furious row and one went for the other with his knife. "Robert rushed in between them and was thrown down," while Pen shrieked and Elizabeth "did the next best and fainted or all but fainted." They had already nearly gone over a precipice and another family had on that same road been robbed by bandits. But the knife had only torn Browning's coat, so they came off pretty well.

Sarianna was the main safety valve for Elizabeth's rage over the neglect of her husband by the English public.

Because of her own success, she wrote:

> I complain more about Robert, only he does not hear me complain. To *you* I may say that the blindness, deafness, and stupidity of the English public to Robert are amazing . . . while in America he's a power, a writer, a poet. . . . "Browning readings" here in Boston, "Browning evenings" there. . . . "It's worth *eating much dirt*" said an Englishman of high family and character here, "to get to Lady ———'s soirée." Americans will eat dirt to get to *us*. There's the difference . . . physicians, dentists, who serve me and refuse their fees . . . friends who give up their carriages and make other practical sacrifices are *not English*—no. . . .

This same neglectful public was ready enough to lionize Browning socially, as an asset in himself and not merely as the husband of the famous "poetess."

Elizabeth had gradually grown more social during the years when she had to persuade her husband that too much solitude was a mistake. It may be that he feared his own appetite for society which, once yielded to, would become enormous. And he was enormously popular, despite his tendency to bring out an intended compliment dangerously in reverse, saying to Mrs. Story, "I had a delightful evening at your house. *I never spoke to you once*"; and to a young artist discouraged over his work, "But, my dear fellow, if you were satisfied you would be so very easily satisfied."

Elizabeth advised·him to avoid compliments and stick to politics, but she wrote to Sarianna "the women admire him everywhere too much for decency." And in Rome, "the most dissipated of places (to which Paris is grave and quiet)," Elizabeth describes her husband as scarcely knowing "if he stands on his feet or his head. . . . Dissipations decidedly agree with Robert there's no denying that, though he's terribly hypocritical, and prefers an evening with me at home, which has grown to be a kind of dissipation also."

The social life of Rome still whirled around them, Elizabeth as well as Robert being caught up in it—the occasional picnic, the frequent drive. Late nights away from her own fireside she avoided. But "We have soirées I assure you," she wrote to Arabel, "of as many as can be packed in our room—I pour out the tea in a corner, and Ferdinando carries it round on a tray." The Storys came and the Eckleys; Motley, the historian; Leighton, the painter; Odo Russell, the Cartwrights, Marshalls, Brackens.

This was in the Bocca di Leone, but it is hard to tell today either there or in the Via del Tritone how much of the present layout was included in their apartment. The Via del Tritone house is now offices, entirely remodeled, and the people there had never heard the name of Browning. But at 43 Bocca di Leone the poets were still a *"bel ricordo"* for their successors in the house that harbored them when Italy was in the making. A plaque on the wall declares immortal the songs in which they had prophetically announced her new destinies.

Put up on the centenary of Browning's birth by the Roman Municipality, it quoted in translation an overquoted verse:

Aprendo il mio cuore vi trovareste inciso Italia.

> Open my heart and you will see
> Graved inside of it, "Italy."

They had here ten rooms of varying sizes, none of them very big, but the sitting room was adequate to accommodate themselves and at least thirteen named guests. It was used early in 1859 for a smaller, more intimate affair.

"We have had a wedding here," writes Elizabeth to Arabel, "and Robert has 'given away' the bride, who is no other than Miss Fox." (This was the Eliza known as Tottie, who described the youthful Browning playing the piano on his birthday while the church bells pealed a greeting.) "Mr. Fox," Elizabeth went on, "had written from England to entreat Robert to take his place at the ceremony." And then they had bride and bridegroom and bride's cousin to dinner with "champagne and everything in order." But alas it did not end there, for Elizabeth felt obliged to agree that Tottie should paint her picture, sadly lamenting as the sittings proceeded that she "began by looking young and coarse like a milkmaid . . . and will end by being old and coarse like a cook."

Elizabeth had, by 1858, reached the peak of her success, but her health was becoming more and more precarious. After one of their broken nights she wrote to Sarianna: "If it had not been that I feared much to hurt him in having him so disturbed and worried, it would have been a very subtle luxury to me, this being ill and feeling myself dear. Do not set me down as too selfish."

But gradually the allusions to her health became less cheerful: "forgive my poor brittle body," she writes to Fanny Haworth, "which shakes and breaks." And to Mrs. Martin "The weight of the whole year . . . seems to have stamped out of me the vital fluid."

They had perhaps been presuming too much on the restored health of so many years—crossing the Alps in November, spending the night on the boards of an open deck, traveling in a cockleshell of a boat. She speaks in her letters of the greatly increased comfort when, thanks to the Kenyon legacy, they need no longer choose the cheapest modes of travel. But after Le Havre the axis of their lives became Florence, Rome, Siena. At Siena, in 1859, the Storys with Edith and two small boys were in a neighboring villa, Isa Blagden in a tiny cabin of a dwelling, and Walter Savage Landor with the Storys until Browning could find a room for him nearby. For he had adopted the old lion, now in his eighties, after his family had either turned him out or had been finally repudiated by him. "I believe," he wrote to Isa in August, 1859, "I am to have the poor dear old man permanently 'added to my portion' as the Methodists phrase it. *You* do the sister-of-charity business generally —and I am bound to act my best on 'Mr. Browning's First and Only Appearance in that Character, at particular Request,'—I hope I may add 'The Performance being exclusively for the Benefit of a distinguished Member of the Company.'"

He began by arranging for Landor's permanent residence, found rooms in Florence and had them decorated "very superiorly," bought furniture and rescued the old man's belongings from his family. Mme. Ferdinando Romagnoli, still spoken of as Wilson, undertook the charge of him and he was gradually being tamed, until only very occasionally would he dash the plate onto the floor if his dinner displeased him, or if she brought it a few minutes late. At Siena in the summer, Browning listened to him patiently, read aloud to him his own poetry, and coaxed the old lion into roaring softly.

Landor, though writing some elegant poetry, had won his chief fame by his *Imaginary Conversations*. "All the culture of the encyclopedists," says Ezra Pound, "reduced to manageable size and full of human life ventilated, given a human body, not merely indexed." Pound selects in *The ABC of Reading* some of Landor's poems which he justly calls "cantabile," and claims that Landor was "so far ahead of his British times that the country couldn't contain him."

But in fact it was not Landor's writing or ideas which drove him from his country, but his misfortunes, quarrels, and vendettas. He was often abominably treated, but he did not make it easy for anyone to treat him well. He wrote of himself: "I strove with none for none was worth my strife." Strange words from a man who had fled abroad to escape an action for slander brought by a clergyman's wife who was, he had hinted, a Lesbian.

Even had they been kind, which they clearly were not, Landor was the last man to endure patiently a life of dependence on his son and his son's wife.

Browning not only loved Landor, but was grateful to him for the poem which compared him to Chaucer on the roads of England—and then in Italy:

> But warmer climes
> Give brighter plumage, stronger wing; the breeze
> Of Alpine heights thou playest with, borne on
> Beyond Sorrento and Amalfi, where
> The Siren waits thee, singing song for song.

There were, too, in Landor qualities of generosity and affection for his friends, brought out in the rather idealized portrait drawn by Dickens. William Rossetti, staying with the Storys, recognized him as Boythorne in *Bleak House*. "He wore a large loose cap around which various flies were weaving their disquieting dance." Though "mildly composed" he said, "in a tone of resolved conviction, 'I have considered the matter, and I find that, of the many vile nuisances existing on the face of the earth, flies are the most strictly intolerable.' "

Elizabeth had no great liking for Landor. He was a burden on "dear darling Robert," who amused her by talking of " 'his gentleness and sweetness. . . .' Of self-restraint he has not a grain, and of suspiciousness many grains." Then, too, he hated Louis Napoleon. "Mrs. Browning," Edith Story recalled, "would be stirred past endurance by these assaults on her hero . . . and would raise her treble voice even to a shrill pitch in protest, until Mr. Browning would come into the fray as mediator."

All three Hawthornes write about the Brownings, who had been introduced to them in 1856 by Monckton Milnes, later Lord Houghton. Milnes's breakfast parties are his chief claim to fame. Carlyle used to say, Froude tells us, "that if Christ came again on earth Milnes would ask him to breakfast and the clubs would all be talking of the 'good things' that Christ had said."

Hawthorne thought Browning "simple and agreeable in manner, gently impulsive—talking as if his heart were uppermost." He was delighted to be told that of all his works *The Blythedale Romance* was Browning's favorite. "I hope I showed as much pleasure at his praise as he did at mine,—for I was glad to see how pleasantly it moved him." Although the two families never became intimate, it was to Browning that Una Hawthorne turned, after her mother's death, for help in deciphering the manuscript of *Septimus*.

Pen dances delightfully in and out of the letters and memoirs of the period. Mrs. Hawthorne meeting him in the passage felt he "looked like a waif of poetry, lovelier still in the bright light of the drawing room." At tea, passing the cakes, he was "graceful as Ganymede."

English visitors and all later biographers dwell on the golden curls and girlish dress, although this was not so startling in the Italy of those years as it seems universally today. In England at the age of six Pen had offered to fight a lad of twelve to show him that he too was a boy. But in Italy, Mrs. Hugh Fraser describes him as "well dressed" and he believed his new jacket had attracted the attention of the Queen of Naples. "I am," he claimed, "one of the sights of Rome!"

He was reading Dumas at nine, playing Beethoven at ten, and "has not given up drawing neither," wrote Elizabeth to Ruskin. But one Christmas, when his presents are recorded just before his ninth birthday, he received (by request) "a sword to dazzle the eyes," a box of tools and a carpenter's bench, and *Robinson Crusoe*. A little later, when told the story of St. John, he decided that the fate of the Apostle on Patmos was just like Robinson Crusoe.

He had been having lessons—Latin and mathematics—from a young Abbé with, said Elizabeth, a secret sympathy for the Risorgimento who came with them from Rome to Siena. Edith Story became his second pupil and Pen worked better, his mother said, not to be disgraced before her. She was many years his senior and he had a great affection for her. Landor spoke of Abelard and Heloise—Pen, not the Abbé, being Abelard.

His father gave him a handsome pony and brought it back to Rome with a groom to take charge of it. "I am supposed to be the spoiler," commented Elizabeth. They had to find some riding companions for Pen. "I object to Hatty Hosmer who has been thrown thirty times," his mother said. Wearing a crimson blouse, Pen was presented to various small Italian princes with whom he talked of ponies and played at leapfrog.

But better than princes or ponies were the Italian *contadini* whose sheep he helped to herd, whose cows he chased, whose games he learned, whose grapes he picked, "driving in the grape-carts (exactly of the shape of the Greek chariots), with the grapes heaped up round him . . . galloping thro' the lanes on his pony the colour of his curls." He read aloud the Venetian poet, Dall Ongaro, to the applauding grape-gatherers in the evening and "ate so many grapes he could eat nothing else whatever."

"*Sono Italiano*," Pen would say, and in his journal his mother read: "This is the happiest day of my hole (*sic*) life, for now dearest Vittorio Emanuele is really *nostro re*."

Getting near eleven, he resolved, he told his mother, to have no toys for Christmas; he would have "a microscope instead and study nature." She sent him to choose presents for some other children and he came back disconsolate. "I know it's foolish of me, Mama, but the shop looked so beautiful and everybody buying . . . and the *passionate* love of the old things came back to me, and I couldn't be *energetic* about the microscope any more." He wanted a toy gun instead. "After all, you see Mama, I am *not* a man yet."[6]

An engaging mixture of boy and child, speaking brokenly four languages, tenderhearted, talented, full of enterprise, but with no natural quality of perseverence and thoroughly spoiled through the best years for learning it, he emerges nonetheless as an entrancing little creature whom one would have spoiled with the rest of them—his parents and Wilson, Ferdinando and the Italian *contadini*—and even the French soldiers. He encountered a regiment on the Pincio, "made friends with ever so many captains," marched in their ranks, talked to some musical ones about Chopin and Stephen Heller, and with all about politics. "He had never been so happy in his life," but it was, indeed, a very happy life altogether. He did not see the shadows darkening. But Elizabeth wrote to Mrs. Martin in December, 1860, "For the first time I have had pain in looking into his face lately—which you will understand."

19 The Pope, Napoleon, and the Rest

"Come with me and deliver Italy!"

PRINCE HOHENSTIEL-SCHWANGAU

THE BROWNINGS had shown their faith in the country's future by investing most of their money in Italy. Arabel, in 1859, wrote inquiring how their "Tuscan funds" were affected by the war. "I said to Robert," Elizabeth answered, " 'Really I never thought of our money till this moment.' 'But I did' he returned. We are neither of us uneasy." Much more interesting to her was the fact of being visited by "Massimo d'Azeglio . . . one of the very noblest men in Italy," who had told them, "It is '48 over again with matured actors."

But a little later she was admitting that the money had depreciated "for the moment." It would be foolish to sell out, "our interests are here just as our hearts are in this cause."

And in another letter deploring the "infamous *lies* of The Times— I say *lies* . . . Arabel . . . I don't say mistakes," she says. "I used to have literal physical palpitations over the newspapers—tears in my eyes, sobs in my throat." Her pain *about England* shows her she is more of a patriot than she had thought.

It is not really surprising that *The Times* was at that date regarded abroad as the voice of England, considering how seriously its reports and articles were taken by the leading statesmen of both parties. Palmerston, the Whig premier, wrote to the editor in 1858, suggesting "less

personal asperity of tone" about Napoleon III, Elizabeth's idol, and in
March 1859 pressed home the danger of exasperating the Emperor until
"French means of aggression and English means of Defence are more
nearly equalized . . ." The Orsini plot to murder the Emperor had been
hatched by political refugees in England, and the bomb unsuccessfully
thrown was made in Birmingham! Like most Englishmen, *The Times*
Editor was friendly to Italy but both he and his correspondent in Paris
detested Napoleon and, although condemning the attempted assassination, hoped that the British government would make no concessions
"immediately after the offensive demonstrations which have been made
in France."

Elizabeth's "patriotism" was not of the same brand as that of *The
Times; Poems before Congress* published early in 1860 would identify
her in British eyes with the "offensive" demonstrators of Paris.

The funds were an excellent excuse for not going to England either
in '59 or '60. They would, wrote Elizabeth, certainly recover, it was only
a question of waiting. The Brownings were, besides, contributing as
much as they could afford to the war effort, and they did not want to
leave Italy at this exciting time. Elizabeth's intimates may have breathed
a sigh of relief, so violently abusive of England had her letters become.
On this subject as on spiritualism, there was a growing imbalance which
in calmer moments she recognized. "Just now," she wrote in March
1859, "I am scarcely of sane mind about Italy. It even puts down the
spirit subject. I pass through cold stages of anxiety and white heats of
rage."

And in July or August '59 to Sarianna "This is to certify that I am
alive after all, yes and getting stronger. Though the sense left to me is
of a peculiar frailty of being; no very marked opinion upon my hold of
life . . ."

In her more fevered states she seems curiously to match the Italian
scene which obsessed her. To the cool observer, however sympathetic,
there is about it all an atmosphere of grand opera: how fitted for the
stage are the declamations of Mazzini, his melancholy face, his unchang-
ing black, the continuing cloak-and-dagger conspiracies, the abortive
risings he inspired which were making him abhorrent to those who had

once ardently admired him. Working underground from England he did not understand the changes in Italy—on the one hand the growing strength of Piedmont, on the other the danger of premature risings. For each revolt was put down by Austria with attendant cruelties and made the solid work harder of building towards a free and united Italy.

Asked by Isa Blagden to help a fund for the Mazzinian Revolutionaries, Browning wrote "every sort of conceivable horror, shootings, burnings and murderings—and all absolutely to no good—to the victims' country, nor to Italy generally: and now that the failure is complete—*subscribe,* shall I?"

The words "cloak and dagger" conjure up the scene of de Rossi's assassination—a scene of grand opera if ever there was one—the young men hiding the murderer with their cloaks and shouting, as it might be singing, "Abasso Rossi, Morte a Rossi." And the scarlet blouse and white horse of Garibaldi; the single gun which could not be fired, but which was ceremoniously dragged along in the Sicilian invasion and, as a "property" of the invincible Garibaldi, struck terror into the opposing forces. Everything about Garibaldi is a little larger than life, but not at all too large for song and stage.

The Pope was back in Rome, and on matters domestic and material was proceeding with reforms. He had disbanded the army hurriedly recruited in 1848, Roman taxes were light and the national debt disappeared. The government was paternal, but the number of lay functionaries much increased. The Pope had been well received in Rome, although elsewhere—and especially in England, now crowded with exiles—his fantastic popularity had disappeared. He was spoken of now with contempt and loathing.

The French ambassador, Rayneval, had written in 1856 to his country's Foreign Minister, praising all that had been done in the line of hospitals, prisons, charitable establishments, expansion of trade, building of houses—and this with a taxation less than half that paid by Frenchmen. He concluded: "the pontifical administration bears the marks of wisdom, reason and progress." It was not what his government wished to hear and he lost his job shortly thereafter. For Napoleon had already begun the rather devious game he was to play between Rome

and Turin, and an attack on papal administration was a necessary pre-
liminary.

The renewal of the Italian struggle in 1858 is more familiar to most
of us than the "dress rehearsal" of ten years earlier. Cavour had worked
steadily, not for the federation wanted by Gioberti and the Pope, but
for a united Italy ruled by the King of Piedmont. He had committed
Piedmont to supplying a small army, drawn from Sardinia, on the side
of France and England in the Crimea. Thus Piedmont could put the
Italian case at the peace table.

As tortuous in his own way as Napoleon, though more single-
minded, he conferred with the Emperor secretly at Plombières; and at
the opening of the Piedmont Parliament in 1859 Victor Emmanuel
spoke of the "*grido di dolore*" reaching him from all parts of Italy. The
Neapolitan ambassador turned pale, those from neutral countries,
England, Prussia, Russia—and France—were deeply impressed. It is
said that Napoleon had suggested these words to Cavour, and he had
already paved the way by his own attitude when the Italian political
refugee, Orsini, had attempted to assassinate him a few months earlier.
The bomb killed eight people in the crowd, but Napoleon expressed
sympathy for a misguided patriot driven to violence.

Cavour now set himself skillfully to irritate Austria that that country
might appear the aggressor, and an Austrian demand for the disarma-
ment of Sardinia, followed by a curt refusal, produced the desired declaration of war. France joined her army to that of Piedmont and they won
in June the victory of Magenta, entered Milan in triumph and won the
double battle of Solferino and San Martino.

And then Napoleon ceased to be the generous ally, and met the
Emperor of Austria at Villafranca to arrange terms of peace.

Perhaps one reason which makes it so difficult to understand Browning's *Prince Hohenstiel-Schwangau Saviour of Society* is that it is almost
impossible to understand Napoleon III. Earlier the Brownings had been
in Paris during the Emperor's *coup d'état* when Mrs. Browning declared
that after all he marched by the will of the people. Browning was at
least doubtful then, but when he began to write about him soon after

Villafranca, he was more doubtful still. When he wrote (or completed) the poem after Sedan, "It is," he wrote to Isa Blagden, "just what I imagine the man might, if he pleased, say for himself."

Whether he *would*—or even could—ever have said it is another question; and doubtless his own moods would vary between self-condemnation and self-defense:

> The universal vote we have: its urn
> We also have where votes drop, fingered o'er
> By the universal Prefect.

Was not that, to be honest, the state of things with most votes when an Emperor had to be considered? A tyrant in France, Napoleon expended all his liberal feelings on Poland and Italy. Cardinal Antonelli had replied sarcastically to one of his demands for reform in the Papal States by asking whether there was so much liberty in France that they wanted to export their surplus. In the private meeting at Plombières, Napoleon had demanded the annexation to France of Savoy and Nice, in return for his services in establishing the Kingdom of North Italy; but Cavour resented bitterly the full price now demanded for a half-done job. At Villafranca, Austria gave up Lombardy, but kept Venice. Tuscany, Parma, Modena and the Roman legations were added to the Northern Kingdom (by plebiscite) in the following year and France could in a sense claim that this was her work. She also claimed that Nice and Savoy were in fact French in composition, but the plebiscite there was held only *after*, and in confirmation of, the annexation. The "universal Prefect" was already a Frenchman!

Napoleon said that he had feared a Mazzinian revolution all over Italy, and certainly Mazzini in the background can never be forgotten. And the Italian populace had on the whole failed to volunteer for his army, while the Pope had been rapturously received on a tour of his States not long before. The Austrians were renowned for the cruelty with which they suppressed revolts; better wait and see, was probably the instinct of most Italians. Writing to congratulate Elizabeth on her lack of patriotism—"we and Prussia chiefly, shall be punished hereafter"—Ruskin lamented the Italian weakness. "It is not life. It is only galvanism—or at least the first staggering motion of a man blind and bound for half his life." As for the payment, it is likely that Browning has caught the varying moods of the Emperor—and his hand on the national pulse of France:

> Come with me and deliver Italy!
> Smite hip and thigh until the oppressor leave
> Free from the Adriatic to the Alps
> The oppressed one! . . .
>   "All for nought—
> Not even, say, some patch of province splice
> O'er the frontier? Some snug honorarium-fee
> Shut into glove and pocketed apace?"
> (Questions Sagacity) "in deference
> To the natural susceptibility
> Of folks at home, unwitting of that pitch
> You soar to . . .
>   . . . but prompt
> To recognize the cession of Savoy
> And Nice as marketable value!"

In the poem Napoleon repudiates this prompting of Sagacity: Let her prompt Metternich, not him; but in brute fact he followed it. "So Italy was free"; and France had made a first-rate bargain.

Italy Napoleon saw as a Federation, a United States of Italy, with the Pope as Chairman of the Board, his spiritual authority unquestioned —a free Church in a free State. Pius hesitated: one wonders what Cavour would have done if he had accepted. For the extremists in the Piedmont Parliament were against giving the Pope any position at all in the new Italy. They wanted the Papal States—the Romagna, Umbria and the Marches—with no question of indemnity for the Pope. And in the Romagna, Cavour was already closing convents.

The Pope's mind was made up when he realized that Napoleon assumed that the Romagna already belonged to Piedmont. He was first to lose a state and then to accept only limited powers over those that remained. He refused—on the strange principle we have noticed. Christ's robe was being torn "which remained whole even on the hill of Calvary," and he must share Christ's sufferings rather than be a party to this desecration.

The Sardinians, not satisfied with the Romagna, determined to invade Umbria and the Marches, while Cavour, not declaring war on Naples, was secretly supporting Garibaldi in his "Crusade of The Thousand"—for this was the tiny army with which he set out to conquer, or liberate, Sicily. "Try to navigate," wrote Cavour to Admiral Persano, "between Garibaldi and the Neapolitan cruisers. I hope you understand me."

More volunteers joined Garibaldi including some of the Sicilian peasants, who ran away at the first noise of guns but presently became useful soldiers. Naples was well and truly hated in the island. Palermo fell, the whole of Sicily was conquered and Garibaldi, without pausing, returned swifty to the mainland, entered Naples, and defeated the Neapolitan armies at the battle of Volturno. With no personal ambitions, he sought only to offer his conquest to Victor Emmanuel as "a new and brilliant jewel" for his crown. He himself would return to his goats and rocks on the island of Caprera.[1]

Meanwhile the Piedmont regular army were advancing against volunteer forces responding from many countries to the Pope's appeal for defenders of the States of the Church: young Irishmen came, sons of most of the French legitimists, Belgians and Poles—all with as great a sense of dedication as Garibaldi's Thousand. Less well led, too briefly welded into an army, they won the admiration of their foes when, greatly outnumbered, they were defeated at the battle of Castelfidardo. Umbria and the Marches were now added to the crown of Piedmont.

Napoleon had gone on a cruise and was inaccessible for the fortnight of this strange swift war. His armies did nothing except keep the Piedmontese from entering Rome and insist they depart from the narrow territory known as the Patrimony of St. Peter.

"So well I was," wrote Elizabeth, "with all the advantages of Rome in me, looking so well, that I was tired of hearing people say so . . . it was the blow on the *heart* about the peace, after all that excitement and exaltation . . . and then the sudden stroke and fall, and the impotent rage against all the nations of the earth— . . . Robert has been perfect to me. For more than a fortnight he gave up all his nights' rest to me, and even now he teaches Pen." And again, "my poor Robert who nursed me like an angel, prevented from sleeping for full three weeks."

And about the same time to Isa Blagden: "I dreamed lately that I followed a mystic woman . . . in white, with a white mask, on her head the likeness of a crown. I knew she was Italy. . . . All through my illness political dreams have repeated themselves, in inscrutable articles of peace and eternal provisional governments." And to Mr. Chorley: "I have been living and dying for Italy."

This was the woman who, discussing her own country, felt that "patriotism in the narrow sense is a virtue which will wear out, sooner or later, everywhere. Jew and Greek must drop their antagonisms; and if Christianity is ever to develop it will not respect frontiers." It was Robert, not she, who had been "frantic" about the horrors of the Crimean war. She "never, at worst, thought that the great tragedy of the world was going on *there* . . . there are more chronic cruelties and deeper wrongs."

Maybe, but one can only agree with the diagnosis of Henry James: "Mrs. Browning's correspondence," he says, "flushes and turns pale" as her letters "reflect her passion, her feverish obsession, with extraordinary vivacity and eloquence; but it is impossible not to feel, as we read, that to 'care,' in the common phrase, as she is caring is to entertain one's convictions as a malady and a doom. . . ." She had lost, James felt, that "saving and sacred sense of proportion," which great poets and geniuses keep "even in emotion and passion, even in pleading a cause and calling on the gods . . . we absolutely feel the beautiful mind and the high gift discredited by their engrossment."

James has a curious half sentence in this analysis "while the pulses of her companion much more clearly throb," which must refer to Browning and is certainly true of him. On this matter of a free and united Italy he was far from the opposition to his wife that marked his attitude on spiritualism. On only one point did he disagree—her curious estimate of Napoleon III. He annoyed her by the remark, "It was a great action; but he has taken eighteenpence for it, which is a pity." And although she admitted that it was "indelicate" to station

French soldiers in Savoy, to oversee the so-called free vote as to whether this people desired to belong to France, she still assumed that it would *be* a free vote. Henry James was in Switzerland at "the hour in which the French Emperor was to be paid by Victor Emmanuel the price of the liberation of Lombardy," and he recalled the "passionate protests" of the terrified Swiss as the power of "enormous and triumphant France . . . to absorb great mouthfuls was being so strikingly exhibited."[2] But Elizabeth was writing: "The wailing in England for the Swiss and Savoyards, while other nationalities are to be trodden underfoot without intervention except what's called *aggression,* is highly irritating to me."

Very different from James's were the reactions of another American, Kate Field, who shared Elizabeth's views and had attached herself to the Brownings two years earlier in Rome. "You are very ambitious," Browning said to her approvingly; and, indeed, both husband and wife immensely appreciated the enterprising young Americans, Margaret Fuller, Hatty Hosmer, Kate Field, who defied convention and risked penury to do good work and win renown. Kate Field sacrificed a fortune by refusing to obey the rich uncle whose heir she was to be if she returned to the States and abandoned some of her social and political views. She wrote for various periodicals and was at this time poorly paid enough. Later she became an immensely successful journalist, running for five years a newspaper entitled *Kate Field's Washington.* And by an extraordinary turn of fate the fortune she had lost was made up for by shares given her by the Bell Telephone Company in gratitude for her skill and grace in demonstrating this marvelous new invention to Queen Victoria! The shares grew to the value of some two hundred thousand dollars, worth today well over a million.

Kate's position in the expatriate world of Italy was certainly not diminished by her radiant good looks. Her auburn hair is described and her blue eyes, which she matched on occasion with dress and hair ribbons. At a party where she showed the quality of her voice, the celebrated actress, Charlotte Cushman, was amazed, urged her to get first-class lessons, and with Isa Blagden welcomed Kate into their group of emancipated women. In the summer of 1860 she was in Florence and relieved both Brownings by sharing the ever-present burden of

Landor. Meeting him at Isa's house, she so entranced him that he told Elizabeth she was "the most charming young lady he had ever seen," "and you know, dear Kate," said Elizabeth, "he has seen a great many."

He offered to teach her Latin. She went daily for her lesson, spoke of him as "chivalry incarnate" and discerned "something of heaven about him." One evening, again at Isa's, as Kate kissed both her hostess and Elizabeth, Landor asked her, "Do you mean to stop there?" Getting a kiss himself he declared it the happiest day of his life. "Had I been sixty years younger you would not have kissed me." Not content with complimenting her in Latin phrase, he wrote a poem about the kiss—

> . . . given me in the sight of more
> Than ever saw me kissed before. . . .
> She came across nor greatly feared
> The horrid break of wintry beard.

At each of his own sallies Landor would "laugh immoderatley." The phrase recurs in the descriptions and one can fancy Elizabeth's relief that the old man should have a worshiping young girl to—yes, positively, to enjoy it![3]

Kate's letters home and letters to her from the Brownings bring again the sense of youth and gaiety at the Casa Guidi so vivid in Harriet Hosmer's memories. But there are two differences. Curiously enough it is the sculptor not the journalist who remembers the style of both Brownings' speech, thus bringing the past to life; but too one feels her past with them six years ago had more life in it. When Elizabeth's *Poems before Congress* were published, a letter from Browning congratulates Kate on being almost alone in understanding that greatly maligned volume. It is an angry and a sad one. The high spirits of the early fifties were chiefly his, they could still break out and did, but Elizabeth's physical ill health and mental misery could not but affect the atmosphere.

Something was happening with the Brownings, especially with Elizabeth, that so often happens as time draws on and acquaintance and admirers multiply. Many, many years later Browning wrote to Mrs. Fitzgerald, likening carelessness about health "to a foolish dancing one's heart over a precipice—and the only hard words my wife ever got from me were just on that account,—when she would run risks, be forgetful of taking meals, allow herself to be talked half-dead by inconsiderate visitors." There had been an occasion when two women were "each determined to sit the other out"—and one does not doubt Browning when he asserts "I used to grow brutal when her poor face began to show suffering."

Kate Field was not of such; she had sensitivity as well as gaiety, a sensitivity responding to what she felt as a "magnetic flood of love and poetry that was constantly passing between husband and wife."

Why, it has been asked, if Browning agreed with Elizabeth on the Italian situation, did he leave her alone to write about it?—it is even asked passionately why he did not speak out against the Emperor—long ago, in Paris, when Elizabeth and Pen were cheering his progress, after the bloody crushing of a popular insurrection. It was, one gathers, an act of treachery to Shelley's memory. Why, indeed, did not this admirer of his die on the barricades?

It is interesting that in fact Browning had in his essay on Shelley answered the question before it could be asked. Shelley's idealism had in youth led him to endeavor "to realise as he went on idealising; every wrong had simultaneously its remedy." And thus he committed himself to "expedients" often misconceived. But "gradually he was raised above the contemplation of spots and the attempt at effacing them, to the great abstract light and through the discrepancy of the creation, to the sufficiency of the First Cause. Gradually he was learning that the best way of removing abuses was to stand fast by truth."

Browning saw his own vocation also as the poet's; there were scores of fields where the social and political reformer must work, but all of them are relative. The poet is a man sent by God. His function is akin to that of the prophet: reading men and nature, proclaiming what he sees, he speaks for the speechless. As Robert Langbaum has pointed out, when Browning gets inside a man in a dramatic monologue, he unlocks the truth—not "by interpreting the facts according to some theory but by restoring to the facts their life, the beating hearts and high-blooded ticking brains of two centuries since." It is not insignificant that, just as he did not consider "Bishop Blougram's Apology" an attack but an Apologia, he was abused and praised later for blackening *and* for whitewashing Napoleon III in *Prince Hohenstiel-Schwangau.*

He was discovering "the most vital form" of the new period in the poetry that he was inaugurating. And like Eliot and Joyce, the former of whom owed him so great a debt, he was working to "dig below the ruins of official tradition to discover in myth an underground tradition, an inescapable because inherently psychological pattern into which to fit the chaotic present."[4]

Was Browning to abandon this effort, never more perfectly achieved than in *Men and Women,* in order to write what in an hour of constantly changing fortunes would be perhaps inappropriate a week after it was written? He was not, as to a large degree his wife was, a poet of the hour. It is fascinating to discover from her letters that he did try, that they had planned to write and to publish jointly. "When I showed him my ode on Napoleon he observed that I was gentle to England in comparison to what he had been, but after Villafranca (the Palmerston Ministry having come in) he destroyed his poem and left me alone, and I determined to stand alone. *What Robert had written no longer suited the moment.*" (Italics mine)

On the major issue of Italy's freedom they agreed totally; about Napoleon, no. It has been suggested that an earlier version of *Prince Hohenstiel-Schwangau* was the poem then "destroyed." This does not seem likely, for in his memory it existed then only as a prose sketch of an idea, "blown out" many years later, and in the light of later events, into a dramatic monologue.

Would it have been worth wounding Elizabeth at this juncture by diminishing the man, in her eyes a "sublime deliverer" lifted "to the level of pure song"? Was there any point in proving or disproving to the public that (in her vivid words) the Pope was "hard to manage even for the Emperor. It is hard to cut up a feather bed into sandwiches with the finest Damascus blade"? Was there much point even in defending England against her unmeasured attacks and trying to show her that the whole situation was more complex than she conceived?

Another factor which must always be remembered is Browning's generous and wholehearted admiration for his wife's work. Often and often he repeated that she, not he, was the poet. And although time has proved him wrong, he was not quite as wrong as changing fashion has for many years decreed. It would, indeed, be absurd to place her beside him, but she was a true poet even if now dated. *Poems before Congress* has in it fine lines which to those living through Italy's great hour must have seemed even finer. For too many years each fortunate nation

> Beside her has dared to stand,
> And flout her with pity and scorn,
> Saying she is at rest,
> She is fair, she is dead,
> And, leaving room in her stead
> To Us who are later born,
> This is certainly best!

Elizabeth's own scorn for England found perhaps unfair but certainly effective expression:

> For where's our blessed "status quo,"
> Our holy treaties, where,—
> Our rights to sell a race, or buy,
> Protect and pillage, occupy
> And civilize despair?

"It's extraordinary," said Odo Russell (British representative in Rome) to Browning, "the sensation your wife's book has made. Every paper I see has something about it."

Comparing their relative standing at that date, Browning may well have been wise to leave speech to his wife in the defense of Italy. When his poem appeared to him outdated, "The poetical devil in me," said Elizabeth, "burnt on for an utterance."

Browning's daimon was a different one. His surviving letters of this period are fewer, their contents so much less rich, than hers, that we are only too apt to view these years through Elizabeth's eyes and to exaggerate, as Browning himself did later, the length of a pause in which he was taking breath after *Men and Women* and was beginning to write *Dramatis Personae*.

20 Mr. Sludge
and Mrs. Eckley

*This trade of mine—I don't know, can't be sure
But there was something in it, tricks and all!*

"MR. SLUDGE, THE MEDIUM"

HOW FAR Elizabeth had in her best days succeeded in freeing herself from the use of morphine it is hard to tell. Certainly she had cut it down, and Browning had written exultingly to her sisters of her courage in giving it up totally during the months before Pen's birth. "Where is one among a thousand 'strongmen' that would have thrown himself on the mercy of an angel, as she did on mine, quite another kind of being?"

In later years, rumors that she had returned to the drug must have got abroad. Julia Ward Howe, furious at hearing that the Brownings did not think much of her own verse, published two rhymed attacks in her next volume. The first began:

> I hear you do not praise me, Barrett Browning, God inspired
> Nor you Robert with your manhood and your angels interlyred.

In curious contradiction to the phrase "God inspired" was the second poem in which she repudiates for herself an inspiration now described as of a very different kind:

> I shrink before the nameless draught
> That helps to such unearthly things,

And if a drug could lift so high,
I would not trust its treacherous wings.

Browning wrote to Isa Blagden that "Mrs. Story seemed to think we must be writhing under such awful blows." But he had called on Mrs. Crawford "in order to show her how much I despised her sister Mrs. Howe."

Maybe he did, but to despise its author did not mean to be indifferent to the publication of what had troubled himself so deeply. Elizabeth wrote quite calmly to Mrs. Eckley: "As to the verses, there is nothing in them which has displeased me ever so little, except just the allusion to the nameless drug . . . which is called a 'nameless drug', dear, and not morphine. . . . Also the imputation is perfectly true so far, that life is necessary to writing, and that I should not be alive except for the help of my morphine."

The "red hood of poppies," the "amreeta draught," which she had earlier called it, suggest a modern enthusiast talking about L.S.D. And despite the fits of depression, the reliance on the morphine, and the increasing physical weakness, all the friends Elizabeth did see testify to her lively interest in them and their affairs and her entire absence of bitterness.

The Eckley family continued to seek out the Brownings with a zeal that became embarrassing. They would arrange their times in Rome, their moves to Florence at the same dates, they were constantly offering the use of their carriages and horses. Browning liked David Eckley with whom he walked or rode in the early morning; and the son, another David, played with Pen. Sophia or Sophie Eckley attached herself fanatically to Elizabeth. She gave her so many presents that Elizabeth returned one, writing, "There's excess dear and extremity— and the beautiful cameo was meant to grow on your own marble throat."

The letters between them began in 1857 and pass rapidly into "Dearest Mrs. Eckley" and thence to "Dearest Sophie." In Rome they were carried by hand and written (often in pale pencil with no date) while the messenger waited.

Sophie's intensity of admiration Elizabeth repudiated: ". . . if indeed you could see the face of my soul . . . you see me high and I am low—light and I am dark—it isn't a phrase of humility—God sees how true it is." But gradually she began to return the rather feverish affection and admiration, writing of Sophie to Fanny Haworth: "Yes isn't she a poetical, pure, lovely creature? She covers the earth with her own white garments and walks clean-footed over dirty places."

The chief attraction was certainly Sophia Eckley's claim that she walked with the spirits of the dead. She kept trying to persuade Elizabeth that she, too, had had experiences, but Elizabeth with all her cravings refused to become self-deceived. "You tell me," she wrote, "you are sure of my having had communication with spirits belonging to me. How can you possibly be sure, if I am not sure? There has been no testimony worth a straw to me—though I kept my mind open and ready." Yet she would like, she said, to wander through chestnut woods "making the third with that strange spirit." It was, I suppose, a union in the spirits that made Elizabeth so strangely call Sophie her dear sister. She was practicing automatic writing with Fanny Haworth, too; and she went on hoping. "A paper and pencil shall be near [she tells Sophie] that 'they' (if they are gracious) may complete their graciousness." One letter speaks of "our séance"; another says "I have the disks ready."

With Browning, however intensely he disliked it, the subject was out in the open, but presumably it was in reference to Sophie's husband that Elizabeth assured her friend that Robert was "safe . . . not a word shall be said . . . be calm."

Did Elizabeth fancy perhaps that her dead brother might be the strange spirit that walked with Mrs. Eckley, or even—now that death had erased the memories of his cruelty—her strange father? (The thought of a spiritual Moulton Barrett, in a toga perhaps or clad in light, seems highly implausible.)

Robert might be "safe," but the subject was again more serious than when they had played with it at Florence. He had written to Isa from Le Havre: "Do you still sit round a table and see who will turn it least apparently? And you have patience still to hear the French spirits speak thro' a young Lady, while the Flemish spirits stick in her throat? How mournful and old-fashioned it all sounds to me."

Spiritualism, madly the fashion in England, was even more so in the United States. Ruskin tells Elizabeth "that he does not laugh at the subject, neither does he believe." The author of *Uncle Tom's Cabin* claimed to have had manifestations, and her letters were comforting to Elizabeth whose own passionate interest was woven of many strands. Any possibility of enlarged knowledge fascinated her, and she had written to Mrs. Jameson years earlier: "I shall never have rest till I know what is to be known" and expecting from spiritualism "the breaking up of some of the deepest and dumbest mysteries of our double Being."

She had no faintest need for reassurance of immortality for herself; but others might achieve it through a greater exploration of the world of spirits. With all her denials to Mrs. Eckley of any contact during their experiments together, she wrote to Henrietta of one experience she did believe herself to have had—a manifestation of Dr. Channing, the Unitarian. "I asked him if he thought differently or the same of the Lord Jesus Christ. The answer was 'God was manifest in the flesh.'" In the spiritual world the realization of immortality had "overwhelmed" him even more than its beauty—immortality and the thinness of the veil *"between that life and this life."* Asked for a message of reassurance he quoted: *"Be of good cheer, your sins are forgiven you"*; asked had he seen the face of God he said, *"No, no, no, Child."*

It is all Elizabeth's own Credo, which seems an obvious explanation of some part of this approach to the world of spirits. But increasingly Elizabeth deemed it a religious science. Results, she held, were trivial only because "We don't bring serious souls and concentrated attention and holy aspirations to the spirits." But also "Death does not teach all things." There are foolish as well as wise spirits; there are spirits who "personate falsely," there may be mediums who cheat, but the power is "a physical faculty." Home is "quite an electric fire."

Her letters do, indeed, "flush and turn pale," not over Italian unity alone but also over this second burning topic, and unfortunately on both subjects Elizabeth seemed driven by a feverish need to convict if she could not convince her correspondents. Browning may have been wise to talk politics rather than pay compliments, but he "lectured" his wife, she admits, when she railed in conversation with Odo Russell against what she called the "ignominy" of England. The word recurs in letters to all her English friends, and it is unlikely that they responded graciously (Harriet Martineau "set me down with her air of serene superiority"). To others, Mrs. Jameson, for instance, the spiritualism appeared even more foolish than the politics. After a long letter to her on the sins of England and the wrongs of Italy, Elizabeth received the news of Mrs. Jameson's death, and every death was a fresh incentive for spiritualist investigations. Robert's heart, she declared, had softened so that he allowed her to get the *Spiritual Magazine* from England. Telling Fanny Haworth of this she begs her to "get to see the 'hands' and the 'bodies' and the 'celestial garments,' " which a mutual friend had "the privilege of being familiar with. *Touch* the hands."

When the *Spiritual Magazine* attacked *Poems before Congress*, Robert confessed to a little malicious pleasure, but in fact he was getting very little pleasure and a great deal of pain during those months. He had got rid of Home, but now at his wife's side, day by day, driving with her, sitting by her was another medium, in closest intimacy. Probably at first he had only thought of Sophie Eckley as a rather silly little woman and was horrified as the picture gradually unfolded.

Looking back, he claimed: "I cried 'poison' at first sniff—and suffered more, from maintaining it, than from any incident in my whole life." This he wrote in 1863, having just received from Story the news that Mrs. Eckley was trying to divorce his friend "poor dear, good, simple David." "I do not believe one syllable of it," he said of her charges. "You know that those inventions about spirits etc. were not at all more prodigious than the daily-sprouting toadstools of that dung-hill of a soul."[1]

How much was this hindsight, stimulated by the thought of his friend's suffering and the memory of his wife's? For Elizabeth certainly did suffer acutely when—how we do not know—she found she had been deceived. To Fanny Haworth she now wrote of Sophie Eckley: "I don't think she knows what truth is, and why it should be cared for. In order to conciliate me she says she has given up her mediumship!! 'Because mediums are always suspected.'" And to Isa Blagden: "I feel inclined to grind my teeth and stamp. She sticks dear, like treacle . . . once I praised the sweetness—now I feel very sick at the adhesiveness . . . if she said she hated me how much easier I should feel."[2]

But it was of little use to get rid of an alleged medium while the all-absorbing topic remained. Browning must have been thinking of, even if not writing, *Mr. Sludge, the Medium,* while he suffered most over his wife's absorption in a difficult, dangerous quest from which he saw no happy issue. The poem expressed what he as well as she believed—that there was "something in it." But coming whence, leading whither? That question they answered differently. Sludge boldly claims:

> As for religion—why, I served it, sir!
> I'll stick to that! With my *phenomena*
> I laid the atheist sprawling on his back,
> Propped up St. Paul, or, at least, Swendenborg! . . .
> Why, of old,
> Great men spent years and years in writing books
> To prove we've souls, and hardly proved it then.

Sludge admits to wide cheating and warms to a keen enjoyment in telling how he cheated, and above all how he was encouraged to cheat by those wanting to be gulled: "If such as came for wool, sir, went home shorn,/Where is the wrong I did them? 'Twas their choice." Yet as the poem goes on he tells, too, of things that no cheating can explain:

> I have presentiments; my dreams come true:
> I fancy a friend stands whistling all in white
> Blithe as a boblink, and he's dead I learn.
> I take dislike to a dog my favorite long,
> And sell him; he goes mad next week and snaps. . . .
> Why, which of those who say they disbelieve,
> Your clever people, but has dreamed his dream,
> Caught his coincidence, stumbled on his fact
> He can't explain, (he'll tell you smilingly)
> Which he's too much of a philosopher

> To count as supernatural, indeed,
> So calls a puzzle and problem, proud of it.

Today few people would question the existence of extrasensory perception, however explained or even if admitted inexplicable. Sludge has discovered in his own strange fashion a spiritual world surrounding and permeating this one, has even discovered (in a very Browning style!) the Creator of both:

> We find great things are made of little things,
> And little things go lessening till at last
> Comes God behind them. Talk of mountains now?—
> We talk of mould that heaps the mountain, mites
> That throng the mould, and God that makes the mites.
> The Name comes close behind a stomach-cyst,
> The simplest of creations, just a sac
> That's mouth, heart, legs and belly at once, yet lives
> And feels, and could do neither, we conclude,
> If simplified still further one degree:
> The small becomes the dreadful and immense!

To believe this need not make the world of spirit fully understandable, still less subject to human manipulation: "I've told my lie,/And seen truth follow, marvels none of mine;/All was not cheating, sir, I'm positive!"

This poem is perhaps the most fascinating example of Browning's power of speaking as, and for, the man most totally repugnant to him. His sympathy with Sludge grows as he goes on, and the chief villain becomes Hiram H. Horsefall, in whom we can perhaps detect Mrs. Eckley. As Sludge says:

> Who finds a picture, digs a medal up,
> Hits on a first edition,—he henceforth
> Gives it his name, grows notable: how much more
> Who ferrets out a "medium"?

The desire to be cheated makes it bit by bit impossible for the medium to refrain from cheating. It is well known that extrasensory perception comes and goes, but the medium must always show himself in possession of it to content his exploiter. He longs to say, "I saw no ghost at all./Inform your friends I made . . . well fools of them,/And found you ready-made."

The "owner" of the medium has a vested interest in convincing his friends. Horsefall pays Sludge liberally to go away and leave them in ignorance that they have been cheated. And what of a rich woman who could both employ mediums and pretend to powers of her own? The Eckleys of this world are worse than the Sludges, but if Browning had written a dramatic monologue in her person, he would, I fancy, have made a case even for Mrs. Eckley.

But he saw one figure in the drama studiously ignored by the other actors, compared with whose absence that of Hamlet would be insignificant. He wrote: "no trick too gross—absurdities are referred to as 'low spirits;' falsehoods to 'personating spirits'—and the one terrible apparent spirit, the Father of Lies, has it all his own way."[3]

21 *The Last Months Together*

The life in me abolished the death of things,
Deep calling unto deep . . .

THE RING AND THE BOOK

A YEAR or so spent on an effort to popularize *Sordello* ended in its remaining pretty much as it was. But by the spring of 1860 Elizabeth could write to an anxious Sarianna: "Robert deserves no reproaches, for he has been writing a good deal this winter—working at a long poem which I have not seen a line of, and producing short lyrics which I *have* seen and may declare worthy of him." There were other creative activities which she had to defend to his sister. "Robert waits for an inclination," she wrote, and this was true of the entire Italian period. He took up drawing, showing remarkable results in a couple of weeks. And then, turning to modeling, he began to work several hours a day in his friend Story's studio. Interestingly his wife, who had a far juster conception than the public of their relative quality, adds, "For me, if I have attained anything of force or freedom by living near the oak, the better for me. But I hope you don't think that I mimic him or lose my individuality."

"*Mr. Sludge, the Medium*" has often been suggested as the "long poem,"—and certainly, if this was written in Elizabeth's lifetime, it seems improbable that Browning would have shown it to her. But two letters, one to William Allingham and another to Mrs. Jameson, suggest a different answer. She wrote to Allingham from Rome in May, 1860: "Robert is writing, not political *poems,* but *a poem* in books, a line of which I have not seen—and also certain exquisite lyrics which I have seen. Neither he nor I have been idle this winter; nor mean to be idle this summer." The description "a poem in books" she gave also to Mrs. Jameson, and it can apply to nothing ·in *Dramatis Personae* except "James Lee's Wife." But part of this had been printed years earlier in the *Monthly Repository* for May, 1836, and Elizabeth must surely have seen it. It is all rather puzzling, and one is reminded of passing remarks of Browning's suggesting that he wrote a good deal of poetry which never saw the light. To Domett he had spoken in his youth of much writing and destroying. And what became of the "drawers full" of lyrics he mentioned to Archbishop Benson?

Improbable perhaps, but is it inconceivable that this poem "in books" was a first draft of something, destroyed then, begun again years later? For Elizabeth nowhere mentions what we learn from *The Ring and the Book,* that it was in 1860 he found on a stall in the marketplace of Florence the old yellow book he was to make so famous.

"That memorable day" he looked for the first time at the sordid detective story which he would lift into greatness, and it was on the terrace of the Casa Guidi that he first began to map out the countryside that had been its theater:

> . . . when hearts beat hard,
> And brains, high-blooded, ticked two centuries since,
> Give it me back! The thing's restorative
> I' the touch and sight.

Presently he would lay it aside for many months; the actual writing of the poem as we have it began only in 1864, but I think we must see his excitement over it, his periodic brooding over it, as underlying much of the time remaining of Browning's Italian life, after that day of the purchase, that walk home, reading as he walked:

> Still read I on, from written title page
> To written index, on, through street and street,
> At the Strozzi, at the Pillar, at the Bridge;

> Till, by the time I stood at home again
> In Casa Guidi by Felice Church,
> Under the doorway where the black begins
> With the first stone-slab of the staircase cold,
> I had mastered the contents, knew the whole truth.

It was in Florence, too, that he began the metal work on the raw gold which would become a ring: "I fused my live soul and that inert stuff,/Before attempting smithcraft."

On that terrace where he and Elizabeth so often walked, walks shortening now as she grew weaker, he paced dreaming and looking out:

> A bow-shot to the street's end, north away
> Out of the Roman gate to the Roman road
> By the river, till I felt the Appennine.
> And there would lie Arezzo, the man's town,
> The woman's trap and cage and torture-place,
> Also the stage where the priest played his part. . . .
> Till Rome itself, the ghastly goal, I reached.
> Why, all the while,—how could it otherwise?—
> The life in me abolished the death of things,
> Deep calling unto deep . . .

Probably he talked little of the Book. Elizabeth did not want even to read it. Of her husband she says "reading hurts him. As long as I have known him he has not been able to read long at a time." *The* Book did not take long to master, but Browning read it eight times before he began to write. This winter he was already investigating the story in Rome and in Arezzo, and although his memory was in later years notoriously inaccurate, there must have been some basis for the story he told Lehmann of his placing twelve pebbles on the parapet to represent "the twelve chapters into which the poem is divided."

Meanwhile there was the modeling, rumors of which had excited Ruskin. "I think it possible," he wrote in December, 1859, "you may find a quite new form of expression of yourself in that direction." After all Rossetti was both poet and painter, Ruskin himself had tried to be both, and rumor soon had it that Browning was revealing a marked talent. "And so," Ruskin wrote in the following year, "Robert has made Cytherea in clay. I've been trying to draw her, so hard, but couldn't. It's very odd we (there's conceit for you) should take the same fancy together." And Elizabeth wrote to Sarianna early in '61: "It is wonderfully done, say the learned. He says all his happiness lies in clay now."

It was Robert's happiness, indeed, that most concerned her. "An active occupation," she told his sister,

> is salvation to him with his irritable nerves, saves him from ruminating bitter cud, and from the process which I call beating his dear head against the wall till it is bruised. . . . The modelling combines body-work and soul work, and the more tired he has been . . . the more he has exulted and been happy. . . . He has the material for a volume and will work at it this summer he says. . . . Oh the brain stratifies and matures creatively, even in the pauses of the pen.
>
> At the same time his treatment in England affects him naturally —and for my part I set it down as an infamy of the public. . . .

With all her hatred of papal rule, her belief in every rumor of the bad behavior of the Swiss Guards, her longing to see the Pope thrown out of the city, Elizabeth went in Rome only to Catholic churches where her prayers went up with the music. She found it all "beautiful and holy." She never had any idea of becoming a Catholic and in Florence they went "the regular proper way to the Swiss Church." But in the prayer and music in Rome, she said, "was the communion of saints."

Death had been crowding around them. Early in 1860 Mrs. Jameson had died quite unexpectedly, "a blot more on the world for me," wrote Elizabeth; but far worse was the blow of Henrietta's illness. She, the strongest of the three sisters, was stricken with cancer and Elizabeth could hardly bear not to rush to her, but knew that "I should just have increased the sum of evil." In another letter she writes almost bitterly of her destiny always "to be entirely useless to the people I should like to help" even "my own darling sister." She tended to suffer always from self-reproach, feeling now that she might have managed to go to England from Le Havre, had perhaps given in too much to her own physical weakness, yet realizing that she grew weaker all the time.

Henrietta died that autumn and Elizabeth wrote to Fanny Haworth: "It is a great privilege to be able to talk and cry; but *I cannot* you know."

Browning had taken every precaution that he should hear the news first and break it to his wife. By her wish he did not show her the poignant letter from Henrietta's husband, but she was haunted by the thought of the three tiny children and of never again seeing her sister on earth.

She had a comforting letter from Harriet Beecher Stowe, who shared her Christian faith and was also convinced of receiving messages from her own dead son. And Robert, Elizabeth writes, had been "most kind and tender" in her grief and had kept people away from her, but anyhow "gloomy lionesses with wounded paws don't draw the public, I thank God."

She believed in the communion of saints and intercessory prayer "not papistically nor with the vulgar purgatorial idea." "She is only in the next room—though for me I cannot see or hear her—others might." She is praying, "Help thou my unbelief. He is sufficient for this insufficiency." But this letter to Arabel goes on in a very shaky hand: "It seems . . . as if the blood of my heart *must* be left in stains on the stones of the road."

That Browning was right in fearing spiritualist "manifestations" for his wife's nerves—and perhaps even for her mental balance there can be no doubt. But whether he was right or wrong in his attribution of these things to the "Father of lies," there is no trace anywhere of their having dimmed Elizabeth's faith. Fanny Haworth had asked what if Christ be taken for a medium? "If," Elizabeth replies, "He walked on the sea as a medium, if virtue went out of Him as a mesmeriser, He also spoke the words which never man spoke, was born for us, and died for us, and rose from the dead as the Lord God our Saviour. But the whole theory of spiritualism, all the phenomena, are strikingly *confirmatory* of revelation . . ."

The forms in which the Christian faith were clad seemed to her outworn. Not Catholic theologians only, but Luther, too, "was a schoolman of the most scholastic sect; most offensive, most absurd." We must cast off these " 'old cerements' to the uttermost. We are entering on a Reformation far more interior than Luther's." And a part of that Reformation was, in her eyes, a getting closer to the spirits of the dead.

Well aware of her own growing weakness, she felt an increasing realization of life's brevity. "You catch the wind of the wheels in your face, it seems, as you get nearer the end," she writes to Mrs. Martin. And "How the spiritual world gets thronged to us with familiar faces, till at last, perhaps, the world here will seem the vague and strange world, even while we remain." And again: "Do not think that *I* think *any bond is broken,* or that anything is lost. We have been fed on the hill-side, and now there are twelve baskets of fragments remaining."

Elizabeth's fluctuations in both health and spirits made it difficult for Browning to realize that she was in fact growing weaker. She was as she said herself "always dying and it makes no difference." After her father's death and again after Henrietta's she went far down, only to pick up in sea air or in the peace and beauty of Siena. After every victory of the Sardinian army she exulted, a setback threw her into despair, and to a quite unusual degree her feelings affected her bodily. The flushing and turning pale, as noted by James, is constantly visible in her letters, but especially in the unpublished ones. "Nobody knows," she had written fifteen years before to Mrs. Martin, "what it is to have so much vital *will* in one and such a deathly impotence all around it"— and "I have naturally a melancholy heart and a merry mind . . . one mocks at the other."

Even if England proved impossible, they planned in 1861 to see Sarianna and the "dear Nonno," and Elizabeth felt confident that Arabel and perhaps her brothers would join them. She wrote to George in ' April: "Just now it is enough for me to gather together my courage for the journey to France—which seems to me very, very far. I feel more fit for going to Heaven sometimes." She had seen in Rome the English consul in whose arms Keats had died, revolting against death: "In ten years," he cried, "I should be a great poet." Elizabeth wrote: "There would be no answer to such 'divine despairs,' if it were not in the facts in which I deeply believe, that life and work, yes, the sort of work

L

suitable to the artist-nature are continued on the outside of this crust of mortal manhood, and that the man will be permitted to completed himself, if not *here, there*."

But nothing ever could go right with Elizabeth's family. Arabel suggested joining some friends of her own to the party in Paris, and one sees the family problem as perhaps never before in Elizabeth's letter to Arabel: "When we are all brought together and rubbed against one another (as it makes my blood run cold to think of) there will be a gritting and grinding from which strangers are better excluded." Yet although not wanting strangers, she craves for her sister; *couldn't* Arabel anyhow come to Italy? "I am made of brown paper and tear at a touch."

To Fanny Haworth she was writing: "The future in this shifting world, what is it? . . . I have a stout pen and till its last blot it will write . . . but if you laid a hand on this heart, you would feel how it stops and staggers and fails."

The passionate interest in Italy kept pace with the personal griefs and the spiritualist speculations. The first new and enlarged parliament met at Turin at the beginning of this year; and the problems were vast in which Victor Emmanuel needed Cavour's statesmanship, and even his rather tortuous diplomacy. Could any Italian city remain indefinitely the capital of an Italy with another state, even a tiny one, cutting it in the midst and a ruler who was there through the support of French bayonets? Could the turbulent people of Naples and Sicily work with a democratic constitution? "I will have no state of siege," Cavour said. "Anybody can govern with a state of siege."

Men of Piedmont used to say, "We have a government, a chamber, a constitution—and the name for it all is Cavour." In the illness that came upon him he was heard to murmur again and again, "No siege." He wanted his king to rule free men.

He hoped for two things: the application of democratic principles throughout Italy and the advent of a younger Pope who would consent to compromise, or rather to accept the principle of a free Church in a free state. Pius was old, he would soon die.

But it was Cavour who died, and his death seems to have been Elizabeth's own deathblow. Her husband, supported by medical opinion, had decided that she was too weak for the journey to France, and in a letter to Sarianna, written from Florence, she laments the decision and tells her of the new and more than personal blow she had just received: "I can scarcely command voice or hand to name *Cavour*. That great soul, which meditated and made Italy, has gone to the Diviner Country. If tears or blood could have saved him to us, he should have had mine."

This letter was posted on June 7. And on June 13 she wrote to Mrs. Story: "I have felt beaten and bruised ever since . . . there's a crêpe on the flag, and the joy is as flowers on graves."

On June 29, Elizabeth died after an illness so brief and so like her customary attacks as hardly to have aroused alarm. Browning had thought her stronger and better and had on the twenty-third rejoiced that they had not been "pleasantly travelling" when the frightening attack came on. "We went immediately to Florence," writes William Story, who with his wife so dearly loved both Brownings. Looking around the desolate familiar room, they read from her portfolio an unfinished letter, "for her dear Italy were her last aspirations. The death of Cavour had greatly affected her . . . perhaps . . . broke her down." The cycle was complete as Browning said, looking around the room: "here we came fifteen years ago, here Pen was born. . . . She used to walk up and down this verandah in the summer evenings. . . . We saw from these windows the return of the Austrians. . . ." They had, he felt looking back over the years, "been all the time walking over a torrent on a straw."

It was well he had these two to help him, and Isa Blagden, who always spoke of that July as her "apocalyptic" month. She gave the only comfort a friend can give by listening to the high poetic utterance alternating with a simply human cry of desolation in which Browning poured out his grief. I suppose it was the poet in both the Brownings that made them so singularly expressive, while both so often said that they could not speak.

But for the first few days Browning was stunned, only writing to his sister and father, a few broken words: "My own Sis; Papa—you know what this means—it is all over—I cannot say more—All unexpected, unintelligible, but with no pain, no knowledge of what was to be. . . .

Don't come, nor send, nor be anxious. I have Peny to live for and attend to with her in him. I could not break this to you—I will write again."

Four days later he could write to George Barrett, and then to Fanny Haworth, and to Forster.

George he asked to forgive him if there was any pain he could have spared him in the telling, "though I am too stupid to tell how;" Elizabeth had been prostrated by Cavour's death, had partially recovered and then caught cold; "the usual attack," she had said, "no worse"; and when the doctor (a stranger) was grave, she had dismissed his fears: "It's only the experience I've had in plenty—they don't understand."

It was not the first time Browning had sat up night after night watching and waiting while his wife passed through some alarming crisis of her mysterious illness, but his letter to George Barrett shows him in that agony of self-questioning which comes always after a calamity. He had felt so strongly an instinct of impending disaster as to watch each night, while Elizabeth supposed he "slept on a sofa." The best doctor in the district had stayed till morning at the beginning of the attack, had indeed been alarmed, fearing an abscess of the lung, but had left saying, "She is certainly better this evening." She had "washed her face and combed her hair without the least assistance," eaten the jelly offered her and "drunk a glass of lemonade, not a quarter of an hour before the end."

All this he tells George, only "to be relieved of your just reproach" had he kept silence in conscious realization of the danger he unreasoningly felt, "for I could explain away every ill symptom."

"She rose every day," he wrote to Forster, "sat in the drawing-room till evening, and so we talked. . . ." They made plans for the future: "we both of us conceived a sudden dislike for this poor Casa Guidi we had been happy in so long. . . . Pen surmised something from the talk—he went to bid her goodnight: 'Are you really better?' '*Much* better.' He asked twice more and was twice so answered. . . . Then I sat there all night. She slept a while with heavy troubled breathing and woke oppressed. At times she would wander a very little in her mind, through the slightly increased doses of morphine acting on the weakness of her body. I would say 'Do you know me'—'know *you*' (And then what I can't write) 'And you know where you are?'—'Why—not quite!' 'And you *feel?*' 'Comfortable—much better.' Only once she said 'Our lives are held by God.' "

Each letter has its own special touches, though there is much of repetition. "At four o'clock," he told Fanny Haworth, "there were symptoms that alarmed me." He sent for the doctor and called the Italian maid, Annunciata. "She smiled as I proposed to bathe her feet. 'Well, you *are* making an exaggerated case of it.' Then came what my heart will keep till I see her and longer—the most perfect expression of her love to me within my whole knowledge of her—always smilingly, happily, and with a face like a girl's—and in a few minutes she died in my arms, her head against my cheek. These incidents so sustain me that I tell them to her beloved ones as their right."

Annunciata had first seen the change and cried out, "The blessed soul has passed away."

"She went like God's child into His presence," Browning told Forster, "with no more apprehension or difficulty than *that!* Dr. Wilson came presently—it was daylight. He says he expected nothing so sudden . . . there could have been no help; there was no pain."

Notes

INTRODUCTION

1 The quotations from Henry James are taken from "Browning in Westminster Abbey" (*The Speaker*, January 4, 1891).

2 I have no doubt that in the vast mass of Browning literature instances can be found of some such wild statements. I am discussing serious criticism, but even this seems all too often to separate poet and thinker and to be seeking weaknesses instead of admiring power and beauty. An interesting book, *The Browning Critics*, has been edited recently by Professors Litzinger and Knickerbocker. In it some of the best criticism in dispraise and in praise of Browning has been collected—the praise being so selected and arranged as to follow and reply to the dispraise.

CHAPTER 1   *The Browning Family*

1 In every known generation of the Browning family the eldest son was called Robert. Confusion seems best avoided by calling the poet alone by the name he made famous, calling his father Mr. Browning, and identifying grandfather and great-grandfather as such on their rare appearances.

2 There is probably an allusion to Cyrus Mason's rather spiteful account of the Browning family in Mrs. Orr's biography of the poet. She feels it important to deny an "assertion" that any relative except his father had given the youthful Browning financial help. Mrs. Orr knew both the poet and his sister intimately. Browning for many years visited her twice a week. She had fuller access to the personal papers remaining in the family than any subsequent biographer. The Mason manuscript is at Baylor University.

3 Both Mrs. Miller and I learned all that can be learned about the Barrett and Tittle backgrounds from Jeannette Marks' book, *The Family of the Barretts*. Miss Marks talked with the grandson of Alfred Barrett (one of Elizabeth's younger brothers), still resident in Jamaica, and investigated both there and at St. Kitts all the available records.

CHAPTER 2   *The Boy Browning*

1 This poem, "Development," was written in Browning's old age and appears in *Asolando*.

2 Browning describes this episode to Richard Hengist Horne, writing from Florence in December, 1848. See *Letters of Robert Browning*.

CHAPTER 3   *Pauline*

1   The assertion, frequently made to-day, that Browning ran away from competition at school and university could not, I fancy, have been uttered within his living memory. For (1) there is no evidence whatever to support it; (2) it is so intrinsically unlikely. The boy and young man who knew Latin, Greek, and French as well as he did (to say nothing of English), and who possessed the immense power of mind displayed in *Pauline*, would hardly have encountered fellow students with whom he would have feared competition; (3) it is "out of character" (as Macready said when he refused to act a part). This I can only hope to show in the course of my two volumes.

2   There is some conflict of opinion between William Sharp (author also of minor poetry under the name of Fiona Macleod) and Mrs. Orr in the accounts of Browning's boyhood. Sharp's biography came first, appearing in 1890, Mrs. Orr's in 1891. She is indignant over the allusion to gypsies and tramps, declaring that at no time would Browning have indulged in "low life pleasures."

3   That Browning thought he had unveiled the time of his darkness is seen in the curious introductory passage from Cornelius Agrippa, with its unwarranted hope that "a great many people" would read the poem. But "some will be dull in thought and slow minded," others

actually hostile and unfavorable to my way of thought . . . not Apollo or all the Muses or an angel from heaven could clear me of their execration. I advise such people not to read what I have written, to give no mind to it, to forget it: it is nox-ious, poisonous: the mouth of Hell is in this book, spewing forth rocks which might smash their heads if they are not careful.

But those of you who come to the reading in all fairness, if you display as much soundness of judgment as bees in gathering honey, may read without fear. I think you will gain some small profit and much pleasure. . . . If I on any matter have spoken too freely, make allowance for my youth: I was barely grown-up when I composed the work. . . .

Cornelius Agrippa, an occult philosopher of the sixteenth century, was also a magician reputed to be able to cause an evil spirit to enter and apparently resuscitate a corpse. Himself companioned by a devil in the shape of a black dog he dismissed it on his deathbed crying, "Begone evil beast, you have utterly destroyed me."

4   Richard Garnett's *Life of W. J. Fox* tells the story of Fox's ministry, his journalism, his marriage and his love for Eliza Flower. A charming description of the Flower-Fox household is given by Mrs. Miller in *Robert Browning: A Portrait*.

5   Caroline Fox had no connection with W. J. Fox. A young Quaker from the country, she describes in *Memories of Old Friends* visiting London, meeting Mill, hearing Carlyle lecture.

6   The copy of *Pauline* annotated by Mill, with Browning's answers, is in the Victoria and Albert Museum, London.

Further books illustrating this period of Browning's life are *Carlyle's Life in London*, edited by J. A. Froude; *Necessary Evil: The Life of Jane Welsh Carlyle* by Lawrence and Elizabeth Hanson; Harriet Martineau's *Autobiography;* and *John Stuart Mill* by Michael St. John Packe.

CHAPTER 4 *Paracelsus*

1 Autograph letters. University of Texas.

2 Edmund Gosse in *Personalia* is illuminating on his conversation with the aged Browning about this period of his youth.

I cannot discover how Browning knew Benkhausen. He destroyed his early letters to his family, so we depend for the account of the Russian journey on the memory of his sister, Sarianna, whom Professor Hall Griffin saw frequently while he was writing about her brother. The vivid descriptions are borne out by Browning's poem, "Ivan Ivanovitch." Mrs. Bronson has told us about Browning and Prince Gagarin ("Browning in Venice," *Cornhill*, 1902).

3 Comte Amédée de Ripert-Monclar, to whom *Paracelsus* was dedicated, had become known to Browning through his half-uncle, William Shergold Browning, of Rothschild's bank in Paris. The count was a sort of unofficial representative of the French Royalists to the exiles in England. A number of Browning's letters to him have recently been discovered, but it is highly tantalizing that until they have been edited and published, a sight of them has been refused me.

4 From "An Epistle Containing the Strange Medical Experience of Karshish, the Arab Physician."

5 *Robert Browning and Julia Wedgwood, A Broken Friendship as Revealed by Their Letters* is chiefly valuable for Browning's later life, but contains also, like Gosse's *Personalia*, some of his own memories of youth.

6 In *Browning: Background and Conflict*, a very useful study of the poet's thought and critical reactions.

L*

7 Mrs. Orr gives the letter to Fox in full. It is dated April 16, 1835.

CHAPTER 5 *Browning and Macready*

1 Autograph letter. Wellesley College collection.

2 It has seemed best in the tangled story of Browning's plays to let Macready have his say as fully as possible. His fascinating 800-page journal is contemporary—and I have used other contemporary records rather than relying on Browning's memory, which in old age was notoriously inaccurate.

Of the quality of Browning's plays there are obviously two opinions—and also of the degree of their failure. For a more favorable one than I have given of either I suggest that the reader examine the plays, and read also the Griffin-Minchin biography (recently reissued in a new edition) particularly in relation to *Strafford*. It was called in the *Constitutional* (probably by Douglas Jerrold) a "noble tragedy," but after four days' success there followed a chapter of accidents: Vandenhoff, acting Pym, was offered an engagement in the States and withdrew with no notice. Instead of a replacement (were there no understudies in those days?) another play *Walter Tyrrel* was put on—a "scarecrow tragedy," with forest scenes, blue fire, moonlight effects—was vehemently applauded, and followed by a series of benefits chosen by the actors, only one of whom chose *Strafford*. This was its end—and the critics in the main had condemned it. But one hardly realizes from the Journal all the elements against which legitimate theater had to contend: live lions on the stage, a coach and six horses, a Burmese chariot drawn by Burmese bulls, followed by elephants, ostriches, circus riders on their horses—besides the exciting blue fire that had cut short Browning's play. Circus, pantomime, and drama were all crowded onto the early Victorian stage and badly needed sorting out.

3 Arnould's letter to Domett is printed in *Robert Browning and Alfred Domett* (p. 64).

4 This letter is in *New Letters of Robert Browning.*

CHAPTER 6   *Sordello into Suspense*

1 Ezra Pound in *The A. B. C. of Reading* selects Browning and Landor among the handful of poets he deals with. But more emphatically does he stress Chaucer (to whom Landor likened Browning), and the poet Sordello. "I see every reason," he says, "for studying Provençal verse." And "There was a period when the English lyric quality, the juncture of note and melody was very high. But to gauge that height, knowledge of Provence is extremely useful."

This, as well as the modern emphasis on Browning's own revelations in *Sordello* of his views on the poet's art, should always be borne in mind.

2 Undated in *New Letters of Robert Browning*, p. 18.

Carlyle is one of the most important figures in Browning's life and will reappear in Volume II. See especially *Letters to John Stuart Mill, John Sterling and Robert Browning*, and "Correspondence between Thomas Carlyle and Robert Browning," *Cornhill* magazine, May, 1915.

3 Autograph letter. University of Texas.

4 Mrs. Bridell-Fox wrote two sketches of her youthful memories: "Robert Browning," in *Argosy* magazine, February, 1890, and "Memories," in *The Girls' Own Paper*, July 19, 1890.

5 Moncure Daniel Conway was an American who succeeded Fox as minister at South Place. He fought for abolition in his own country despite his heritage of land and slaves in the South. He went gradually from a liberal Christianity, through Unitarianism, into free thought, and wrote an Autobiography from which the quotation is taken and in which he records Browning's expressions of faith, interpreting them as furious efforts to maintain an impossible position.

6 For Browning's feelings of perplexity and discouragement during this period see *Robert Browning and Alfred Domett*, from which the quotations are taken.

7 Told vividly in Garnett's *Life of Fox*.

CHAPTER 7   *Elizabeth Barrett*

1 The unpublished letters quoted in this chapter are in the Berg Collection—and also a copy of that rare volume: *Elizabeth Barrett Browning, Poems and Stories, with an Inedited Autobiography*.

2 Elizabeth's anguish is interpreted by Mrs. Miller as a haunting knowledge that she had wished for her brother's death: there was "a hidden rivalry buried so deep that she was ready to deny its existence"; the slain "familiar" was Bro.

Any imaginary horror is, of course, possible in a dream, especially if opium-induced. The psalmist speaks for all humans of "the terror of the night . . . the pestilence that stalks in the darkness." And that terror may well be of the dark world inside the self. But it is the torment, *not* the revelation, of a person. Elizabeth had loved her brother supremely; she had offered what money she had to facilitate his marriage, but she felt that her near-idolatry, keeping him at her side, had caused his death. Is Mrs. Miller's sinister interpretation of a nightmare necessary to account for her abiding grief?

3 See *Elizabeth Barrett to Miss Mitford*, edited by Betty Miller.

CHAPTER 8 *Robert and Elizabeth*

1 Santayana's "Poetry of Barbarism" can be found in his *Essays in Literary Criticism*. But the essence of his treatment of Browning is included in *Robert Browning: A Collection of Critical Essays* edited by Philip Drew, London 1966. Edwin Muir's essay is in the same book. Hoxie Fairchild's remarks are taken from his *Religious Trends in English Poetry*.

2 From Kenyon Typescript (British Museum), a copy of all the letters contained in Kenyon's *Letters of Elizabeth Barrett Browning*—and some letters and passages that he eventually decided not to print.

3 *The Letters of Robert Browning and Elizabeth Barrett Browning 1845–1846* were published in 1898. Robert Barrett Browning (Pen) their only son, thought "the correspondence should be given in its entirety." The book is almost unedited, has been reprinted several times, and is now very rare. I have used the pocket edition of 1913.

4 Leslie Stephen's remark is taken from *Studies of a Biographer* in

which he has many penetrating things to say of Browning.

5 See "New Light on the Brownings" by Edward Snyder and Frederick Palmer (*Quarterly Review* 1937).

6 Kenyon Typescript.

CHAPTER 9 *One Winter and Then . . .*

1 Autograph letter. Wellesley College Library.

2 See *Letters of Elizabeth Barrett to B. R. Haydon*. Elizabeth Barrett was a sensitive as well as a brilliant letter writer; she never failed to sympathize with her correspondents. Although in these letters she tried to cure Haydon of his attitude of mistrust and suspicion, she also gave him some reason to hope that her admiration for his writing might overcome her objections to his attitudes—that she might really edit his book.

3 After writing this I realized that I must have unconsciously borrowed from Chesterton whose use of the same line from *Clive* I had forgotten.

CHAPTER 10 *Married in Italy*

1 Mrs. Jameson's letters are in The Pierpont Morgan Library, New York, but a great part of them have been printed in "From Paris to Pisa with the Brownings," *New Colophon*, 1950.

2 The daily life of the two poets in Italy is immensely documented, chiefly by Elizabeth. Only a small proportion of Robert's *Collected Letters*, *New Letters*, and *Dearest Isa* cover the years before his wife's death—besides those published in other people's writings, *e.g.*, Wil-

liam Allingham and Harriet Hosmer, or scattered unpublished in libraries. Moreover Elizabeth was as much his superior in prose as he was hers in poetry. The letters to Arabel in the Berg Collection, the canceled letters and passages in the Kenyon typescript, usefully and more intimately supplement the many volumes of her collected letters (for which see the Bibliography). She gives an immensely vivid picture. The great mass of surviving Browning letters belong to the years after his wife's death.

CHAPTER 11   *Italian Background*

For notes on this see Chapter 19.

CHAPTER 12
Life, Death and Danger

1 Browning's comments are quoted from a book entitled *From Robert and Elizabeth Browning: A Further Selection of the Barrett-Browning Family Correspondence.* Introduction and Notes by William Rose Benet. The book is of small importance and may be regarded as a supplement to *Letters to Her Sister* which with the Kenyon Collection (published and unpublished) are the chief sources for this chapter.
2 Kenyon Typescript.
3 Kenyon Typescript.
4 The first edition of *Sonnets from the Portuguese* appeared in 1850. But in 1894 Edmund Gosse spoke of a small private edition printed at Reading in 1847 and edited by Miss Mitford. Gosse said that Browning had "made a statement *to a friend*," telling with vivid detail how Elizabeth had first shown him the sonnets at Pisa! Wise, the fa-

mous bibliographer, making this private edition known, spoke of Browning having told the story to Gosse. This sheer invention by Wise has led to endless discussion— the conclusion usually reached being that of an astonishing failure in Browning's memory or a hardly less surprising confusion on the part of Gosse.

Finally the Reading edition of *Sonnets from the Portuguese* itself came into question among a growing collection of modern first editions. Hall Griffin pays warm acknowledgement to Wise, De Vane calls his the "standard" bibligraphy of Browning's work "in spite of the inclusion of forgeries." Wise (with Nicoll) compiled the admirable *Literary Anecdotes of the Nineteenth Century.* To him we owe the great Ashley Collection at the British Museum. Yet, when doubt was cast on pamphlets in Wise's list claimed as first editions of Ruskin, Tennyson, Morris, Swinburne, both Brownings, etc., it seemed to John Carter and Graham Pollard important to investigate. Their findings are related in *An Enquiry into the Nature of Certain Nineteenth Century Pamphlets* (published in London and New York 1934).

The two most obvious lines were an examination of the paper and the type—and this alone was, as concerned the *Sonnets,* sufficiently convincing. Neither paper nor type were of a kind used before 1860. No history of any of these pamphlets could be traced back behind 1890. They were *too* clean, *too* unmarked, and uninscribed. Shocked at first by Wise's carelessness in not making such inquiries as "commonsense, let alone bibliographical duty, plainly demanded," they became more shocked by the fact that Wise had "engaged his full powers as bibliographer and authoritative collector in the establishing of his finds."

It looked increasingly as though all these forgeries came from the same hand. But with the Reading edition of *Sonnets from the Portuguese* a climax was reached: "we can," they said, "trace no alternative source than Wise for any copies of this forgery."

The great bibliographer was himself responsible for the forgeries.

5 The three above quotations are from the Kenyon Typescript.

CHAPTER 13
Christmas-Eve and Easter-Day

1 These poems, at the peak of Browning's religious thought, have been surprisingly little analysed. Using different terms he and Newman a century ahead of their age are thinking along the same lines, are approaching the supreme Reality in the same fashion, not by a process of verbal ratiocination but by an act of the whole being. A discussion of any modification in his position belongs to my second volume.

J. Hillis Miller in *The Disappearance of God* gives a brilliant sketch of the universality of Browning's poetry and a comment on the contrast between his approach and that of other Victorians. "Only in Browning," he says, "of the writers studied here, are there hints and anticipations of that recovery of immanence which was to be the inner drama of twentieth century literature . . . being and value lie in *this* world, in what is immediate, tangible, present to man in earth, sun, sea, in the stars in their courses, and in what Yeats was to call 'the

foul rag and bone shop of the heart.' " Yet fascinatingly, when "Anima" is surely at work, Miller can only see Browning "stretched on the rack of a fading transcendentalism" reaching "a precarious unity only by the most extravagant stratagems of the spirit." But Browning's is the Christian God, at once immanent and transcendent.

While the force of *Christmas-Eve and Easter-Day* can be conveyed only by a great deal of quotation, it is quite peculiarly difficult to quote. Besides an amount of punctuation that would today be unusual, Browning puts in quotation marks thoughts belonging to *the time of the Experiences* and, in " Easter Day," one side of the long arguments which I believe to be the expression of two elements in himself. Also in quotation marks are the words spoken by the supernatural voice. To a lesser degree this problem of quotation recurs elsewhere in Browning's poetry.

2 See Chapter 6 for a discussion of the conception of Anima and Animus. The theme has been developed by Henri Bremond, Paul Claudel, and E. I. Watkin.

CHAPTER 14 *Two Checkered Years*

1 See *Letters of Owen Meredith to Robert and Elizabeth Browning.*

2 Browning and Carlyle are apt to speak constantly of and to one another—probably both felt and enjoyed what Carlyle called the "curious difference" between his own gloom and Browning's cheerfulness. He gives a delightful picture in the volume published as *Last Words of Thomas Carlyle* (which covers this visit to Paris), and the correspond-

ence between them was collected in an article by Alexander Carlyle in *The Cornhill* for May, 1915. Other letters are in the volumes *Letters to John Stuart Mill, John Sterling and Robert Browning* and in *New Letters of Thomas Carlyle.*

3   *The Times* of July 2, 1852 reporting COURT OF QUEEN'S BENCH Thursday, July 1 (Sittings at Nisi Prius at Guildhall, before Lord Campbell and a Special Jury, Von Müller v. Browning).

4   Apart from the unpublished letters to Arabel these two years are best reflected in *The Letters of Elizabeth Barrett Browning*, edited by Frederic G. Kenyon from which most of the quotations in this chapter are taken.

CHAPTER 15
An Anglo-American Circle

1   This entertaining group of friends and the atmosphere in which they lived can be caught in many books of the period—available in libraries even if, sadly, so often out of print. Perhaps first comes Henry James' *William Wetmore Story;* but the gossiping of Anne Thackeray Ritchie in *Records of Tennyson, Ruskin and Browning,* the *Letters to William Allingham* and Allingham's *Diary,* the memories of all three Hawthornes, Harriet Hosmer's *Letters and Memories,* and *Letters from Owen Meredith to Robert and Elizabeth Browning*—all these make delightful reading. Above all, of course, are the collected *Letters of Elizabeth Barrett Browning,* and her letters to her sister Henrietta. (See bibliography for full titles.) A more recent book is *Browning to his American Friends,* edited with an

excellent introduction by Gertrude Reese Hudson. This book, however, belongs in great part to my second volume.

2   The letter to Milsand is quoted in the Griffin-Minchin biography, that to Forster is in *New Letters of Robert Browning.*

3   *Letters from Owen Meredith.*

4   *Letters of Elizabeth Barrett Browning.* A strange letter to Mrs. Jameson of February 24, 1855, calling such work as nursing a "retrograde" step in the question of women's rights.

CHAPTER 16   *Men and Women*

1   One or two critics, however, see Browning as Andrea—*kept from the fulfilment of his genius* by his *too*-religious wife, as earlier by his mother. I suppose the basic disagreement lies between their view and that of those who hold with Rossetti, Carlyle, Swinburne, André Gide, Ezra Pound, Robert Lowell, and others of their quality, that his was a genius richly fulfilled, ranking him as Landor claimed close to Chaucer.

2   This is Mrs. Miller's view of the poem. In his very interesting book *Amphibian* H. C. Duffin analyses in a long Appendix his reasons for calling her *Robert Browning: A Portrait* a "perverse book . . . it sets out to debunk, to denigrate and manipulates material to that end . . . chooses facts and omits others . . . a number of minute but significant distortions."

An unpublished letter of this period in the Kenyon typescript, quoted by Mrs. Miller, is one of Mr. Duffin's pieces of supporting evidence. Writing to Fanny Haworth, Elizabeth sympathises with a friend whose marriage has gone wrong: "Tell me if your friend recovers her dreams again. I can conceive of a strong attachment recovering from the shock of unexpected points of difference, and of two souls growing together after all." This Mrs. Miller calls "significant" in relation to Elizabeth's own feelings. But she does not quote the sentence with which the letter ends. "You are right. There is poetry in my life—the ideal overflowed into life when I least hoped for it. But there is always poetry in life—is there not?—where there is love."

3 See *The A. B. C. of Reading*.
4 Oscar Wilde in *"The Critic as Artist."*

   But Yeats comments: "Browning says that he could not write a successful play because interested not in character in action but in action in character."

   Yeats himself needed "in lyric or in dramatic poetry, in some sense character in action; a pause in the midst of action perhaps, but action always its end and theme." (Quoted from *Essays and Introductions*, Clarendon Press, 1965, p. 530.)
5 See *The Poetry of Experience*.
6 See *Robert Browning: a Collection of Critical Essays*.

CHAPTER 17 *Conviction So Like Despair*

1 All letters to Harriet Hosmer are taken from her book *Letters and Memories*.
2 Henry James, *The Middle Years*, pp. 104–6.
3 Browning described with some disgust how Home, a rather large young man, behaved with his host and hostess like a fond child "kissing them abundantly." Mrs. Miller sees his disgust as arising from the caricature this presented of his own attitude to his parents. She sees a similar resemblance in the medium's cheating and the poet's "confidence trick." There is no evidence that Browning's behavior to his parents—even as a child—was other than that of any Victorian son. Kissing, says his cousin, was infrequent with him. Mrs. Miller's misreading of *Pauline* explains the theory that Browning himself is speaking through the mouth of Mr. Sludge the Medium and that a sense of "the loss of his own integrity" is visible in his revulsion from Home.

4 The letters to Edward Chapman are in *New Letters of Robert Browning*.
5 *Letters to William Allingham*. It is a pity that these, the Ruskin and Hosmer letters are in no Browning collection.
6 In W. G. Collingwood, *Life and Work of Ruskin*.
7 Printed for private circulation by Baylor University. One hesitates to recommend for further reading Ruskin's Works in thirty-six volumes! But the volumes are admirably indexed and delightful to browse in. An excellent biography is *Ruskin the Great Victorian*, by Derrick Leon.
8 Unpublished letter. Baylor University.
9 In *Letters of Thomas Carlyle to John Stuart Mill, John Sterling and Robert Browning*.

CHAPTER 18
Friends, Family and Frustration

1 The most illuminating reading for this chapter is *Dearest Isa*, a collection of Browning's letters to Isabella

Blagden. Only thirty-nine out of the hundred and fifty-four letters belong to the period before Elizabeth's death, but they are of prime importance through their detailing of Browning's day-to-day life with its cares and anxieties from 1857 to 1861. Both husband and wife wrote constantly to Isa, and the quotations in this chapter are taken from *Dearest Isa.*

2 Kenyon Typescript, August 10, 1858.

3 *Letters to Her Sister,* August 15, 1857.

4 *Letters of Robert Browning,* October 6, 1857.

5 Diary of William Allingham. Thackeray was then editor of the *Cornhill Magazine.*

6 Kenyon Typescript. Letter to Mrs. Martin, December 29, 1859.

CHAPTER 19
The Pope, Napoleon, and the Rest

1 Considerations of space have obliged me to deal too briefly with the whole Italian background— above all with the fascinating figures of the leading characters. Hales's *Pio Nono,* Albert Guérard's *Napoleon III,* Trevelyan's *Garibaldi and the Thousand* are all fascinating reading. Although there are more recent books, Trevelyan's three still remain the most vivid record of the period. *The Leopard* by Lampedusa, although dealing with a later generation helps to explain the very real problem of an Italy historically and

ethnically so various as to have made Napoleon III as well as Pio Nono desire a federation of states rather than a unity dominated by a single one. These books also help us to a further understanding of why Browning was reluctant to set down anything approximating to a newspaper day-to-day commentary. My second volume will contain a further treatment of *Prince Hohenstiel-Schwangau.*

2 Henry James, *William Wetmore Story* and *Autobiography.*

3 See Lilian Whiting, *Kate Field: A Record,* and J. Forster, *Walter Savage Landor.* Also, for Landor's now underrated poetry, see Ezra Pound, *The A. B. C. of Reading.*

4 The quotation is from *The Poetry of Experience.* Note also the two recent volumes of essays collected by Doctors Litzinger and Knickerbocker and by Philip Drew (see Bibliography).

CHAPTER 20
Mr. Sludge and Mrs. Eckley

1 See *Browning and His American Friends* for his feelings about Mrs. Eckley expressed in his letters to William Wetmore Story.

2 Kenyon Typescript, May 10, 1860.

3 This letter of Browning's is not in any of his collected volumes. It was written to Miss de Gaudrion and is quoted in *The Family of the Barretts.* On the main subject of this chapter see Katharine Porter's *Spiritualism in the Browning Circle.*

Selective Bibliography

THE Broughton-Northup-Pearson Browning Bibliography, with its supplement, lists under "Biography and Criticism" close to five thousand items, of which I do not claim to have read a quarter. Of those I have looked at some are entirely worthless, others more valuable than I had anticipated. There is, too, an indispensable minimum of reading about the world which surrounded Robert and Elizabeth Browning and the men and women who influenced them.

I have listed here, helpfully, I hope, for the student, a selection of books and articles covering the first half of Robert Browning's long life. There will be another bibliography for Vol. II.

WORKS OF ROBERT BROWNING

Essay on Chatterton. Edited by Donald Smalley. Harvard: Oxford, 1948.
An Essay on Percy Bysshe Shelley. Published for the Shelley Society by Reeves and Turner, 1888.
The Poetical Works of Robert Browning. John Murray, 1951. (First definitive edition Smith, Elder, 1896.)

BIOGRAPHIES

Browning, Elizabeth Barrett, Hitherto Unpublished Poems and Stories with an *Inedited Autobiography.* Boston, Bibliophile Society, 1914.
Burdett, Osbert, *The Brownings.* Constable, 1928.
Chesterton, G. K., *Robert Browning.* English Men of Letter Series, Macmillan, 1903.
Dowden, Edward, *The Life of Robert Browning.* Everyman's Library, J. M. Dent, 1904.

Griffin, W. Hall, and Minchin, H. C., *The Life of Robert Browning. With Notices of His Writings, His Family, and His Friends* (revised edition). Archon Books, 1966.
Hewlett, Dorothy, *Elizabeth Barrett Browning: A Life*. Cassell, 1953.
Hovelaque, Henri Léon, *La Jeunesse de Robert Browning*. Paris, Les Presses Modernes, 1932.
Miller, Betty, *Robert Browning: A Portrait*. John Murray, 1952.
Orr, Mrs. Sutherland, *Life and Letters of Robert Browning* (1891). New edition, revised and in part rewritten by Frederic G. Kenyon. John Murray, 1908.
Sharp, William, *Life of Robert Browning*. Walter Scott, 1890.
Taplin, Gardner B., *The Life of Elizabeth Barrett Browning*. John Murray, 1957.
Whiting, Lilian, *The Brownings: Their Life and Art*. Little Brown, 1911.

LETTERS

The Letters of Robert Browning and Elizabeth Barrett Barrett. Smith, Elder, 1899.
Robert Browning and Alfred Domett. Edited by Frederic A. Kenyon. Smith, Elder, 1906.
Letters of Robert Browning. Collected by Thomas J. Wise. Edited with an Introduction and Notes by Thurman L. Hood. J. Murray, 1933.
Robert Browning and Julia Wedgwood. A Broken Friendship as Revealed in Their Letters. Edited by Richard Curle. John Murray and Jonathan Cape, 1937.
New Letters of Robert Browning. Edited with Introduction and Notes by William Clyde de Vane and Kenneth Leslie Knickerbocker. John Murray, 1951.
Dearest Isa: Robert Browning's Letters to Isabella Blagden. Edited by Edward C. McAleer. University of Texas Press: Nelson, 1952.
Browning to His American Friends: Letters Between the Brownings, the Storys, and James Russell Lowell (1841–1890). Bowes & Bowes, 1965.
Learned Lady: Letters from Robert Browning to Mrs. Thomas Fitzgerald 1876–1889. Edited by Edward C. McAleer. Harvard University Press: Oxford, 1966.
From Robert and Elizabeth Browning: A Further Selection of the Barrett-Browning Family Correspondence. Introduction and Notes by William Rose Benét. John Murray, 1936.
Letters of the Brownings to George Barrett. Edited by Paul Landis. University of Illinois Press, 1958.

Letters of Elizabeth Barrett Browning Addressed to Richard Hengist Horne. With Comments on Contemporaries. Edited by S. R. Townshend Mayer. Richard Bentley, 1877.
The Letters of Elizabeth Barrett Browning. Edited with biographical additions by Frederic G. Kenyon. Smith, Elder, 1898.
Elizabeth Barrett Browning: Letters to Her Sister, 1846–1859. Edited by Leonard Huxley. John Murray, 1929.
Letters from Elizabeth Barrett to B. R. Haydon. Edited by Martha Hale Shackford. Oxford University Press, 1939.
Elizabeth Barrett to Miss Mitford. Edited by Betty Miller. J. Murray, 1954.

GENERAL

(*a*) *Books.*

Adams, Sarah Flower, *Vivia Perpetua.* With a Memoir of the Author by E. Bridell Fox. Privately printed, 1893.
Allingham, Helen, and Williams, E. B. editors. *Letters to William Allingham.* Longmans, 1911.
Allingham, William, *A Diary.* Edited by H. Allingham and D. Radford. Macmillan, 1907.
Bates, Gerardine (Mrs. R. MacPherson), *Memoirs of the Life of Anna Jameson by Her Niece.* Boston, Roberts Brothers, 1878.
CARLYLE, THOMAS
   Last Words of ——, Longman's, 1892.
   Letters of —— *to John Stuart Mill, John Sterling and Robert Browning.* Edited by Alexander Carlyle. Stokes, 1923.
   New Letters of ——. Edited by Alexander Carlyle. John Lane, 1904.
   Reminiscences of ——. Edited by J. A. Froude. London, 1887.
Carr, J. Comyns, *Some Eminent Victorians.* Duckworth, 1908.
Carter, John, and Pollard, Graham. *An Enquiry into the Nature of Certain Nineteenth-Century Pamphlets.* Constable, 1936.
Clarke, Helen Archibald, *Browning's Italy: A Study of Italian Life and Art in Browning.* Baker Taylor Co., 1907.
Chesterton, G. K., *A Handful of Authors.* Sheed and Ward, 1953.
Clough, Arthur Hugh, *Correspondence of* ——. Edited by F. L. Mulhausen. Oxford, 1957.
Cobbe, Frances Power, *Life of* ——. Houghton Mifflin, 1894.
Collingwood, W. G., *Life and Works of Ruskin.* Methuen, 1893.
Conway, Moncure Daniel, *Autobiography, Memoirs, and Experiences.* Cassell, 1904.
Corkran, Henriette, *Celebrities and I.* Hutchinson, 1905.

Crosse, Cornelia, *Red-Letter Days of My Life*. Richard Bentley, 1892.

DeVane, William Clyde, *A Browning Handbook*. Bell, 1956.

————, *Browning's Parleyings: The Autobiography of a Mind*. Yale University Press, 1927.

Dowden, Edward, *The Life of Percy Bysshe Shelley*. Revised Edition, Kegan, Paul, 1896.

Drew, Philip (Edited). *Robert Browning: A Collection of Essays*. Methuen, 1966.

Duckworth, F. K. G., *Browning—Background and Conflict*. Ernest Benn, 1931.

Duffin, Henry Charles, *Amphibian: A Reconsideration of Browning*. Bowes & Bowes, 1956.

Duffy, Sir Charles Gavan, *Conversations with Carlyle*. Low, 1892.

Elwin, Malcolm, *Walter Savage Landor*. Macmillan, 1841.

Fairchild, Hoxie Neale, *Religious Trends in English Poetry, Volume IV*, Columbia University Press: Oxford, 1957.

Fox, Caroline, *Memories of Old Friends*. Smith, Elder, 1882.

Fraser, Mrs. Hugh, *A Diplomat's Wife in Many Lands*. Dodd, Mead, 1913.

Froude, James Anthony, *Thomas Carlyle: Story of His Life in London 1834–1881*. Longmans, 1919.

Garnett, Richard, *The Life of W. J. Fox*. John Lane, 1910.

Gosse, Edmund, *Robert Browning: Personalia*. Fisher Unwin, 1890.

Guérard, Albert, *Napoleon III*. Howard University Press, 1943.

Hales, E. E. Y., *Pio Nono*. Eyre, 1956.

Hanson, Lawrence and Elizabeth, *Necessary Evil: The Life of Jane Welsh Carlyle*. Macmillan, 1952.

Hare, Augustus, *The Story of My Life*. G. Allen, 1896.

Hawthorne, Julian, *Shapes That Pass*. Houghton, Mifflin, 1928.

Hawthorne, Nathaniel, *French and Italian Notebooks*. Strahan, 1871.

————, *Passages from English Notebooks*. Fields, Osgood, 1870.

Holloway, John, *The Victorian Sage*. Macmillan, 1953.

Home, Daniel Dunglas, *Incidents in My Life*. Longmans, 1871.

Horne, R. H., *A New Spirit of the Age*. Smith, Elder, 1844.

Hosmer, Harriet, *Letters and Memories*. Edited by Cornelia Carr. Moffat, Yard, 1912.

James, Henry, *Essays in London and Elsewhere*. Osgood, McIlvaine & Co., 1893.

————, *The Private Life and Other Tales*. Osgood, McIlvaine & Co., 1893.

————, *William Wetmore Story and His Friends*. Blackwood, 1903.

————, *Italian Hours*. Heinemann, 1909.

————, *The Middle Years*. W. Collins, 1917.

————, *Autobiography*. Scribner's, 1917.

Jones, Sir Henry, *Browning as a Philosopher and Religious Teacher*. Macmillan, 1891.

Kenyon, F. G., *Robert Browning and Alfred Domett*. Smith, Elder, 1906.

King, Roma, Jr., *The Bow and the Lyre: The Art of Robert Browning*. University of Michigan Press: Cressett Press, 1965.

Knight, W. A., *Retrospects*. Smith, Elder, 1904.

Langbaum, Robert, *The Poetry of Experience*. Chatto and Windus, 1957.

Leon, Derrick, *Ruskin the Great Victorian*. Routledge and Kegan Paul, 1949.

Litzinger, Boyd, and Knickerbocker, K. L., *The Browning Critics*. University of Kentucky Press, 1965.

Lounsbury, T. R., *The Early Literary Career of Robert Browning*. Scribner's, 1911.

Lubbock, Percy, *Elizabeth Barrett Browning in Her Letters*. Smith, Elder, 1906.

Macpherson, Mrs. R. *See* Bates.

Macready, William Charles, *Diaries 1833–1851*. Edited by William Toynbee. Chapman and Hall, 1912.

Marks, Jeannette, *The Family of the Barretts: A Colonial Romance*. Macmillan, 1938.

Marriott, J. A. R., *The Makers of Modern Italy: Mazzini, Cavour, Garibaldi*. Clarendon Press, 1895.

Matthiessen, F. O., *The James Family*. Knopf, 1947.

Meredith, Owen (Lytton, E. Robert Bulwer), *Letters to Robert and Elizabeth Browning*. Edited by Aurelia B. Harlan and J. Lee Harlan, Jr. Baylor Browning Interests, 1936.

Mill, John Stuart, *Autobiography*. Columbia U.P.; Oxford, 1924.

Miller, J. Hillis, *The Disappearance of God*. Harvard U.P.: Oxford, 1964.

Minchin, H. C., *Walter Savage Landor: Last Days, Letters and Conversations*. Methuen, 1934.

Nicoll, Sir William Robertson, and Wise, Thomas, *Literary Anecdotes of the Nineteenth Century, Vol. I*. Dodd Mead, 1896.

Orr, Mrs. Sutherland, *A Handbook to the Works of Robert Browning*. Bell, 1885.

Packe, Michael St. John, *The Life of John Stuart Mill*. Secker and Warburg, 1954.

Pastor, Ludwig von, *History of the Popes. Volume XXXII*. J. Hodges, 1940.

Pearson, Hesketh, *Dickens, His Character, Comedy and Career*. Methuen, 1949.

Porter, Katharine H., *Spiritualism in the Browning Circle*. University of Kansas Press, 1958.

Pottle, F. A., *Shelley and Browning: A Myth and Some Facts*. Pembroke Press, 1923.

Pound, Ezra, *The A.B.C. of Reading*. Faber, 1962.

Quarles, Francis, *Emblemes Divine and Moral*. T. Tegg, 1845.

Ray, Gordon N., *Thackeray: The Age of Wisdom*. Oxford University Press, 1908.

Renton, R., *John Forster and His Friendships*. Chapman and Hall, 1912.

Ritchie, Anne Thackeray, *Records of Tennyson, Ruskin and Browning*. Harper, 1892.

———, *From Friend to Friend*. Murray, 1919.

Rossetti, William Michael, *Some Reminiscences*. Scribner's, 1906.

———, *Rossetti Papers, 1862–70*. Sands, 1903.

———, *Pre-Raphaelite Diaries and Letters*. Hurst & Blackett, 1900.

Rudman, H. W., *Italian Nationalism and English Letters: The Risorgimento and Victorian Men of Letters*. Allen & Unwin, 1940.

Saintsbury, G., *Corrected Impressions*. Dodd Mead, 1895.

———, *History of English Prosody, Vol. III*. Macmillan, 1906.

Santayana, George, *The Poetry of Barbarism*. Scribner's, 1900.

Sotheby's Catalogue, "The Browning Collections," 1913.

Steegmuller, Francis, *The Two Lives of James Jackson Jarves*. Yale University Press: Oxford, 1953.

Super, R. H., *Walter Savage Landor: A Biography*. Calder, 1957.

Symons, Arthur, *An Introduction to the Study of Browning*. Revised edition. J. M. Dent, 1906.

Trevelyan, George Macaulay, *Garibaldi and the Thousand*. Longmans, 1948.

———, *Garibaldi and the Making of Italy*. Longmans, 1948.

Untermeyer, Louis, *Makers of the Modern World*. Simon and Schuster, 1955.

Wanley, Nathaniel, *The Wonders of the Little World*. T. Basset, 1678.

Whiting, Lilian, *Kate Field: A Record*. Little Brown, 1899.

Whitla, William, *The Central Truth: The Incarnation in Browning's Poetry*. Toronto, 1953.

Wilde, Oscar, "The Critic as Artist" in *Intentions*. Methuen, 1948.

Woodham-Smith, Cecil, *Florence Nightingale*. McGraw-Hill, 1951.

Woolf, Virginia, *Flush: A Biography*. Hogarth, 1933.

Woolner, Amy (editor), *Thomas Woolner, His Life in Letters*. Chapman & Hall, 1917.

(*b*) *Articles.*

———, "Robert Browning at College," *New York Times*, December 31, 1960.

Baddeley, Sir Vincent, "The Ancestry of Robert Browning," *Genealogists' Magazine*, March, 1938.

Boyce, G. K., "From Paris to Pisa with the Brownings." *New Colophon,* 1950.

Carlyle, Alexander, "Correspondence between Thomas Carlyle and Robert Browning," *Cornhill,* May, 1915.

Fairchild, Hoxie Neale, "Browning the Simple-Hearted Casuist," *University of Toronto Quarterly,* April, 1949.

Field, Kate, "Elizabeth Barrett Browning," *Atlantic,* September 1861.

Fox, E. Bridell, "Robert Browning," *Argosy,* 1890.

———, "Memories," *Girls' Own Annual,* 1890.

Furnivall, F. J., "Browning's Footman Ancestor," *Academy,* April 12, 1902.

Gosse, Edmund, "Edmund Gosse on Browning," *The Critic,* March 14, 1896.

Hudson, Gertrude Reese, *Robert Browning and His Son.* Publications of Modern Language Association, 1946.

Huxley, Leonard, "A Visitor to the Brownings at Casa Guidi from material supplied by O. S. Holt," *Cornhill,* January, 1924.

James, Henry, "Browning in Westminster Abbey," *Speaker,* January 4, 1891.

Kinney, Mrs. Elizabeth C. L., "A Day with the Brownings at Pratolino," *Scribner's Monthly,* December, 1870.

———, Italian Reminiscences, edited by Laura Stedman and G. J. Gould "With the Brownings at Florence," *Neal's Monthly,* January, 1913.

Miller, Betty, "The Child of Casa Guidi," *Cornhill,* Spring, 1949.

———, "This Happy Evening," *Twentieth Century,* CLIV, 1953.

———, "The Seance at Ealing," *Cornhill,* CLXIX, 1957.

Snyder, Edward, and Palmer, Frederick, "New Light on the Brownings," *Quarterly Review,* July, 1957.

Stephen, Leslie, "Browning's Casuistry," *National Review,* December, 1962.

Index